MW00763272

Where
Wear ^{to}
2004

THE INSIDER'S GUIDE TO
SHOPPING IN ITALY

Fairchild & Gallagher

NEW YORK • LONDON

PUBLISHERS
Jill Fairchild & Gerri Gallagher

WRITERS
ROME Logan Bentley & Barbara Lessona

MILAN JJ Martin

FLORENCE Arabella Yerburgh

COPY EDITOR
John Graham

DESIGN / PRODUCTION ARTIST
Jeff Baker

COVER DESIGN
Richard Chapman

CARTOGRAPHER
Candida Kennedy

PREVIOUS WRITERS
ROME Alessandra Signorelli

MILAN Heather O'Brian

FLORENCE Lucie Muir

DISTRIBUTION, SALES AND MARKETING
The Julie Craik Consultancy

Where to Wear, Italy, 2004 Edition
ISBN 0-9720215-5-8

Copyright © 2003 Fairchild & Gallagher
Printed and bound in the United Kingdom.

All rights reserved.
Every effort has been made to ensure the accuracy of the information
in this book. However, the publisher and authors make no claims to,
and accept no liability for, any misrepresentations contained herein.
No part of this book may be used or reproduced in any
manner whatsoever without written permission, except in the
case of brief quotations embodied in critical articles and reviews.
For information, contact Where to Wear in New York or London at:

666 Fifth Avenue
PMB 377
New York, NY 10103
TEL 212-969-0138
TOLL-FREE 1-877-714-SHOP (7467)
FAX 212-315-1534
E-MAIL wheretowear@aol.com

10 Cinnamon Row, Plantation Wharf, London SW11 3TW
TEL 020 7801 1381
E-MAIL wheretowear@onetel.net.uk

www.wheretowear.com

Table of Contents

Introduction

Dear Italy Shopper,

Welcome to *Where to Wear*, the world's most detailed and authoritative directory of clothing and accessory stores. At *Where to Wear* we annually update our collection of global guides, making your travels through the world's fashion cities a breeze. We pioneered in 1999 with *Where to Wear New York*, and we have since added London, Paris, Los Angeles, San Francisco. Our guide to shopping in Italy covers Florence, Milan and Rome.

This second edition of *Where to Wear Italy* has all the information you'll need to look and feel great. We describe over 450 different clothing and accessories stores, ranging from the global celebrity names of the Via Condotti and the Piazza della Repubblica to out-of-the-way treasure-houses. *Where to Wear* shows visitors where to begin and Florentines, Milanese and Romans where to go next. If you want the best vintage value or the bonniest baby boutique, you'll find them here.

Where to Wear is the only shopping guide written by a team of top fashion journalists. We have our fingers on the pulse of the ever-changing fashion world. We've tromped through each and every store to discover what's fabulous, functional, frumpy, fancy or frightful in them this season. We tell you what the store and its merchandise are all about and who its target customer is, and we list the address, phone number and opening hours. We've marked those stores that merit special consideration with an asterisk (☆), and occasionally we have something sweet (or not so sweet) to say about the staff's helpfulness or attitude. Please let us know if you disagree.

And to make your life even simpler we have included two separate indexes grouping the stores both by category and by location. Shopping has never been easier! In addition, you'll find the best addresses for beauty treatments, fitness studios, day spas, couture dry cleaners, shoe repair shops, specialty stores (for beads, ribbons, etc) and much else.

Life is not all shopping, of course, so you will also find a list of in-store restaurants and other delightful lunch spots. It's an eclectic list, chosen by our experts for your fun and convenience.

So rev up your credit card and get going, and make sure to keep *W2W* in your handbag, briefcase or backpack.

—Jill Fairchild & Gerri Gallagher

Jill Fairchild Melhado , daughter of fashion world legend and *W* magazine founder John Fairchild, worked as an intern at *Glamour* magazine, *GQ* and *Vogue*. Ms Fairchild has also worked for Ailes Communications, a television production company, and in the late Eighties she founded and ran her own accessories company.

Gerri Gallagher is a Condé Nast editor who has lived in Europe for 15 years. She was the managing editor of Fairchild Publication's *W Europe* from 1990 to 1993 and is currently associate editor of *Tatler* magazine in London.

Julie Craik , *Where to Wear* partner and director of sales, marketing and distribution has worked in publishing for 20 years. Before joining *W2W*, she was associate publisher of *Tatler* magazine and had previously worked for the National Magazine Company.

Clothing & Shoe Size Equivalents

Children's Clothing

American	3	4	5	6	6X
Continental	98	104	110	116	122
British	18	20	22	24	26

Children's Shoes

American	8	9	10	11	12	12	1	2	3
Continental	24	25	27	28	29	30	32	33	34
British	7	8	9	10	11	12	13	1	2

Ladies' Coats, Dresses, Skirts

American	3	5	7	9	11	12	13	14	15
Continental	36	38	38	40	40	42	42	44	44
British	8	10	11	12	13	14	15	16	17

Ladies' Blouses and Sweaters

American	10	12	14	16	18	20
Continental	38	40	42	44	46	48
British	32	34	36	38	40	42

Ladies' Hosiery

American	8	8.5	9	9.5	10	10.5
Continental	1	2	3	4	5	6
British	8	8.5	9	9.5	10	10.5

Ladies' Shoes

American	5	6	7	8	9	10
Continental	36	37	38	39	40	41
British	3.5	4.5	5.5	6.5	7.5	8.5

Men's Suits

American	34	36	38	40	42	44	46	48
Continental	44	46	48	50	52	54	56	58
British	34	36	38	40	42	44	46	48

Men's Shirts

American	14	15	15.5	16	16.5	17	17.5	18
Continental	37	38	39	41	42	43	44	45
British	14	15	15.5	16	16	17	17.5	18

Men's Shoes

American	7	8	9	10	11	12	13
Continental	39.5	41	42	43	44.5	46	47
British	6	7	8	9	10	11	12

Italy Map

MILAN

Verona Venice

Parma

Genoa Modena Ferrara

Bologna

N
W   E
S

FLORENCE Rimini

Ancona

Livorno

Sienna

Tuscany

Perugia

Umbria

Orvieto Terni

Lazio

ROME

Latina

KEY

Shopping areas

Places of interest

Parks (rural areas)

Hospitals

Churches

Villa
Borghese

City Center

PAGES 74–75 PAGE 76

PAGE 77

The
Vatican

ROME

The
Colosseum

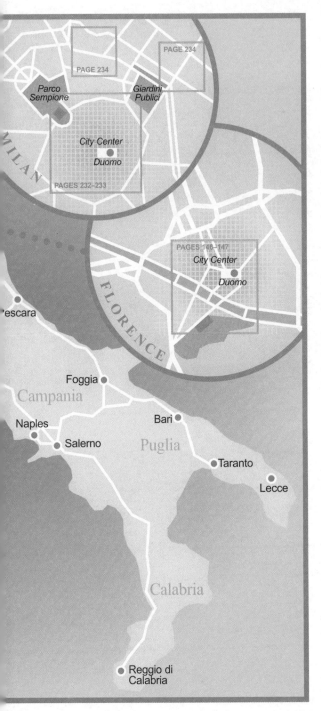

PAGE 234

PAGE 234

Parco
Sempione

Giardini
Publici

MILAN

City Center

Duomo

PAGES 232-233

PAGES 146-147

City Center

Duomo

FLORENCE

escara

Foggia

Campania

Naples

Bari

Salerno

Puglia

Taranto

Lecce

Calabria

Reggio di
Calabria

Where to Wear Rome 2004

Best Picks

In-Store Restaurant

Restaurants

Rome Best Picks

Abiti Usati
Alberta Ferretti
Arli Cashmere
Arsenale

AVC by Adriana Campanile
Barilla
Battistoni
Belsania 19

Bottega Veneta
Brioni
Brugnoli
Camiceria Albertelli

Corner
Costume National
Dalco
De Clerq e De Clerq

Degli Effetti
Edo City
Emanuel Ungaro
Etro

Fendi
Fratelli Vigano
Galassia
Gallo

Gucci
Il Portone
Josephine de Huertas

Josephine de Huertas & Co
Kristini Ti
Laltramoda
La Perla

Le 3 C
Le Gallinelle
Loro Piana
Luna & L'Altra

Mada
Marina Rinaldi
MaxMara
Narciso Rodriguez

Nia
Nia & Co
Nicol Caramel
Nuyorica

Omero & Cecilia-
   Vestiti Usati
Passion
Prada

Prada Sport
Puma Store
Saddlers Union
SBU

Tad
Thé Verde
Valentino Boutique

Rome In-Store Restaurant

Tad   **06-3269 5123**
Via del Babuino 155a

Rome Restaurants

PIAZZA DI SPAGNA AREA

Café Romano   **06-6998 1500**
Via Borgognona 4b
Italian, seemingly always open

Dolci & Doni   **06-6992 5001**
Via delle Carrozze 85b
international, snack bar

Fiaschetteria Beltramme   **(no telephone)**
Via della Croce 39
wine bar

Gran Caffé la Caffetteria   06-321 3344
Via Magutta 61
Italian, a huge theatrical place

Gusto   06-322 6273
Piazza Augusto Imperatore 9
international, pizzeria

Hamasei   06-679 2134
Via della Mercede 35-36
Japanese

Il Bolognese   06-361 1426
Piazza del Popolo 1-2
Italian (Marcello Mastroianni's favorite, and ours; ask for Signor Tomaselli, the owner)

L'Enoteca Antica di Via della Croce   06-679 0896
Via della Croce 76b
wine bar

Le Pain Quotidien   06-6880 7727
Via Tomacelli 24-25
salads

Margutta Vegetariano   06-3265 0577
Via Margutta 118
vegetarian

Naturist Club   06-679 2509
Via della Vite 14
vegetarian

Nino   06-679 5676
Via Borgognona 11
Italian

Rokko   06-488 1214
Via Rasella 138
Japanese

Settimio all'Arancio   06-687 6119
Via dell'Arancio 50
Italian

Shaki   06-679 1694
Via Mario de' Fiori 29a
salads, wine bar

Vini e Buffet   06-687 1445
Piazza della Torretta 60
salads, wine bar

PANTHEON AREA

La Rosetta   06-686 1002
Via della Rosetta 8
fish

Maccheroni   06-6830 7895
Piazza delle Coppelle 44
Italian

Quinzi & Gabrieli   06-687 9389
Via delle Coppelle 5-6
fish

CAMPO DE' FIORI AREA

Al Galletto   06-686 1714/686 5498
Piazza Farnese 102
Italian

Al Sampietrino   06-6880 2474
Piazza Campo de' Fiori 48
soups, salads

Ditirambo   06-687 1626
Piazza della Cancelleria 74-75
Italian

Grappolo d'Oro   06-689 7080
Piazza della Cancelleria 80
Italian

L'Insalata Ricca   06-6880 3656
Largo dei Chiavari 85-86
salads

Monserrato   06-6880 4095
Via Monserrato 96
fish

Pierluigi   06-686 8717 / 686 1302
Piazza dei Ricci 144
Italian

PIAZZA NAVONA AREA

Antico Caffé della Pace   06-686 1216
Via della Pace 3-7
coffee bar

Cul de Sac   06-6880 1094
Piazza Pasquino 73
Italian

Da Francesco   06-686 4009
Piazza del Fico 29
pizzeria

L'Insalata Ricca   06-6830 7881
Piazza Pasquino 72
salads

Santa Lucia   06-6880 2427
Largo Febo 12
Italian

VIA NAZIONALE AREA

Fish   06-4782 4962
Via dei Serpenti 16
international seafood house

Hasekura   06-483 648
Via dei Serpenti 27
Japanese

Valentino   06-488 0643
Via del Boschetto 37
Italian

PARIOLI

La Scala   06-808 4463
Viale Parioli 79d
Italian

TRASTEVERE

Trattoria da Augusto   06-580 3798
Piazza de' Renzi 15
Italian

Rome Store Directory

Newcomers to Italy's proudest cities may be amazed to discover that many stores close during the lunch hour, and in some cases the "hour" is in practice two or two and a half hours. Don't despair, they will re-open! It's just that having invented one of the world's greatest cuisines, they see no reason why they shouldn't enjoy it. Our advice is to join them, and for each of the cities in this book we have provided a select list of restaurants, sidewalk cafés, salad bars, pizzerias etcetera, ideal for your shopping excursions.

We have also listed the opening hours for each store, though these may vary considerably; to avoid frustration, we recommend checking by telephone if in doubt. And finally, while Italian fashion and Italian clothing stores are among the most stylish in the world, you may be disappointed if you plan your shopping in August. The Italians have a special relationship with August (which is often fiendishly hot), and are happy to forsake retail in favor of the beach. To the regular astonishment of workaholic Protestant-ethic northern Europeans and Americans, many Italian stores happily close for weeks—yes, weeks!—at a time. It's a Mediterranean thing…

☆ Abiti Usati

Don't be deceived by the somewhat dishevelled appearance of this musty cave-like shop. Buried in the heaps of merchandise piled along the walls are real treasures such as Seventies Burberry coats, pastel-colored Lacoste polo shirts, cashmere jumpers by Braeman or Ballantyne, Hermès ties, Celine silk scarves and Levi's jeans that would have Japanese collectors frothing at the mouth. Not to mention snakeskin cowboy boots, leather biker jackets, and the occasional original Gucci or Louis Vuitton bag, all at amazingly affordable prices. If overwhelmed by such abundance, ask owner Michele Salvatore for advice…he's a real expert on the ever-changing subject of vintage cool.

Piazza Navona area

Via del Governo Vecchio 35   **06-6830 7105**
00186 Rome   Mon-Sat 10-8

Age d'Or (clothes)

Dedicated to dressing children from 0 to 12 years, and very elegant. See the knitted ribbed-cotton sweater with matching diaper cover (coprifasce) for newborns, overalls from well-known brands such as Pappa e Ciccia and Petit Bateau, and refined cardigans and sweaters in wool or cotton from Paula. Also find stretch jumpsuits, dresses, shirts, pants, Husky-type jackets from Il Gufo (quilted microfiber in colors such as pink, green and blue)—all for the discriminating mother who wants the most elegant clothes for her children. You can have special outfits made to measure for boys and girls for weddings (pages and flower girls), baptisms and first communions. Since the shop is in a residential area not usually frequented by tourists, most of the clients are upper-class and very picky.

Parioli

Via Nino Oxilia 6-8   **06-807 6840**
00197 Rome   Mon 4-8, Tues-Sat 9:30-1, 4-8

Age d'Or (shoes)

Children will feel right at home here, with a gingerbread house and goldfish swimming in his bowl in the window, clouds painted all over a sky-blue ceiling, stepping-stones that wind to an arch surrounded by a trompe l'oeil house and trees leading to the stock. The most adorable shoes for infants to size 38 are displayed: party shoes, Mary Jane slippers with soft suede soles, tiny trainers, jelly sandals for splashing among the rocks at the beach as well as spiffy daytime shoes. Just for fun there are a few small Converse T-shirts and jackets.

Parioli

Viale Parioli 37   **06-807 9621**
00197 Rome   Mon 4-8, Tues-Sat 9-1, 4-8

☆ Alberta Ferretti

Follow Nicole Kidman's lead and head to Ferretti when in search of femininity-boosting clothes. Her ethereal creations would transform even a Sumo wrestler into the most delicate porcelain doll. Silk chiffon dresses have the consistency of petals, flowery see-through camisoles look like they could be blown away by a mild breeze, and pretty puffed sleeves, cute ruching and sweet embroidery are everywhere…on slim coats, delicate sleeveless knits, microcardigans or even silk evening bags and featherweight sandals. Fabrics are made to caress the skin: silk, silk velour, cashmere, soft wool, suede and leather. Colors are subtle, like dusty pink, duck-egg blue or blush beige. This immaculate store has a hushed quality, as if loud sounds could shatter the clothes. www.aeffe.com

Piazza di Spagna area

Via Condotti 34	**06-699 1160/679 7728**
00187 Rome	Mon 2:30-7, Tues-Thurs 10-7
	Fri-Sat 10-7:30, Sun 11-1:30, 3-7

Alexander

Classy attention-grabbers of the female gender get the tools of their trade here, clothes that are sexy without being garish. Lacy or ribbed tops, lace-up bustiers and cotton jersey bodies or stretchy denim skirts and trousers are all by the French company Anti-Flirt, which despite its name is very flirty indeed. The store's own range of stretch faux leather, made of fitted vests, sleeveless shirts, zipped jackets or miniskirts in colors that go from deep aubergine or chocolate brown to silver gray and powder pink, has the peculiarity of changing color once on the body. And Sylvie Schimmel's distressed leather and shearling coats are perfect examples of seductive hippy-chic style.

Piazza di Spagna area

Piazza di Spagna 49	**06-679 1351**
00186 Rome	Mon 2-7:30, Tues-Sat 9:30-7:30

Angelo di Nepi

Black might be back, but Angelo di Nepi doesn't think so. This Roman designer likes his colors, and with a vengeance: his stores resemble the brightest of rainbows, with red, orange, turquoise, emerald green or shocking pinks screaming from silk taffeta shirts, tweed jackets and coats, little beaded tops, long skirts or scarves. This year, designs express an African mood and a contagious joie de vivre. Great to shake off the blues on a cold rainy day. www.angelodinepi.com

Campo de' Fiori area

Via dei Giubbonari 28	**06-689 3006**
00186 Rome	Mon 12:30-8, Tues-Sat 9:30-8

Piazza di Spagna area

Via Frattina 2	**06-678 6568**
00187 Rome	(opening times as above)

Via Cola di Rienzo area

Via Cola di Rienzo 267a	**06-322 4800**
00192 Rome	(opening times as above)

9

☆ Arli Cashmere

A treasure trove for cashmere lovers, Zoran style, hides behind a glass door in an anonymous building. This former auto repair shop has been transformed into a large modern space with a very high ceiling. Glass tables and shelves hold cashmere sweaters stacked neatly, illuminated by large modern aluminum lamps hung from the ceiling. There are cashmere jumpsuits or pajama-like tops and bottoms, sweaters, polos, skirts, turtlenecks, capes…all in the yummiest colors. Everything has a comfortable chic look. Sabrina, who is usually on hand for advice, does the design. Four workers in the back produce the garments with their knitting machines while you watch. The little jumpsuits for infants are irresistible. You can order any style in any color and size; the wait is from three to five weeks but it's well worth it, as is the 10 euro taxi fare from Piazza di Spagna.

Parioli

Via Giorgio Vasari 10	**06-3600 4107**
00196 Rome	Mon-Sat 8:30-7:30
	(Sat 8:30-12:30 in summer)

Armani Jeans

Everybody, from politicians to Sophia, came to toast Giorgio at his megastore's opening in July 2002, confirming that whatever the Master does, even just jeans, causes great expectations. The high-ceilinged space is neat and straightforward like his designs, and hosts the Armani jeans collections both for him and for her. Casual/play styles include thick ribbed sweaters, leather jackets, corduroy shirts, cotton tees and tweed coats; and, of course, piles of those metal-eagled jeans in all shades, shapes and washes.

Piazza di Spagna area

Via Tomacelli 137	**06-6819 3040**
00187 Rome	Mon 3-7:30, Tues-Sat 10-7:30, Sun 2:30-7
Via del Babuino 70a	**06-3600 1848**
00187 Rome	(opening times as above)

☆ Arsenale

Opened 10 years ago by Roman designer Patrizia Pieroni, Arsenale was very avant-garde at the time, specializing in ethnic-chic and furnished in New York loft style. New York magazine editors love the place. The atmosphere is that of an atelier, where saleswomen offer you their wares, and the clothes look best on size 10 and under. Signora Pieroni is the best advertisement for her own creations and is always on hand to offer advice if requested. She was one of the first to carry Robert Clergerie's shoes and she has a gift for helping you put together your own individual look, combining things that don't seem to work together but look great because most are in dark, ultra-sophisticated, recherché fabrics. You'll see a client enter wearing the über-classic look, and leave in a rather outrageous but utterly flattering outfit that Signora Pieroni has created, often much to the client's surprise. For her favorite clients, she will pull out vintage pieces from the back of the store that she loves but will let you buy if you really swoon for them.

Piazza Navona area

Via del Governo Vecchio 64	**06-686 1380**
00186 Rome	Mon 3:30-7:30, Tues-Sat 10-7:30

☆ AVC by Adriana Campanile

Adriana Campanile's children's shop is small, painted a cheerful yellow with wood paneling. The assortment of shoe styles and sizes is ample, from newborn to size 38, say 10-12 years old. Adriana Campanile stocks everything from classic British-type suede sandals with tiny cut-outs in the front and straps around the back to moccasins, pastel metallic mules, ballerinas and Mary Janes, in every pretty color you can imagine. There are some sport shoes, belts, hats and swimsuits.

Piazza di Spagna area

Via Vittoria 18	**06-361 3691**
00187 Rome	Daily 10-1:30, 3:30-7

☆ AVC by Adriana Campanile

The walk-in shop window holds an enormous selection of shoes, from ballet shoes to high and low boots, from walking shoes to sandals, from Chanel slingbacks to evening shoes. Adriana Campanile designs and produces her own range, recreating classic and trendy styles from all over the world with her own twist. Heels go from flat to nine centimeters (three and a half inches) and the shoes come in a variety of colors and leathers, plus some other fabrics. Prices start at 80 euros and are mostly around 100—and it's not easy to find such a variety at that price. Campanile started with a small shop in Parioli…now she's right smack in the middle of Rome's golden triangle for luxe shopping.

Piazza di Spagna area

Piazza di Spagna 88	**06-6992 2355**
00187 Rome	Mon-3:30-7:30, Tues-Sat 10:30-7:30
	Sun 10:30-2:30, 3:30-7:30

Bagheera

Bagheera is one of the glitzy Pariolines' strongholds—Pariolines are female residents of this exclusive neighborhood, Parioli—where they replenish their insatiable wardrobes with million-dollar looks. Seductive brands include Miu Miu, Alessandro Dell'Acqua, Plein Sud and Chloé. But the real catch is young designer Francesca Jori's (daughter of the store's owner) Jorando line, a boho-chic feminine collection with hints of Chloé and Voyage. The fresh minidresses, cropped tops, or tie-dyed T-shirts are made from Italian fabrics and embellished by hand in Asia with embroidery, sequins, Swarovski crystals and ribbons; silk slippers come decorated with intricate beading. A small bucket bag, in two shades of pink woven leather, is modelled on Indonesian women's shopping baskets. Deliciously exotic.

Parioli

Via G.Antonelli 26　　　　　　　　　　**06-807 4401**
00197 Rome　　　　Mon 4-8, Tues-Sat 9:30-1, 4-8

Bagheera Accessori

Following the main store's credo, this smaller boutique gathers shoes and accessories from hip international designers. Whether you're after René Caovilla's super-glam evening styles, Miu Miu's cheeky pumps or the girlish round pointed boots and court shoes by Marc Jacobs, this pastel shop has it all. Other styles include Rodolphe Menudier's pointy denim shoes, Antonio Berardi's amazing slave-chic suede sandals and boots, and O L'Autre Chose military-green fabric boots and camouflage mules.

Parioli

Piazza Euclide 30　　　　　　　　　　**06-807 0046**
00197 Rome　　　　　　　　　　Mon-Sat 9-1, 4-8

Bally

Imagine the nerd at school, turning out years later to be a stunner. This Swiss company, under the creative direction of Scott Fellows, has undergone a similar transformation and the prestigious location in Via Condotti, amongst the heavyweights of fashion, is here to prove it. Gone are the amorphous bland shapes of the past, replaced by modern adventurous lines and bold colors like apple-green or orange, on everything from shoulder bags to loafers, sport shoes to leather jackets. What next? Birkenstock-mania?　　　　　　　　　　www.bally.com

Piazza di Spagna area

Via Condotti 38-40　　　　　　　　　　**06-699 0236**
00187 Rome　　　　　　　　　　Daily 10-7 (Sun 2-7)

Banchetti Sport

For those who like themselves classic, even when it comes to sports, this old Roman store is the obvious choice. If we are talking skiing, tennis, camping or aerobics Banchetti's gear is traditional and reliable, like an old Swiss watch. Ski jackets are from ultra-stylish French brand Moncler, a cult name on the jet-setty slopes, and tennis gear is by Italian label Sergio Tacchini. Bathing suits? By Speedo of course, and also by Colmar. When it comes to sport shoes, Superga, those ultra-flat canvas shoes so loved by chic ladies worldwide, are the first choice. Another fixed feature? The evergreen Lacoste polo shirt in all its rainbow of colors and in men's, women's and children's sizes.

Pantheon area

Via Campo Marzio 38　　　　　　　　　　**06-687 1420**
00186 Rome　　Mon 3:30-7:30, Tues-Sat 9:30-1, 3:30-7:30

Barbara Gregori

A neighborhood boutique that caters to a very specific clientele of Roman matrons who want to look chic but not like fashion victims. Some of the designers sold here are

Maska, Hilton, Allegri (wonderful raincoats and jackets) and Federico for pants. The look is mostly classic, in beige, cream or black and mostly Italian names. The decor is unadorned—white walls, parquet floors, light-colored wooden cabinets and shelves. Complete your look with beautiful accessories with a slight ethnic look.

Piazza di Spagna area

Via Vittoria 57a   **06-322 1818**
00187 Rome   Mon 3:30-7:30, Tues-Sat 9:30-7:30

☆ **Barilla**

Just down from Rocco Forte's Hotel de Russie on Via del Babuino, now Rome's trendiest street, is one of the few stores in Rome selling fashionable shoes under 100 euros. In the Eighties Barilla produced shoes for the high fashion collections, as well as very expensive shoes made to measure—they were famous for their Chanel slings in many combinations of colors. This shop was opened for their own less expensive line, though they also carry other brands such as Lumberjack and Stone Heaven. The tourist who wants an inexpensive sandal (29 euros), the executive secretary who follows the trends, the fashionista watching her budget…all are catered for here. The staff allow you to browse without breathing down your neck, but are most helpful when asked. Ask for Alessandra or Melina.

Piazza di Spagna area

Via del Babuino 33a   **06-3600 1726**
00187 Rome   Mon-Sat 9:30-8, Sun 10-7:30

☆ **Battistoni**

Get a whiff of old-world chic in these classy boutiques gathered around a magnificent courtyard. Battistoni has been a famous tailor for many decades, as his clients' address book, a Who's Who of celebrities, can testify. Instead of the standard black-clad shop assistants, sophisticated, elegant ladies greet you at the door of the woman's boutique, a breezy teak-lined affair with very high ceilings. Distinguished gentlemen stand behind the desks in the historic men's store, where rare works of art hang on the walls and antiques are used as furniture. Their pride and joy? Impeccable custom-made suits, for both men and women. But there is also ready-to-wear of the highest quality, made of silk and cashmere knits, suave linen styles, and leather by the best artisans. Men's sportswear, new this year, observes this same painstaking dedication to quality. The after-service assistance is their pride, with in-house tailors often altering garments deep into the night.

Piazza di Spagna area

Via Condotti 60-61a   **06-697 6111**
00187 Rome   Mon 3-7, Tues-Sat 10-7

BBC

This upper-crust designer emporium dispenses trendy looks to the yuppie-chic crowd of this highly residential area. Boys can toy with vintage James Deanish Levi's jackets and jeans, Paul Smith knits and the store's own line of high quality T-shirts, ordinary shirts and suits. Girls can go crazy on Paul Smith lines, Vanessa Bruno's tees, Hervé Chapelier's famous nylon bags in camouflage or leopard print and Robert Clergerie shoes. Look also for groovy sneakers, Acqua di Parma cologne and bath products, and a selection of exotic objects for the home.

Parioli

Viale Parioli 122   **06-808 3680**
00197 Rome   Mon 3:30-7:30, Tues-Sat 10-2, 3:30-7:30
                                       Sun 10:30-2, 3:7:30

BBC Jeans

This tiny shop, younger brother of the Parioli megastore, is where the same hip clientele get their sporty and casual-chic attire. Think Levi's vintage distressed leather biker jackets, Paul Smith's Pink and Blue lines sweatshirts and minidresses, Vanessa Bruno's ultra-thin cotton tees in various shapes and colors, and funky accessories.

Piazza di Spagna area

Via Vittoria 3a   **06-361 1379**
00187 Rome Sun-Mon 3:30-7:30, Tues-Sat 10-2, 3:30-7:30

☆ Belsiana 19

Classy chaps with a palate for fashion, but an allergy to excess, find in this classic store clothes that are modern, high-quality, but never showy. Exté and Alberto Aspesi suits, for instance, are traditional and contemporary at the same time. Ralph Lauren's buttoned-down cotton shirts or long-sleeved polo shirts are an absolute must for that outdoor-chic look that makes you think of weekends in Maine or Aspen. Paul Smith's jeans or striped shirts are perfect for the careless British look. And Ballantyne's jumpers are like a joker, they go well with everything. There is also a small collection for girls, featuring casuals by Polo Ralph Lauren and DKNY Jeans.   www.belsiana19.com

Piazza di Spagna area

Via Belsiana 94   **06-678 0529/678 5423**
00187 Rome   Sun-Mon 3:30-7:30, Tues-Sat 10-7:30

Benetton

The Treviso company is Italy's undisputed casualwear king. The Benetton family's stores sprout like mushrooms in every possible location, train and underground stations included. Finding someone who hasn't stepped into a Benetton store at least once is like finding an Italian who doesn't drink coffee. The store on Via del Corso houses all the collections, including children's and maternity. If you're looking for a basic item, you'll find it here. But arm yourself with patience…roaming around these vast rooms can be exhausting.   www.benetton.com

Piazza di Spagna area

Via del Corso 423   **06-6810 2534**
00187 Rome   Daily 10-8 (Sun 11-8)

Piazza di Spagna 67-69   **06-675 8241**
00187 Rome   (opening times as above)

Campo de' Fiori area

Corso Vittorio Emanuele II 77-79   **06-6880 3577**
00186 Rome   Sun-Mon 12-7:30, Tues-Sat 9:30-7:30

Via Nazionale area

Via Nazionale 174   **06-679 1555**
00184 Rome   Mon-Sat 10-8, Sun 11-7:30

Via Cola di Rienzo area

Via Cola di Rienzo 197-209   **06-322 7171/320 2802**
00192 Rome   Mon-Sat 10-8, Sun 11-1, 3-7:30

Blunauta

Back in the Seventies when China first opened its trade to Italy, the seven Greco brothers and sisters, well-connected young Romans, ordered garments made there to their specifications in pure cotton, cashmere and silk. The styling is strictly Italian, with flattering fits and attentive detail. Scoop-necked T-shirts that curve in at the waist and are trimmed with tiny buttons appeal to the slender Italian woman. You reach the shop in Piazza di Spagna on an inner courtyard via a passageway from the street. Here are night-gowns and pajamas (mostly in silk), sweaters, blouses, suits and casual eveningwear. Twinsets in cotton or a mix of cotton and silk and in too many colors to count can be worn on any occasion. Embroidered silk wraparound skirts pair with tiny Indian-style raw silk embroidered tops. If the airline loses your luggage, stock up here with everything from sporty daytime clothes to cocktail chic.

Piazza di Spagna area

Piazza di Spagna 35   **06-678 9805**
00187 Rome   Mon-Sat 10-7:30

Cola di Rienzo area

Via Cola di Rienzo 303   **06-3973 7336**
00193 Rome   (opening times as above)

Bonpoint

This place will make you wish you could regress to your tod-dler years and do your own shopping. Why didn't our mothers get us the sublime creations of this Parisian house that caters to all kids, from newborns to 14-year-olds? The clothes displayed on tiny racks in an immaculately elegant boutique with gilded mirrors and crystal chandeliers are good enough to eat: mini tweed coats with velvet collars, tiny silk and linen cardigans in sorbet shades, cute cotton smocked dresses in floral patterns à la Laura Ashley, and supersoft leather loafers. The name is a status symbol in kindergartens all across Europe.

Piazza di Spagna area

Piazza San Lorenzo in Lucina 25　　　　　**06-687 1548**
00186 Rome　　　Mon 3:30-7:30, Tues-Sat 10-2, 3:30-7:30

Borini

It might not look like much from the outside (crumbling walls, graffiti), but this tiny unassuming shop is one of Rome's best kept secrets. Owned by the Borini family since 1940, it features the latest styles in footwear, impeccably executed and at remarkably reasonable prices. Pointed slingbacks, mules, flats, stilettos, over-the-knee or cowboy boots, platform shoes, gladiator sandals, odalisque slippers…they've got them all. No wonder the cubicle space is always crammed with punters fighting for attention. Snap up what you like, sizes disappear at the speed of light.

Campo de' Fiori area

Via dei Pettinari 86-87　　　　　　　**06-687 5670**
00186 Rome　　　　Mon 3:30-7:30, Tues-Sat 9-1, 3:30-7:30

Borsalino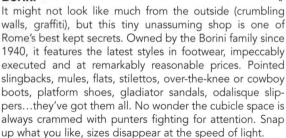

The French even made a movie with Alain Delon in honor of this venerable manufacturer of men's and women's hats. The fedora comes in many variations and colors, and the large assortment of styles includes many classics such as the panama and the pork pie-style cousin of the fedora as worn in his youth by Frank Sinatra. The newsboy's puffed hat with visor comes in a check or plaid. Women with a sense of style will love the straw or felt cloches with amusing trims, and woven straw caps resemble the ones worn by Tatum O'Neal in *Paper Moon*. Ask for Rita.

Piazza di Spagna area

Piazza Fontana di Trevi 83　　　　　　**06-678 1015**
00187 Rome　　　Mon 3:30-8:30, Tues-Sat 9:30-8:30

Piazza del Popolo 20　　　　　　　　**06-3265 0838**
00187 Rome　　　　　　　　　　　　Daily 10-8

Pantheon area

Via Campo Marzio 72a　　　　　　　**06-679 6120**
00186 Rome　　　　　　　　Daily 9:30-1:30, 3-7:30

☆ Bottega Veneta

Mega leather brands beware! Bottega Veneta's ascent to super-cool status seems unstoppable. Since the Gucci group snapped up the 50-year-old northern Italian company and gave its creative direction to Tomas Maier (previously at Hermès) the brand has been flying high. Their first Roman store (500 square metres in a 17th-century convent) has all their trademark products, already modern classics: from the limited edition woven Kabat bag that needs two people's craftsmanship and two days to make, to the fringed Veneta shoulder bag in suede and velvet and the chic new-colonial cotton and leather clutch bag. The glove-soft, king-size alligator bag gives luxury a new meaning.

Piazza di Spagna area

Piazza San Lorenzo in Lucina 7-13   **06-6821 0024**
00186 Rome   Mon 3-7, Tues-Sat 10-7

Boutique Versace

Versace fans won't be disappointed by this majestic, lavish boutique with its marble floors and rococo decor, so in step with the sumptuousness of the clothes and accessories. Donatella has definitely made her own mark with daring, sexy, ultra-feminine designs that transform women into gorgeous new millennium Bond girls. Yellow, fuchsia, luscious leather, bold prints, gold touches, side-splits, vertiginous hemlines…all her key elements can be found here. And those stunning lacy micro-dresses….bet Liz Hurley has already a couple of them hanging in her closet, waiting for the next premiere. Service is extremely nice and friendly, always a big plus.   www.versace.com

Piazza di Spagna area

Via Bocca di Leone 26-27   **06-678 0521**
00187 Rome   Mon-Sat 10-7

Boutique Versace Uomo

Guys might have less to play with (than girls) when it comes to clothes, but not in the world of Versace. Pop into this majestic boutique and you'll see why. Take shirts: they come in see-through lace, audacious prints, and also in pink, turquoise, mauve, yellow, orange, and daring combinations of the above. Talking suits and jackets? Expect them sequined, in damask, and printed leather. Jewelry is chunky and golden, and so are belt buckles. Even knits come with crazy patterns or funky gothic writing. For fearless blokes only.   www.versace.com

Piazza di Spagna area

Via Borgognona 24-25   **06-679 5037**
00187 Rome   Mon-Sat 10-7

Bozart

Some of the most beautiful fantasy costume jewelry in Italy comes from Bozart. The entire collection can be seen at their shop and you'll be hard-pressed to resist buying something. Classic pearls come in many different lengths, with colorful stone clasps. In summer, necklaces with shells and coral or turquoise paste would dress up any bathing suit. There are several different collections, including one made of semi-precious stones such as amethyst, cornelian, rock crystal and aquamarine. Colorful small evening bags have unusual decorations.

Piazza di Spagna area

Via Bocca di Leone 4   **06-678 1026**
00187 Rome   Mon 3:30-7, Tues-Sat 10-7

☆ Brioni

Want to look as if your name is Bond, James Bond? Do as Pierce Brosnan does and get suited at Brioni, at your service since 1945. Browse in the changing-room of their main store and you'll discover that the current 007 is only the latest of a bunch of stars, John Wayne and Clark Gable included, who have ordered their suits here. And we're not talking ordinary suits: classic cuts, attention to detail, use of natural fibers only (for padding) and fabrics like cashmere make them top of their class. Have your measurements taken and you're set for life: they'll send you samples of materials and you can order your suit or jacket from anywhere in the world. Want quick satisfaction? Grab something from their ready-to-wear collection, featuring sport jackets, blazers, shirts, jerseys and, of course, suits.

Piazza di Spagna area

Via Barberini 79   **06-484 517**
00187 Rome   Mon-Sat 10-1:30, 3:30-7:30

Via Condotti 21a   **06-678 3428**
00187 Rome   Mon-Sat 10-7:30

Via Veneto 129   **06-478 22119**
00187 Rome   (opening times as above)

☆ **Brugnoli**

This classic, slightly old-fashioned shoe store carries a large assortment of brands as well as their own line. Men will find Allen Edmonds, Edward Green, Church's, Alden, Trekkers and Crocket Jones. For women there are Car Shoes, Pura Lopez, Pedro Garcia, and Claudio Orciani. For both men and women, Sabelt (high-top Formula 1 drivers shoes) and Merrell are available, also Stewart leather jackets and Moncler rainproof jackets. The owners are extremely helpful—when we say old-fashioned we include the concept of service. Ask for Luigi.

Parioli

Viale Parioli 108 (men only)   **06-807 0751**
00197 Rome   Mon 3:30-7:30, Tues-Sat 10-7:30

Piazza di Spagna area

Via del Babuino 57   **06-3600 1889**
00187 Rome   Mon 3:30-7:30, Tues-Sat 10-7:30
                                     Sun 2:30-7:30

Bruno Magli

This Bologna-based family company was recently bought by the Opera group dominated by Bulgari, and the new owners have created a new logo and a new look with a red, white and gray motif. The Via Condotti store opened last May, near the Spanish Steps and sandwiched between Dior and Bulgari. The decor is spare, with cream-colored marble floors covered here and there with beige rugs, wood paneling on the walls and leather chairs in the shoe department. Shoes dominate, of course—people still talk of O.J.Simpson's Bruno Maglis—but there are leather garments as well, mostly coats and jackets. The styles are innovative and great care is taken over quality; the stock is still made in Magli's factories.

Piazza di Spagna area

Via Condotti 6-6a **06-6920 2264**
00187 Rome Mon 3-7, Tues-Sat 10-7

Cambalache

With the collapse, in fashion, of geographical borders, European capitals are filled with what look like Indian dervishes (probably a bunch of Parisian duchesses), Romanian gypsies (some London It-girls?) or Peruvian shepherds (possibly employees of the bank around the corner). Rome is no exception, as this petite store testifies. Brainy girls-who-shop and models get basic items here at unbelievably friendly prices, and create east-meets-west looks that are exclusive and original. Find anything from thin cotton Indian tunics and delicate embroidered silk slippers to simple raffia and coconut-shell sandals (from Thailand) and cropped silk Jaipur-inspired tops in silver and gold patterns. A fixed feature? The slouchy bag in fabrics that range from sari material to alpaca wool.

Campo de' Fiori area

Via dei Chiavari 30 **06-686 8541**
00187 Rome Mon-Sat 11-8

☆ Camiceria Albertelli

How can you go wrong if you have your shirts made by the man who personally tailors Valentino? Piero Albertelli is the heir to a dynasty of shirtmakers who have, at different times, served everybody from Diana Vreeland to Catherine Deneuve, from Henry Fonda and Kirk Douglas to Robert De Niro. The fabrics, from high-quality Italian brands like Tenenti Riva, Albini and Ortolina, are first cut to measure, then washed to test eventual shrinking, and finally fitted on the customer at two different times to guarantee an impeccable and lasting fit. Orders can be shipped everywhere around the globe.

Pantheon area

Via dei Prefetti 11 **06-687 3793**
00186 Rome Mon 3:30-7:30, Tues-Sat 9:30-1:30, 3:30-7:30

Carla G.

This immaculate sliver of a store showcases Bolognese designer Carla G's simple and wearable essentials, in a basic color palette with occasional concessions to red, pink or light blue. Cuts are body-skimming and at times Pradaesque, as in the lean jackets and coats or the pantsuits in neutrals. Find also blouses (currently ethnic), wool and cotton jerseys, leather jackets, shoes and accessories. Ideal for uptown girls on a budget.

Piazza di Spagna area

Via del Gambero 24 **06-679 1210**
00187 Rome Mon 3:30-7:30, Tues-Sat 10-8

Via del Babuino 121 **06-679 3158**
00187 Rome Sun-Mon 3:30-7:30, Tues-Sat 10:30-7:30

Via Cola di Rienzo area

Via Cola di Rienzo 134   **06-324 3511**
00192 Rome   Mon 3:30-7:30, Tues-Sat 9:30-7:30

Carpisa   ♂ ♀

For the young at heart (and in pocketbook) this cheery shop is part of a Neopolitan chain with stores all over Italy and a turtle for a logo. Their bags and small leather accessories come in pretty colors with decorative appliqués or tiny beads or rhinestones that spell fashion at a decent price. Leather wallets cost from 18 to 25 euros, in canvas from 11 to 15; smart nylon body bags in black and beige are 16 euros, money belts 6. Carpisa offers some of the best value for money in Rome.

Piazza di Spagna area

Via Belsiana 59   **06-678 6101**
00187 Rome   Sun 1-7:30, Mon 2-7:30, Tues-Sat 10-7:30

Celine   ♀

Yet another example of a successful makeover. Resuscitated from oblivion, thanks to Michael Kors's magic touch, the French company Celine has become so hot that international high-maintenance babes, Gwyneth Paltrow included, can't live without it. Sporty-chic items, like the ski-style striped-sleeve turtleneck and the ubiquitous leather Boogie bag, have become must-haves. Current pièces de résistance include inverted pleated trousers, gold-accented exotic tops, low-slung cropped boleros and those mattress-thick cashmeres that will make you wish you'd won the lottery. Start saving now.   www.celine.com

Piazza di Spagna area

Via Condotti 20a   **06-678 7586**
00187 Rome   Mon-Sat 10-7

Cesare Paciotti   ♂ ♀

If shoes could kill, Paciotti's would do it instantly, no blood spilled, as these styles are seriously, scorchingly hot. Points tend to be extremely long, to resemble the dagger that is the brand's symbol; heels are slim and skyscraper high. Wear them and you'll at once feel sexier, taller and bolder; you will also discover your inner acrobat, as strutting at these heights requires considerable agility and balance. The highlights of the fall season? An Andy Warhol-inspired collection with Paciotti's face shining out from a number of patent-leather styles. See it to believe it.   www.cesare-paciotti.com

Piazza di Spagna area

Via Bocca di Leone 92   **06-679 6245**
00187 Rome   Mon 3-7, Tues-Sat 10-7

Chanel   ♀

Chanel boutiques worldwide are approached with a certain kind of reverence. After all, these are the temples of that certain je ne sais quoi, Coco's special flair that never loses its appeal. Take the Chanel jacket, that looks good even on ripped jeans and has been a passport to jet-set chic for decades. Or the black patent-leather gilt chain bag, still carried by ladies-who-lunch around the globe. The Roman boutique has it all, plus an enchanting view of an exotic courtyard with a palm tree.   www.chanel.com

Piazza di Spagna area

Via del Babuino 98-101   **06-692 070**
00187 Rome   Daily 10-7

Christian Dior

Get a fix of that punk-rock-chic Dior's designer John Galliano does so well. The clothes and other gear speak of endless glam nights and a universe where early wake-up calls are a no-no. The location is hyper-strategic, in pole position on über-fashion street Via Condotti, facing Prada and ahead of Gucci and with windows framing the stunning view of the Spanish Steps. Styles are glittery and opulent, with lots of unusually woven fur, laced-up leather and a mood that goes from Russian princess to Peruvian babe. Patchwork leather pants are a staple, as well as shoes with studded leather straps, and of course the saddle bag which comes in all sizes and materials from croc to denim. New this season are corset dresses and zipped tank tops, and even an extended line for kids. Isn't that a frightening thought?

Piazza di Spagna area

Piazza di Spagna 73-75   **06-6992 4489**
00187 Rome   Daily 10-7 (Sun 1-7)

Cisalfa

Nothing much compared to some giant sport stores abroad, but as good as it gets here in Rome. This three-story shop is totally devoted to casuals and sports equipment. The ground floor boasts an array of casualwear from Lacoste to Henry Cotton, Lee, Levi's and Colmar. The basement has a selection of sneakers by Puma, Adidas and Converse; tracksuits by Freddy and Champions; and bathing suits, tennis gear and rollerblades. The third floor, adorned with pictures of the greatest soccer stars, is devoted entirely to Nike products and soccer gear.

Piazza di Spagna area

Via del Corso 475   **06-3265 1519**
00186 Rome   Mon 4:15-8, Tues-Sat 10-8
                                            Sun 11-1:30, 3:30-8

Coin

This is a rare specimen of the department store, a breed that is not yet proliferating in Rome. Despite being one of the biggest and best, it won't take your breath away. It has just two floors (plus basement) and no hyper-exciting merchandise to speak of. But a few cool labels can still be found. On the ground floor, in cosmetics, look out for Make-up Forever and MAC's line, whose basics are already classics. In casualwear, dig out funky little things by Dolce & Gabbana's diffusion line "&", and Ralph Lauren's Polo Jeans cute cotton sweaters and shirts. In the basement, besides a supermarket, there is a Moda Bambini (kids' fashion) section, where you can finally let the younger generation loose.   www.coin.it

Via Cola di Rienzo area

Via Cola di Rienzo 173   **06-3600 4298**
00192 Rome   Daily 9:30-8 (Sun 10:30-8)

☆ Corner

Have you ever dreamed of clothes that are clean-cut, simple, classic, and right for every scene, from office to street to cocktail party? Milanese designer Alberto Aspesi, with a cult following in Italy, is the answer to your prayers, and this shop stores all his seven lines. His bestsellers are tweed, plain wool or velvet coats and jackets, cut close to the body to create an elongated silhouette; down sport jackets pretty enough to become city gear; and super-light waterproof nylon jackets, ideal in winter when riding the ubiquitous motorino (scooter), Rome's favorite accessory.

Piazza di Spagna area

Via Belsiana 97   **06-679 5020**
00187 Rome   Mon 12-7:30, Tues-Sat 10-7:30

☆ Costume National

Gutsy modern city chicks love this brand's graphic clothes, which have attitude and a touch of eccentricity. Sleek tailored jackets, masculine trousers, pencil skirts and sharp suits come with a lot of seaming and detail and in neutrals like black, brown, beige, tan and white. Leather jackets and coats are lean and fitted and patent-leather shoes and boots essentially designed in extreme shapes, very round or very pointed. The highlight of this season is the ultra-sexy, richly patterned silk off-the-shoulder dress, very Cannes.   www.costumenational.com

Piazza di Spagna area

Via del Babuino 106   **06-6920 0686**
00187 Rome   Mon 3:30-7:30, Tues-Sat 10-7:30

☆ Dalco

Back in the Sixties they made all the shoes for Valentino's high fashion shows, and you couldn't find anything like them anywhere else in Italy. Ordinary folks could buy the shoes (at a price) at their shop on Via di Porta Pinciana. Then in 1987 Nives Dalco moved her shop to Via Vittoria in the golden triangle. The shop is small but very refined, with unique models in the window and nothing under 400 euros. This is one of those rare places where an artisan wearing a white smock comes downstairs to take measurements of your foot—the experience alone is worth the price if you've

Rome Directory

never indulged before in the luxury of made to order. Spiritual relatives of Imelda Marcos will feel they've died and gone to heaven here. Ask for Signora Dalco herself or her daughter Silvia.

Piazza di Spagna area

Via Vittoria 65   **06-6994 0682**
00187 Rome   Mon 3:30-7:30, Tues-Sat 10-7

Dancing Duck

If you cried while watching *Save the Last Dance*, chances are you'll adore this ministore full of all things dancy. Join a constant stream of Julia Styles wannabes in search of cult items such as Dimensione Danza's low-waisted sweatpants (with logo'd waistband), for which there is a long waiting list. And check out Dancing Duck's own line of leggings, bras and leotards in stretchy Lycra wool and cotton. They also offer an in-house design service, irresistible to the true dance fanatic.

Piazza di Spagna area

Via Belsiana 96b/c   **06-679 4378**
00187 Rome   Mon 3:30-7:30, Tues-Sat 10-7:30

D&G

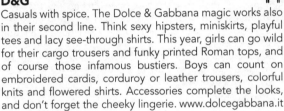

Casuals with spice. The Dolce & Gabbana magic works also in their second line. Think sexy hipsters, miniskirts, playful tees and lacy see-through shirts. This year, girls can go wild for their cargo trousers and funky printed Roman tops, and of course those infamous bustiers. Boys can count on embroidered cardis, corduroy or leather trousers, colorful knits and flowered shirts. Accessories complete the looks, and don't forget the cheeky lingerie. www.dolcegabbana.it

Piazza di Spagna area

Piazza di Spagna 93   **06-6938 0870**
00187 Rome   Daily 10-7:30 (Sun 11-7:30)

Davide Cenci

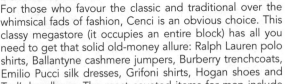

For those who favour the classic and traditional over the whimsical fads of fashion, Cenci is an obvious choice. This classy megastore (it occupies an entire block) has all you need to get that solid old-money allure: Ralph Lauren polo shirts, Ballantyne cashmere jumpers, Burberry trenchcoats, Emilio Pucci silk dresses, Grifoni shirts, Hogan shoes and Tod's handbags. The most coveted items for men include Brooks Brothers shirts, Church's shoes, Aquascutum coats and Cenci's own classy suits, shirts, shoes and ties, all strictly made in Italy.

Pantheon area

Via Campo Marzio 1-7   **06-699 0681**
00186 Rome   Mon 3:30-7:30
     Tues-Fri 9:30-1:30, 3:30-7:30, Sat 10-8

☆ De Clerq e De Clerq

Diane and Evelyn De Clerq are famous for the variety of colorful stripes in their handcrafted knitwear in cotton, cashmere, cashmere/silk and linen. This is the Prada of knitwear—just one item, even a small scarf, is enough to mark you as an elegant woman. The clothes are cut close to the body…imagine a Parisian wearing De Clerq and riding her bicycle in St. Germain to display her metropolitan sporty look. There is nothing under 200 euros and not much on display except what's in the window—almost everything is kept in drawers. The owners are helpful but a bit snobbish, secure in their success. Ask for Veronique or Diane on Saturdays.

Piazza di Spagna area

Via del Carozze 50   **06-679 0988**
00186 Rome   Mon 3:30-7:30, Tues-Sat 10-7:30

☆ Degli Effetti

Retailer Massimo Degli Effetti, a veritable pioneer in the Roman fashion scene, opened his first (men's) shop in 1981, introducing designers such as Gaultier, Comme des Garçons and Yamamoto to the local fashion arena. Later he expanded to a woman's store and a "Millennium" space, and the pioneering spirit remains the same. Prepare to marvel at products by very now Belgian-American brand Casey-Vidalenc, where garments are lined with authentic antique kimonos, or Project Alabama's handstitched (by Alabama women) revisited vintage. And find la crème de la crème of contemporary fashion: Prada, John Galliano, Jil Sander, Martin Margiela, Helmut Lang, Dries Van Noten, and avant-garde names Rick Owens and Carol Christian Poell. But be prepared: cool, at this level, doesn't come cheap.
www.deglieffetti.com

Pantheon area

Piazza Capranica 75,79 & 93   **06-679 1650**
00186 Rome   Mon 3:30-7:30, Tues-Sat 10-2, 3-7:30

De Grillis

The Rome branch of Florence's boutique par excellence Luisa Via Roma, De Grillis is just two blocks from Via Nazionale but off the tourist track and something completely different. There's a salon atmosphere, and many clients who live in the area like to stop by in the morning for a coffee or fruit juice. Not only do they have a very eclectic selection of shoes (including René Caovilla, Chloé, Vicini, St. Laurent, Giuseppe Zanotti) and clothes (Roberto Cavalli, Antonio Marras, Alessandro dell'Acqua, Guerriero), but if you want to check your e-mail or see photos of the collections there's a handy computer. If the store doesn't have the model in your size or preferred color, it will be sent from Florence for next-morning arrival.

Via Nazionale area

Via Campo Carleo 25   **06-678-7557**
00184 Rome   Daily 10-8

Demoiselle

You might not think of stopping at this somewhat old-fashioned-looking lingerie shop but it could be worth it, especially if you're looking for swimwear. Find Blumarine and La Perla, and also the young Roman designer Delfina (Delfina Swimwear) who is sold at Barneys in New York and Principessa in Houston and who made it to the annual swimwear issue of *Sports Illustrated*.

Piazza di Spagna area

Via Frattina 93	**06-679 3752**
00187 Rome	Daily 10-8

Diesel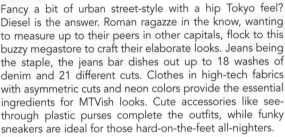

Fancy a bit of urban street-style with a hip Tokyo feel? Diesel is the answer. Roman ragazze in the know, wanting to measure up to their peers in other capitals, flock to this buzzy megastore to craft their elaborate looks. Jeans being the staple, the jeans bar dishes out up to 18 washes of denim and 21 different cuts. Clothes in high-tech fabrics with asymmetric cuts and neon colors provide the essential ingredients for MTVish looks. Cute accessories like see-through plastic purses complete the outfits, while funky sneakers are ideal for those hard-on-the-feet all-nighters.

Piazza di Spagna area

Via del Corso 186	**06-678 3933**
00186 Rome	Mon-Sat 10:30-8, Sun 3:30-8

Via Cola di Rienzo area

Via Cola di Rienzo 245-249	**06-324 1895**
00192 Rome	(opening times as above)

DM

A typical neighborhood boutique that caters to a well-heeled and discriminating clientele (think upper east side in New York or Belgravia in London) with a simple, fresh, elegant decor to match the merchandise. In the rear a comfortable couch faces the spacious dressing-room, and the designers include Lawrence Steele and Alberto Aspesi, with shoes by Robert Clergerie and Spaniard Tony Mora and bathing suits by Les Tropeziennes. Definitely worth a visit if you're shopping in Parioli—the owners are as chic as the clothes and most helpful.

Parioli area

Via Antonelli 10a	**06-807 4350**
00197 Rome	Mon-Sat 10-1, 4-7:30

Dolce & Gabbana

Want to look smart in a suit, but still be so damn sexy? Leave it Domenico & Stefano, the Italian wonder boys who, since their debut on the fashion circuit in 1985, have reinvented the concept of seductive-chic. Their inspiration? Sicilian housewives, neo-realist actresses, Madonna and voluptuous Italian bombshells like Monica Bellucci. The result is explosive. Think slim severe black suits with silk push-up bras peeking from the décolletage. Or lean tailored coats with a printed slip-dress underneath with matching bra. Silk leopard linings refine elegant suits, pointy slingbacks and even military jackets. Slip this stuff on and you'll literally hear the paparazzi chasing you. Men can get that gangster-chic look with pinstriped suits, skinny jersey tops and tight ribbed sweaters. Huge clay urns with giant cactuses and baroque gilded chairs in multicolored velvet tapestry are scattered around the store, adding to the steamy atmosphere.   www.dolcegabbana.it

Piazza di Spagna area

Via Condotti 51-52   **06-6992 4999**
00187 Rome   Mon-Sat 10-7:30

Du.Du.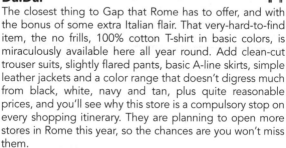

The closest thing to Gap that Rome has to offer, and with the bonus of some extra Italian flair. That very-hard-to-find item, the no frills, 100% cotton T-shirt in basic colors, is miraculously available here all year round. Add clean-cut trouser suits, slightly flared pants, basic A-line skirts, simple leather jackets and a color range that doesn't digress much from black, white, navy and tan, plus quite reasonable prices, and you'll see why this store is a compulsory stop on every shopping itinerary. They are planning to open more stores in Rome this year, so the chances are you won't miss them.

Piazza di Spagna area

Via della Croce 78b   **06-679 5192**
00187 Rome   Mon 1-7:30, Tues-Sat 10-7:30, Sun 12-7:30

Via delle Carrozze 44a-45   **06-6992 3434**
00187 Rome   Mon 1-7:30, Tues-Sat 10-7:30

Eddy Monetti

Out on a posh yacht? Strolling in an exclusive resort? Après-skiing in a designer chalet? You wouldn't want to commit a fashion faux pas and this store, dating from 1887, provides key items that will have you gliding smoothly through those crucial moments. Fay (by Tod's Diego Della Valle) down and nylon jackets, for instance, are practical and so now, and Burberry coats and jackets add that touch of British sporty-chic. Malo cashmere sweaters are classy but understated and Ralph Lauren polo shirts timeless, if a bit obvious. Add Etro's paisley-print handbags and you'll be all set.   www.eddymonetti.com

Piazza di Spagna area

Via Borgognona 35 (women)   **06-679 4389**
00187 Rome   Mon 3:30-7:30, Tues-Sat 10-7:30

Via Condotti 63 (men)   **06-678 3794**
00187 Rome   Mon-Sat 9:30-3:30

☆ Edo City

If you're a fan of all things Japanese (and not just a sushi/sashimi monster), this monochromatic store is definitely the place for you. Try to keep your cool in the presence of one-off silk kimonos from the Twenties and Thirties, precious evening pochettes from the Forties and Fifties, bright getas (the Japanese equivalent of our flip-flops) from the Sixties and Seventies, and antique silk or nylon scarves. In other words, Japanese vintage at its best. There are some contemporary items, like the classic featherweight Japanese schoolgirl shoulder bag in colorful nylon, but the emphasis is always on creating classic items using tradition-al methods and materials. Look out for the frequent exhibi-tions of funky new artists in the back room.

Campo de' Fiori area

Piazza del Paradiso 18   **06-6819 2659**
00186 Rome   Mon 4-8, Tues-Sat 10:30-1:30, 4-8

Eleonora

"Death to understatement, the Eighties are back!" screams this bright and flashy megastore with a taste for the theatri-cal. Two tanned black-clad bodyguard types greet you at the door, loud techno-music runs non-stop and the lighting comes from rotating movie-set spotlights. The decor relies on black, white and blood red, with inserts of leopard print (on couches). These are presumably included to match some of the clothes, like Cavalli's exotic animal-printed coats and jackets, or Dolce & Gabbana's leopard-print silk dresses or coats. Other merchandise seems to assail you visually from the shelves, like Sophie Le Maitre Kelly bags on acid, decorated with colored drawings and mega-Swarovski. Also represented are John Galliano (clothes and accessories), Simonetta Ravizza (leather and fur coats) and Jean Paul Gaultier, new this year. As for the shop assistants, they tend to descend on you in packs and shadow you like the best detectives. If it's too much, our advice is to retreat and relax in the small bar area where interesting coffee-table books are on display.   www.eleonoraboutique.it

Piazza di Spagna area

Via del Babuino 97   **06-679 3173**
00187 Rome   Mon 1-7:30, Tues-Sat 10-7:30

☆ Emanuel Ungaro

Voilà, a designer who truly adores women and proves it year after year in his collections. His classy boutique with oriental touches opened its slick doors in September 2002 and joined the roster of mega names in Fashionland's ritzy Via Borgognona. His prêt-à-porter collection, here dis-played in full, confirms that Ungaro makes women look like women, no matter the time of day. Touches of vaguely folk-loric embroideries, ruches, volants, embellished tailored dresses, coats or jackets make every garment a dangerous tool of feminine seduction. Handle with care.

Piazza di Spagna area

Via Borgognona 4b-4c   **06-6992 3345**
00187 Rome   Mon-Sat 10-7

Emporio Armani

Nothing particularly fancy about this vast store, one of the oldest in this ultra-hip street. No cozy little bar serving espresso, no magazine racks with the trendiest fashion mags, no wall of supergroovy chill-out CDs. We're talking basic, a long beigy space where Armani's more affordable lines for both sexes are on display. Expect the signature elements: soft shapes, neutral matte colors, and quality materials on basics as well as accessories that go from travel bags to umbrellas.

Piazza di Spagna area

Via del Babuino 140   **06-322 1581**
00187 Rome   Mon 3-7:30, Tues-Sat 10-7:30

Energie   ♂♀

Local surf dudes—who, in the absence of surfing beaches, strut their stuff in Via del Corso, a shopping street that on Saturday becomes a sort of streetwear catwalk—get their gear at this huge garage-like store pumping with high-energy music. The ground floor is devoted to boys, with piles of Hawaiian shirts, logo'd tees, shorts and T-shirts by specialist brands such as O'Neill, Sundeck, No Fear and Franklin & Marshall. Nike vintage sportswear is the big draw this year, with unisex accessories including sneakers by Puma, Adidas and Converse, sunglasses by Arnette and rucksacks by Eastpack also tempting the kids in off the streets. Girls can get some funky outfits on the mezzanine, where a good selection of Miss Sixty's jeans and casuals are on display.

Piazza di Spagna area

Via del Corso 486-487   **06-322 7046**
00186 Rome   Mon-Sat 9:30-8, Sun 10:30-1:30, 4-8

Via Cola di Rienzo area

Via Cola di Rienzo 143   **06-320 2493**
00192 Rome   Daily 10-8

Ethic   ♀

A new kid on the block in the universe of casualwear, this Italian company (a sort of Benetton meets London's The Cross) encourages personal and unique style and displays an astonishing array of looks (often outside the current trends) with an eye to the ethnic and a fondness for natural Indian fabrics. Frilly embroidered shirts, sequined tops, neo-romantic velvet coats, classic twinsets, leather military coats, silver Afghan jewelry…anything goes in the world of Ethic. With this extremely modern philosophy, no wonder it's a big hit. Add the fact that it is cheap and cheerful, and you'll see why everybody, at one point or another, shops here.   www.ethic.it

Piazza di Spagna area

Via del Carozze 20   **06-678 3352**
00187 Rome   Daily 11-8

Campo de' Fiori area

Piazza Cairoli 11-12   **06-6830 1063**
00186 Rome   Daily 10-8 (Sun-Mon 12-8)

Via del Corso 85   **06-3600 2191**
00186 Rome   Mon 3:30-8, Tues-Sat 9:30-8

Pantheon area

Via del Pantheon 46-47   **06-6880 3167**
00186 Rome   Mon 3-7:30, Tues-Sat 10-7:30

☆ Etro

The warm atmosphere of this wood-paneled gallery-like store is perfectly in tune with Etro's sunny, chic fashion: the colors are those of a Mediterranean sunset, ideally viewed in Capri, Panarea, or from a Tuscan country house. They are gathered in Etro's signature paisley print, and ever-present on cashmere scarves, shirts, ties and an entire collection of bags. Shirts come in bold prints and colored stripes, horizontal or oblique. The clothes are made from raw silks, velvets, tweeds or suede and have a vaguely eastern feel, as in the beautiful silk caftans. A curiosity? The original orangey-red chairs made from two giant sandwiched Foot bags, Etro's most popular style of handbag.

Piazza di Spagna area

Via del Babuino 102   **06-678 8257/679 3777**
00187 Rome   Mon 3-7, Tues-Sat 10-7

Expensive

Expensive? Not. Which explains why young fashion victims seasonally raid this flashy store packed with runway looks reproduced to perfection. And although fabrics are sometimes lacking in the quality department, prices are very low-budget friendly. So let yourself loose on the goods: they might fall apart by the end of the season, but that's all the more reason to go shopping again the next one, isn't it? www.expensive-fashion.it

Piazza di Spagna area

Piazza di Spagna 36   **800-311 678**
00187 Rome   Daily 10-8 (Sun 11-8)

Via del Corso 129 & 405   **(telephone as above)**
00186 Rome   (opening times as above)

Fabindia

The large windows may draw you in, with their display of tunics, shirts, caftans and pants for both men and women made from Indian fabrics in raw silk, shantung and light cotton. You can also buy the fabrics.

Piazza Navona area

Via del Banco di Santo Spirito 40   **06-6889 1230**
00186 Rome   Mon 3-7:30 Tues-Sat 10-1:30, 3-7:30

☆ Fendi

Lose yourself in the temple of leathery furry things, products of the timeless art of the famous Fendi sisters. The brand responsible for the worldwide Baguette epidemic dishes out cult items season after season. Take the oblong Ostrik bag, for example, spotted hanging from more than one starry shoulder. It comes in three sizes and a variety of textures that is truly amazing: just think of the sequined

Rome Directory

gilded one, the painted leather one, the hand-engraved metal-plated one and, last but not least, the most eccentric of all, decorated with suede pompoms. Find also the mini Baguette embroidered with corals and seed pearls and the mini Mother Baguette, a micro version of the maxi Baguette. Confused? Move on to the Selleria line, a timeless classic, where the edges are handsewn and the leather is supersoft: it includes all types of slouchy bags, but also chic loafers and cuddly leather coats. Explore the store's various floors, where beautiful, luxurious clothes collections are artfully displayed. And take your time wandering around the spectacular space (no pesky shop assistants here) where the iron-gray floors, dark wooden tables and spotlights all create the impression of an interactive museum…where the creations are displayed to be touched, felt, experienced. A new store due to open on Largo Goldoni is expected to carry the whole accessories collection, leaving the original store with the men's and women's ready-to-wear and the home collection.

Piazza di Spagna area

Via Borgognona 36-37   **06-696 661**
00187 Rome   Daily 10-7:30 (Sun 11-7)

Fiore Argento

If the daughter of a very famous film director becomes a fashion designer, a certain amount of publicity ensues. In the case of Fiore Argento, a Parson's School of Design graduate and daughter of master of suspense Dario Argento, she's also got real talent and, like the rest of her family, a strong personality that she conveys in original, urban-contemporary, feminine clothes. Add the fact that Fiore's muse and favorite model is sister Asia, one of Italy's most exciting young actresses, and the success story in guaranteed.   www.fioreargento.com

Campo de' Fiori area

Vicolo del Malpasso 12   **06-687 6391**
00186 Rome   Mon 10-1, Tues-Sat 10-1, 4-7

Fogal

Want to funk up a little black dress? Or add that crucial touch to a somewhat bland outfit? Fogal tights and stockings provide the solution to style dilemmas that give fashionistas sleepless nights. See their scrumptious flowery tights that come in an orange-red or orange-pink combination: you could walk around naked in them and still look dressed up. Or their fishnet tights in bright ice-creamy shades…they'll give you that French flirty air of careless chic, while their ultra-sheer black stockings with thick back seams will transform you into a Helmut Newtonish sexy German nanny. Add lingerie to be seen in, and cute little tops, and you'll see why this cheerful little store is definitely worth a visit.   www.fogal.com

Piazza di Spagna area

Via Mario de' Fiori 73
00187 Rome

06-678 4566
Mon 1-7, Tues-Sat 10-7

Fonderia

Unusual designs, flawless cuts and friendly price tags are this little boutique's impressive assets. Brothers Stefano and Paolo Angelico come from a family of bespoke tailors, hence their extreme attention to shapes, their knowledge of fabrics that tend to be natural (linen, cotton and pure wool) and their attention to detail. The garments are funky, modern and very wearable: see the wraparound double skirt in contrasting fabrics (a bestseller), or the chemise dress in shantung or striped cotton, best worn on top of flared pants. This season, the pair have headed east and gone wild for the kimono. Fresh and original.

Campo de' Fiori area

Via dei Balestrari 9
00186 Rome

06-689 3265
Mon 4-8, Tues-Sat 10-1:30, 4-8

Foot Locker

Sneakermaniacs from all walks of life flock to this store to get that vital 10th (or more) pair of sport shoes. The space is overflowing with punters most of the day, so get ready to elbow your way through to get a glimpse of these objects of desire which keep getting funkier, brighter and lighter. In the battle for the most popular, Nike still reigns, closely followed by Adidas, Le Coq Sportif from France and, naturally, Puma, whose Mostro ultra-flat model is currently sported by some of the coolest feet in Rome. Service is swift but the shop assistants are always busy, so make sure you grab one if he or she comes anywhere close or you might wait forever.

Piazza di Spagna area

Via del Corso 39-40
00186 Rome

06-3600 2063
Daily 10-7:30 (Sun 11-1:30, 4-7:30)

Fratelli Rossetti

Milanese Rossetti is another classic Italian footwear manufacturer's name nestling in this mega shopping street. The conservative store, masculine with wood paneling and floors, boasts the company's traditional shoe styles, as well as bags, belts and leather jackets. Their pride and joy, and their most publicized creation of the last decade, is undoubtedly the Flexa, a featherweight sport shoe equipped with extractable arch support and a rubber sole made of the same stuff used on some astronauts' shoes. And since their sailing Flexa has been adopted by Italian America's Cup crews, you can bet it's good. www.rossetti.it

Piazza di Spagna area

Via Borgognona 5a
00187 Rome

06-678 2676
Mon 3:30-7:30, Tues-Sat 9:30-7:30

Via del Babuino 59a	**06-3600 3957**
00187 Rome	Tues-Sat 10-7:30

☆ Fratelli Vigano

This is the last bastion of the Roman aristocratic gentleman, who has been catered for here since the 1920s. The owners are a bit eccentric, opening and closing when they feel like it—don't even try to go before 11am—and threatening to close for years. But if you do pass through the hallowed doors you'll be amazed: knitted wool ties, Borsalino hats, genuine panamas, Loden coats, classic tweed jackets that can withstand a blizzard, and British raincoats. If you didn't have time to stop by a gentleman's shop in London (in Jermyn Street, say), this favorite of the Roman upper classes smelling slightly of mothballs will be just your cup of tea.

Piazza di Spagna area

Via Minghetti Marco 8	**06-679 5147**
00187 Rome	Tues-Sat 10:30-1

Furla

There is something about this company that has secured it a dedicated and enthusiastic following. It is called simplicity. Their designs of leather goods, bags, purses, travel bags, wallets and shoes tend to be clean, unfussy, unpretentious. Leather is top quality, of the kind you know will last. Colors are sunny and cheerful—pink, orange, red, shocking pink—and prices are within most wallets' reach. Not surprisingly, Pradaesque rectangular wallets are already a cult item. The only downside, in our view, is that the Furla logo is engraved in letters too big on some of the handbags. But no one's perfect.

Piazza di Spagna area

Via Condotti 55-56	**06-679 1973**
00187 Rome	Daily 10-8 (Sun 10:30-8)
Piazza di Spagna 22	**06-6920 0363**
00187 Rome	Mon-Sat 10-8
Via Tomacelli 136	**06-687 8230**
00187 Rome	Mon-Sat 10-7:30
Via del Corso 481	**06-3600 3619**
00186 Rome	Mon-Sat 10-8, Sun 10:30-2, 3-8

Via Nazionale area

Via Nazionale 54-55	**06-487 0127**
00184 Rome	Mon-Sat 9:30-7:30

Via Cola di Rienzo area

Via Cola di Rienzo 226	**06-687 4505**
00192 Rome	Mon 4-8, Tues-Sat 10-8

☆ Galassia

If in need of a major fashion fix, head to this store which has specialized in edgy labels since its birth 20 years ago. Jean Paul Gaultier's various lines are a fixed feature (think tulle stretchy printed T-shirts and tubular dresses), as well as Issey Miyake's and Vivienne Westwood's first lines.

Newcomers include The People of the Labyrinth with their tie-dyed nylon and spandex dresses. Fans of Yohji Yamamoto's cult Adidas sneakers will find the whole collection here.

Piazza di Spagna area

Via Frattina 20-21   **06-679 7896**
00187 Rome   Mon-Sat 10-7:30

Galleria Mignanelli

Simona Romagnoli, a young Roman designer, has created a drawing-room atmosphere from a deconsecrated church for her clients who like to lounge on a sofa, drink a cup of tea and discuss their wardrobe. She specializes in using the most beautiful textiles such as dévoré velvets, silks, satins, brocades and damasks. There's an ethnic influence in the reds and golds used as well as in the oriental patterns. Iridescent fabrics are used for caftans and kimono-stoles that mould themselves to the body. Soft cashmere turbans wrap around the head, leather garments have inlaid work, and dresses for evening are cut low in the front. Special clothes for special women.   www.simonaromagnoli.it

Piazza di Spagna area

Rampa Mignanelli 10   **06-6920 0864**
00187 Rome   Mon-Fri 11-7

☆ Gallo

Gallo is one of Italy's oldest manufacturers of stockings and yarns, for all genders and ages. Chic Roman women love to wear their horizontally striped knee socks (in a bevy of color combinations) with moccasins and slacks. Men's socks come in solids or stripes, wide or narrow. There are clothes for infants (0-3), including tiny bathrobes, dresses, sweaters, cotton stretch jumpsuits and tights in a very soft yarn at 11 euros. Handy for wearing around the house are the colorful velvet slippers with rubber soles from the Veneto known as Friulani, and their double-face fine cotton knit bikinis in two colors you won't find anywhere else.

Piazza di Spagna area

Via Vittoria 63   **06-3600 2174**
00187 Rome   Mon 3:30-7:30, Fri-Sat 10-7:30

Gente

More than one supermodel visiting the Eternal City has been spotted in this somewhat sterile shop in the ever-trendier Via del Babuino. Not surprising, as some of the hippest names in the fashion spectrum are represented here: Helmut Lang with his denim collection, Maharishi with pants and T-shirts, Miu Miu with her girly tops and dresses, and ultra-hip Marni with his divine vintagey pieces. There is a men's section on the second floor and an eveningwear department boasting gowns by John Galliano, Antonio Marras, Ann Demeulemeester and Jil Sander. The accessories section is packed with shoes and bags signed by big names like Marni or Jimmy Choo.

Piazza di Spagna area

Via del Babuino 80-82
00187 Rome

06-320 7671
Mon-Sat 10-7:30

Via Frattina 69
00187 Rome

06-678 9132
(opening times as above)

Via Cola di Rienzo area

Via Cola di Rienzo 277-279
00192 Rome

06-321 1516
(opening times as above)

Geox

Mario Moretti Polegato produces "The Shoe That Breathes" with a ventilated but waterproof rubber or leather sole. Terrific, especially in summer, for those who are willing to sacrifice super-chic for elegant but comfy. There are classic lace-up city shoes for men as well as moccasins and sneakers, and models with low, medium or high heels for women. Colors tend to be subdued, but the 90-130 euro price range is reasonable (in a country where everything seems to have doubled in price since the introduction of the euro). Ask for Signora Marina, one of the directors.

Piazza di Spagna area

Via Frattina 3
00187 Rome   Mon 3:30-7:30, Tues-Sat 10-7:30 Sun 3:30-7

06-699 0480

Giorgio Armani

Armani reopened his shop in mid-summer, completely reorganized and redecorated with the collaboration of architect Claudio Silvestrin. The decor struck one Italian fashion journalist as cold, but who cares? The theme may be black and white—black ebony, white St. Maximin stone—and Giorgio does seem to be on something of a black and white bender: the women's collection for winter 2003-04 is dominated by black and white, with a cropped red wool jacket with turned-back cuffs about the only colorful garment. Of the three floors, the ground floor is dedicated to the men's collection (in keeping with the US tradition that men hate to have to go up several floors to find their clothes); Armani Woman is on the second floor, and a complete line of accessories for both sexes is on the third.   www.giorgioarmani.com

Piazza di Spagna area

Via Condotti 77
00187 Rome

06-699 1460
Mon-Sat 10-7

Giuseppe Messina

If Dalco is the epitome of luxe for made-to-order shoes, this tiny cubbyhole looks like something out of the 1920s and Giuseppe and his wife like people in a Fellini movie. Initially we were sent away by Giuseppe's wife—she interprets for Giuseppe as he is hard of hearing, but they had no interest in being listed in a guidebook—but we persevered and recommend you do too. If you're staying in Rome for a while or want to order some divine white satin court shoes for your wedding, you won't be sorry. We ordered a pair of

Capri sandals for 80 euros, and Signora Messina carefully drew around each foot on paper. We plan to have a pair of Ralph Lauren granny boots copied, "but don't come back until September," she warned. "We don't make winter shoes in the hot weather."

Piazza di Spagna area

Vicolo della Torretta 6   **06-687 2902**
00186 Rome   Mon-Sat 9-2, 4-8

Givenchy

With the young British designer Julien Macdonald at the helm, this legendary French house, famous for being Audrey Hepburn's favorite, seems to be sailing in uncharted waters. The look is still classy and slightly opulent—expect beautifully cut pantsuits, glossy leather jackets, thin knits in gold or draped jersey dresses—but funkied, with a touch of English eccentricity. Details surprise, like strings of wooden balls on suit jackets, or the lace-up front of a classic leather bag, or the bizarre sort of dust cover of tapestry fabric on another traditional leather purse. And who would have thought that a simple pumpkin could be raised to the dizzy heights of must-have handbag inspiration?   www.givenchy.com

Piazza di Spagna area

Via Borgognona 21   **06-678 4058**
00187 Rome   Mon-Sat 10-7:30

☆ Gucci

Feel the energy of pure greed when pushing the slick doors of this megastore: an ever-present cool-looking crowd eyes the goods rapaciously, the G sign imprinted on their irises. Gucci, since Tom Ford has put his hand to it, has become as cool as it gets, both on this and the other side of the planet judging by the crowd of slant-eyed babes cramming the store. Scan the ground floor for jewelry, belts and purses and lots of those coveted bags. Climb to the first floor for those luscious clothes (for her and him), classic shoes, and curious paraphernalia such as the Gucci saddle and cap (Gucci horse line), the black or white motorcycle helmet, and the leather or logo'd fabric teddy bear (baby Gucci), perfect to amuse designer kids in their designer cradles.   www.gucci.com

Piazza di Spagna area

Via Condotti 8   **06-678 9340/679 0405**
00187 Rome   Sun-Mon 2-7, Tues-Sat 10-7

Gucci (accessories)

This Gucci accessories store is particularly popular with its Roman clientele who like the personal service provided and prefer to avoid the tourist crowds in the flagship store on Via Condotti. Decor is in the minimalist style Tom Ford uses all over the world, with a lot of dark gray and white, though he has not touched the frescoes on the ceiling of the upper floor—the building was once the stables of the Palazzo

Torlonia. There are no shoes or clothes here, but a good selection of luggage, bags, ties, scarves, attaché cases, small leather goods, jewelry and watches. Ask for Alberto Vitti.

Piazza di Spagna area

Via Borgognona 7b   06-6919 0661
00187 Rome   Sun-Mon 2-7, Tues-Sat 10-7

Gucci (jewelry)

The first store in the world dedicated just to Gucci fine jewelry and watches. The collection includes the Flat Chain line, the Cabochon line and a medium-priced line designed personally by Tom Ford. A heavy wide ring consisting of a square-ish band of pink tourmaline is lined on either side with a rounded band of white gold. If you can't resist showing your love for Gucci there's a wide 18-karat white gold band sculpted with the double GG and decorated with small sunken diamonds. Small square modern earrings cost as little as 400 euros: blue topazes, amethysts or diamonds set in white gold; garnets, citrine quartz or peridot set in yellow gold.

Piazza di Spagna area

Via Condotti 68a   06-6978 8266
00197 Rome   Sun-Mon 2-7, Tues-Sat 10-7

Via Borgognona 7d
00197 Rome   (opening times as above)

Hermès

Although many are trying, no one seems to have been able, so far, to get Hermès's exact recipe for its 100% unpolluted chic. Take the Kelly bag: it has inspired thousand of variations, but none equals the original. Or those printed silk scarves: throw one on, and you'll feel like a French actress from the Fifties. Or even those rectangular porcelain ashtrays: they could make a formica table look modish. This store has a lot of cult items, from the enamel bracelets to those H belts or divine leather diaries and purses. Not to mention a small women's and men's clothing collection, made up of luscious cashmere coats and jumpers, luxuriant leather jackets, printed silk shirts and cashmere knits with metal buttons, all seemingly designed for life in a world where there are no regular homes, only châteaux.

Piazza di Spagna area

Via Condotti 67   06-679 1882
00187 Rome   Mon 3-7, Tues-Sat 10-7

Hogan

Hogan has moved into the old Tod's store, keeping the same decor as before but now carrying only shoes, boots, and bags branded Hogan. Diego Della Valle's son Emanuele got the idea for the new winter line, Hogan Riders, when he visited his pal Nick Ashley's shop for cycle accessories in London. "I thought about the philosophy of bike riders, which is similar to the style of Hogan, so I asked Nick to work with our design team," he says. The result: jackets, gloves and knapsacks are now in the pipeline to complement the boots, shoes and bags. The Motorcycle boots for the coming winter recall those Marlon Brando wore in *The Wild Ones*, including a polacchino that rises above the ankle with a 4cm heel and a buckle across the back; another version hits mid-calf, and the classic Interactive boot gives men a lift with its 6cm heel. The women's version comes almost to the knee with a cuff on the top. Hogan's Britney bag in three sizes has been flying off the shelves, as well as the Pan American in an updated version.

Piazza di Spagna area

Via Borgognona 45   **06-678 6828**
00187 Rome   Mon-Sat 10-7:30

Hugo Boss

Men who know this brand will be happy to find the store with its decor familiar from other Hugo Boss stores around the world. Known for well-cut, well-made garments, they are good value for money. The Orange Label tends to sporty, where the Black Label is classic, both dress and casual. A man can dress from head to toe here, including underwear and socks, and even those who like to dress a bit trendy will find something to their taste. Tailors are on hand to make alterations.   www.hugoboss.com

Piazza di Spagna area

Via Frattina 146   **06-678 6173**
00187 Rome   Mon 3:30-7:30, Tues-Sat 10-7:30, Sun 2-7

Il Baco di Seta

Paola Albanozzo has created an airy open space with white floor and walls and enormous windows. The clothes are minimalist, essential and comfortable, mostly with a loose but not sloppy fit. There are white linen tunics and pants and summer skirts in brown or beige. Accessories include silk purses, silk shantung duffel bags, straw baskets and Bensimon sport shoes. Signora Albanozzo repeats her classic lines season after season, and most are cut large enough to fit up to size 18 or 20.

Piazza di Spagna area

Via Vittoria 65   **06-679 3907**
00197 Rome   Mon-3:30-7:30 Tues-Sat 10-2, 3:30-7:30

☆ Il Portone

Young men have been buying their socks and underwear here for years (if their mothers haven't already stocked up for them). The boxer shorts come in colorful patterns and stripes, and there's a wide variety of pajamas and dressing-gowns. Ready-to-wear shirts, known for wide and narrow stripes in many colors, provide a classic look for around 75 euros, or you can have them made to order from the fabric of your choice. There are also some shirts and sweaters for women.

Piazza di Spagna area

Via del Carozze 73   **06-679 3355**
00187 Rome   Mon 3:30-7:30, Tues-Sat 10-7:30

Indoroman   👩

Gaia Franchetti travels to India and brings back rich fabrics—silks, shantungs, cottons—to be made into dresses,
skirts, pareos and pants, as well as quilts, tablecloths and
mats for the home. Her husband's family is from Venice,
where they became friends with Hemingway, and when
Hemingway saw the shop for the first time it reminded him
of a Venetian fondaco, the ground floor of the palaces
where the merchants returned from the orient displayed
their wares. Gaia also takes wide grosgrain ribbons to India
and has them embroidered with Indian motifs to use as borders for dresses, skirts, curtains or whatever.

Piazza di Spagna area

Via Gregoriana 36   **06-6919 0908**
00187 Rome   Mon-Fri 9-7

Intimissimi   👨👩

Lingerie so cute you'll want to wear it on the beach, and so
sensual you wish you had a date every night? Intimissimi is
just that, plus it's within every wallet's reach. Some styles are
classic and demure, but others are fresh and funky, like the
dark pink and blue lacy bra-knickers ensemble with matching camisole, or the Sixties flowery yellow and orange one
with matching slip-dress. Of course fabrics are not up to La
Perla's, but they're soft on the skin and not stiff and scratchy
as some can be. Find also great stretchy tees and cute
nightgowns and pajamas. Boys can look for cotton tee-
underwear ensembles in bright unusual tones.

Piazza di Spagna area

Via del Corso 167   **06-6992 4132**
00187 Rome   Daily 10-8 (Sun 11-8)

Campo de' Fiori area

Via dei Giubbonari 42   **06-6830 1784**
00186 Rome   (opening times as above)

Via Nazionale area

Via Nazionale 189   **06-484 638**
00184 Rome   Mon-Sat 9:30-8

Via Cola di Rienzo area

Via Cola di Rienzo 159-161   **06-324 3137**
00192 Rome   Mon 1-8, Tues-Sat 9:30-8
                                    Sun 11-1:30, 3:30-8

I Vippini   👦

The baroque shop window, the complete opposite of minimalist chic, hides a classic children's store with refined
clothes and a large assortment of shoes including a wonderful spectator model in brown and white. Vippini makes
outfits for baptisms and first communions, and the party
dresses in ice-cream-colored shantungs will make any girl
feel like a princess.

Piazza di Spagna area

Via Fontanella di Borghese 65   **06-6880 3754**
00187 Rome   Mon 3:30-7, Tues-Sat 9:30-1, 2-7

☆ Josephine de Huertas

Roman It-girls with a fashion sense choose this cute boutique when in need of clothes with flair and a sense of humor. French owner Josephine de Huertas, herself a fashion designer, has a penchant for garments by Paul Smith (her bestseller), as well as Ginka, Joseph, Diane von Furstenberg and Yoshiki Hishinuma, whose one-off polyester and rubber dresses, worked with laser rays, are real works of art and will definitely make you stand out at a party. Look out for the cute accessories by emerging young European designers, and the wonderful selection of oriental purses by Emmanuelle Zysman.

Piazza Navona area

Via del Governo Vecchio 68   **06-687 6586**
00186 Rome   Mon 3:30-7:30, Tues-Sat 10-7:30

☆ Josephine de Huertas & Co

De Huertas's original store, opened in 1988 with fellow fashion designer Mauro Crachi, is a sure bet when it comes to wearable classy essentials. Here a clientele of regulars, including young movie actresses and trendy Roman princesses, stock up on Vanessa Bruno's cotton tees, Roberto Collina's wool and cashmere jerseys, Paul & Joe coats and jackets, and shoes by classic Italian label Lario. Discover Gianfranco Ferré's GFF line, whose shirts and suits feature the same impeccable cut as the first line but are easier on your bank account. And don't miss his supersoft black leather jacket that should be compulsory in every wardrobe.

Piazza Navona area

Via del Parione 19-20   **06-6830 0156**
00186 Rome   Mon-Sat 10-2, 3-7:30

Just Cavalli

The store opening a year ago, in a prime location facing the Spanish Steps, drew a large crowd, proving the Florentine designer's growing popularity. Cavallistas can get all the basics of his second line here, made mostly of stretch printed denim. Jeans are ripped and sewn and printed in Cavalli's beloved exotic animal prints, visible also on changing-room curtains, carrier bags, purses, bustiers and watch straps. The first floor hosts a men's collection displaying similar styles, plus oversize wool jumpers and long printed leather coats. Fashion victims with real tans (still popular here), huge sunglasses and spiked hairstyles roam the rooms with the greedy look of kids in a candy store.

Piazza di Spagna area

Piazza di Spagna 82-83   **06-679 2294**
00187 Rome   Mon 1-7:30, Tues-Sat 10-7:30

☆ Kristina Ti

Imagine clothes so light you could pack closets of them in a single suitcase, and so soft you could powder your nose with them: Kristina Ti's teensy silk chiffon dresses and blouses, wool or cashmere tees, and even leather and shearling jackets do the job. The clothes are fresh and feminine, flirty and sophisticated in an understated way. No wonder Italian uptown girls as well as international jet-set ladies shop here with a passion (Catherine Deneuve is a fan). Designer Cristina Tardito, whose family owns a lingerie company, trained as a bikini designer, so don't miss her sublime silk, chiffon or tulle ensembles; even the shoes and boots are so light and ethereal they seem designed for angels.   www.kristinati.it

Piazza di Spagna area

Via Mario de' Fiori 40c-41   **06-6920 0170**
00187 Rome   Mon 3-7, Tues-Sat 10-7

Krizia

Count on designer Mariuccia Mandelli to keep you on your toes. Her designs can look plain and even baggy on the hangers, but put them on and the clever cuts will get to work on your body. Styles range from the ladylike to the intellectual, bordering on the avant-garde. Take a plain black sleeveless wool dress: a ruched front gives it a Comme des Garçonish spin. Some items, like the gilded armor-like top, are bold and rich; others, such as the ought-to-be-illegal short skirts, are fresh and modern while clear plastic sandals with neon glints are outright funky. And you can always count on her soft luxurious knits, in flattering shapes. The store is cozy and relaxed, and there is a living area on the first floor equipped with a coffee machine and a stunning view of the square below.

Piazza di Spagna area

Piazza di Spagna 87   **06-679 3772**
00187 Rome   Mon 3-7, Tues-Sat 10-7

La Cicogna

An upscale version of Prenatal, essentially a department store for infants, children up to 14 and mothers-to-be. The children's clothes come from a bewildering number of famous names: Armani Junior and Armani Baby, Replay, Diesel, Versace, Monnalisa, Blumarine, La Perla, Burberry, Donna Karan, Timberland, Calvin Klein, Kookaï, La Fornarina, Napapijri and others. Expecting mothers will find a good selection in La Cicogna's own clothes. The staff know their merchandise and are very helpful—many of them speak English. Ask for Signora Angela.

Piazza di Spagna area

Via Frattina 135   **06-679 1912**
00187 Rome   Mon 10:30-2, 3-7:30, Tues-Sat 10-7:30
                              Sunday 10-7:30 (winter only)

Via Cola di Rienzo area
Via Cola di Rienzo 268   **06-689 6557**
00192 Rome   Mon 4:15-8, Tues-Sat 10-8

☆ **Laltramoda**
This Italian company hit the jackpot when it opened its first stores 11 years ago. Its credo is quality, good cuts, medium prices and styles that only flirt with current trends. The result is clothes that are easy, versatile and that at the end of the season don't end up at the back of the closet or in the Oxfam bag. Some examples? Beautiful knits in cotton, angora wool, silk or cashmere, basic tees in all colors and shapes, embroidered wool or shearling coats and city-slick leather suits. Enjoy.

Piazza di Spagna area
Via Frattina 113   **06-679 2987**
00187 Rome   Mon 3:30-7:30, Tues-Sat 10-7:30
Via Borgognona 42b   **06-678 4444**
00187 Rome   (opening times as above)
Via Cola di Rienzo area
Via Cola di Rienzo 54-56   **06-321 1622**
00192 Rome   Mon 4-8, Tues-Sat 9:30-8

☆ **La Perla**
It may have been diamonds in Marilyn's day, but currently a woman's best friend is La Perla lingerie. This Italian brand's sexy, classy, luxurious and so so flattering creations are on every body-conscious female's wish list. All their lacy silky styles are on display in this immaculate and newly refurbished shop. Prices are steep, but the good news is that the second line's (Malizia) yummy ensembles have prices that won't require previous weeks of starvation. To pile temptation on temptation, La Perla has also ventured into luscious eveningwear, and swimwear that comes sequined, embroidered in Swarovski and smocked.   www.laperla.com

Piazza di Spagna area
Via Condotti 79   **06-6994 1934**
00187 Rome   Mon 3-7, Tues-Sat 10-7

La Rinascente
While elsewhere department stores are winning hands down the battle against small shops, in Rome the boutiques are holding their ground. So don't be surprised if the capital's main department store, La Rinascente, is far from impressive. The ground floor hosts the toiletries section (but don't expect any new, funky makes), leather goods, costume jewelry and hats; the next two floors are devoted to men's fashion and casualwear, and the last two to women's. Again, don't hold your breath, no heart pumping brands are represented. The best bet is the lingerie section in the basement, where coquettish Dim ensembles, racy D&G animal-print ones, or those Calvin Klein lacy tulle bras seen peeking from Madonna's shirts make for a pretty good selection.

Piazza di Spagna area

Piazza Colonna   **06-679 7691**
00186 Rome   Mon-Sat 9:30-10, Sun 10:30-9

Piazza Fiume   **06-884 1231**
00198 Rome   (opening times as above)

Laura Biagiotti   ♀

Prepare to be amazed upon entering this elegant, high-vaulted, beautifully lit shop where soft classical music creates a serene mood. At the beginning of the last century it was a theatre, and it retains a stagey atmosphere ideal for displaying the captivating creations of Signora Biagiotti, a veteran who recently celebrated 30 years in the Roman fashion scene. Cashmere and silk, both plain and embroidered, and the Dolcetto, a mixture of the two, are some of her materials of choice to create eastern-inspired layered ensembles made of long floaty cardigans, shirts, dresses, pants and skirts. Her pretty white linen Bambola dresses, for instance, are worn with slim pants underneath. A bestseller? The striped multicolored maxi-cardigan, made with leftovers of cashmere.

Piazza di Spagna area

Via Borgognona 43-44   **06-679 1205**
00187 Rome   Mon 3:30-7:30
                  Tues-Fri 10-1:30, 3:30-7:30, Sat 10-7:30

☆ Le 3 C   ♀

Do you like your sandals flat, chic, and possibly handmade? Le 3 C, a small shop with a big following, will certainly seduce you. Their Capri-style sandals come in all types and colors of leather, but don't underestimate other styles, such as the French Pare Gabia handstitched espadrilles with rope soles and tops that vary from striped fabric to raffia, very Brigitte Bardot. Or Parini's ultra-soft and ultra-light handmade slippers, the Rolls-Royce of the slipper world. Not to mention the shoe accessories department, creams, pomades, sprays and brushes so good-looking you'll want to place them on every shelf in your bathroom.

Piazza di Spagna area

Via della Croce 40   **06-679 3813**
00187 Rome Mon 3:30-7:30, Tues-Sat 9:30-1:30, 3:30-7:30

Leam   ♂

Dragging your tired feet from one flagship to another? Relax in this designer emporium (for men only) that aims high and doesn't want to waste your time (since most men and shopping don't get on). It features only the hippest styles from the hippest labels, from Gucci, Prada and Dolce & Gabbana to Marni, Yves Saint Laurent and Dior. Cult items from each season, as seen on the catwalks, will no doubt end up here: think Prada's America's Cup sport shoes, Gucci's magnificent white shearling coat, the Dolce faux-vintage one, Puma sneakers by Jil Sander and Helmut Lang's latest jeans. Find also Y3, Yohji Yamamoto's hotter than hot collaboration with Adidas.   www.leam.com

Piazza di Spagna area

Via Bocca di Leone 5 **06-678 7853**
00187 Rome Mon 3:30-7:30, Tues-Sat 10-7:30

☆ **Le Gallinelle**

A real gem of a store, whose address is passed around in cognoscenti circles by word of mouth. Impossible not to be seduced by designer/owner Wilma Silvestri's sublime creations, inspired by real life, where vintage, ethnic and contemporary fabrics are mixed to create wonderfully modern clothes, one-offs with a soul. Her latest styles include hypersexy corsets in bold printed African fabrics, Turkish-style floaty pants in cotton or flower-patterned moleskin, and Eighties-inspired puffed-sleeved cotton shirts. Glittery gold, green and blue bikinis, designed by Wilma's daughter, are also new this year and guaranteed to get you noticed. And for fall there are stretch wool Forties-style suits in emerald green, indigo or cobalt red, as well as fab vintage pieces and accessories. A real treat. www.legallinelle.it

Via Nazionale area

Via del Boschetto 76 **06-488 1017**
00184 Rome Mon 3:30-8, Tues-Sat 10-1, 3:30-8

Lei

Enter this store any time of year and you'll feel like you've stepped into a clear spring day, birds chirping and all. The clothes seem chosen for an elegant picnic in the park, or a cocktail party where a fruit cocktail is served and the air is scented with jasmine. Frilly silk floral dresses are from the Belgian Chine collection, fresh linen ones in pastel shades from Italian-made 120% Lino, and slim feminine coats come from Britain's Tara Jarmon. There are bright patterned tees signed Custo of Barcelona, and the accessories include flirty Brazilian beach bags and sexy shoes by Kallisté and Katharine Hamnett. Refreshing.

Campo de' Fiori area

Via dei Giubbonari 103 **06-687 5432**
00186 Rome Mon 3:30-7:30, Tues-Sat 10-2, 4-8

Via Nazionale area

Via Nazionale 88 **06-482 1700**
00184 Rome Mon 3:30-8, Tues-Sat 10-7:30

Le Ragazze Gold

Babes with attitude to spare come here for hi-voltage party gear that won't fail to get them noticed, no matter how big the room. The pink and white boutique with sparkly black marble floors is the perfect theatre for sassy styles including exotic animal-printed chiffon dresses, sequined strappy tops and shorts, perky stretch jersey minidresses, swanky denim half-cup corsets and brassy Lycra overalls, mostly by Florentine designer Adele Fado. Find also a sportier line by an Italian brand appropriately called Sexy Woman. Not for the fainthearted.

Piazza di Spagna area

Via del Corso 500   **06-361 2364**
00187 Rome   Mon 3:30-7:30, Tues-Sat 10:30-7:30

Loco   👤👩

Since opening seven years ago this funky store (loco means crazy in Spanish) has become a reference point for the adventurous in footwear. Styles (by Italian designers such as Moma, Gianni Barbato or Les Tropeziennes) vary from the slick and sexy to the eccentric, weird, and plain surreal. No wonder rock stars (like Skunk Anansie), Hollywood actors and costume designers all come here. Also find vintage-style distressed leather bags by Gias, and punk-chic silver jewelry by Roman designer Iosselliani. The laid-back shop assistants and warm copper and wood decor make shopping here a delightful experience.   www.loco.it

Campo de' Fiori area

Via dei Baullari 22   **06-6880 8216**
00186 Rome   Mon 3:30-8, Tues-Sat 10:30-8

☆ Loro Piana   👤👩

For a jolt of pure self-indulgence immerse yourself in the pampering atmosphere of this temple of things soft and cuddly. 100% cashmere shawls in all weights and colors, thick cashmere jumpers and socks, airy linen suits, ultra-soft cashmere and wool blazers, and silk and linen robes and nightgowns speak of a padded world with no worries, except, maybe, how the stock market is going to turn. Breathe in deep, even the air has a cashmerey feel.

Piazza di Spagna area

Via Borgognona 31   **06-6992 4906**
00187 Rome   Mon 3:30-7:30, Tues-Sat 10-7:30

Louis Vuitton   👤👩

It's true they've been around forever, but those LV bags just can't go out of fashion. This elegant store, in this delicious piazza, dispenses all the classic line (those magnificent travel trunks included) as well as the latest models, like the Takashi Murakami collaborative totes whose interpretation of the logo is as playful as the waiting list is long. Shoes, like the buckled leather boots or the fabric sneakers, are modern and hip, and clothes by Marc Jacobs mirror the luxury brand's philosophy. Expect beautifully cut pastel-colored leather jackets with metal buttons and matching miniskirts, soft wool coats with printed silk linings, and très chic cashmeres in multicolored stripes.   www.vuitton.com

Piazza di Spagna area

Piazza San Lorenzo in Lucina 36   **06-6880 9520**
00186 Rome   Mon-Sat 9:30-7:30, Sun 11-7:30

Via Condotti 15   **06-6994 0000**
00187 Rome   Daily 9:30-7:30 (Sun 11-7:30)

Luisa Spagnoli   👤

We all know some 30% of the female population of the US wears over size 18, but somehow the marketing geniuses seem to have forgotten them. Not so Luisa Spagnoli, who makes her styles in sizes up to 52 Italian, equivalent to an American size 22. There are thin cotton twinsets, flirty dresses with flounces, dresses and jackets for work, and pants. Not as expensive as Marina Rinaldi; for those with a selective eye.

Piazza di Spagna area

Via Frattina 84	**06-699 1706**
00187 Rome	Mon-Sat 10-8, Sun 11-2, 4-7
Via del Tritone 30	**06-6992 2769**
00187 Rome	(opening times as above)
Via Veneto 130	**06-4201 1281**
00187 Rome	(opening times as above)

Via Cola di Rienzo area

Via Cola di Rienzo 191	**06-3600 3335**
00192 Rome	Mon-Sat 10-8

☆ Luna & L'altra

Diehard fashionistas worship this shop, packed with the latest designs by international giants such as Martin Margiela, über-Jap Issey Miyake, nomad-chic master Dries Van Noten and French garçon maudit Jean Paul Gaultier. The 20-year-old shop, a compulsory stop on Rome's fashion path, is the brainchild of husband-and-wife Biba Canella and Luigi D'Alessia, who act as advisers to an array of clients that includes actors, artists and wannabes in search of status-symbol pieces. New this year are accessories by French designer Jamin Puech and jewelry by Monis, whose intriguing use of natural products make even the most die-hard city chick want to go a bit earthy. Check out the façade, too: this historical palazzo dates from 1600.

Piazza Navona area

Via del Governo Vecchio 105	**06-6880 4995**
00186 Rome	Mon 3:30-7:30, Tues-Sat 10-2, 3:30-7:30

☆ Mada

Don't be fooled by the unobtrusive appearance of this store almost on the corner of Via del Corso, where you'll find as many food shops as fancy boutiques; there's a treasure trove inside. The three ladies who own Mada typify the elegance of the shop and are so savvy and helpful they could have written the book on bon ton. Their devoted followers, from 18 to 80, will find styles unavailable elsewhere. (Two years ago we found a pair of classic "Ghillies" that have now made a big comeback.) Elegance is the watchword, from the traditional man's wingtip for the woman who dresses English country style to the French label Accesoire, Pedro Rodriguez from Spain, Lario and many other brands that are classy and trendy at the same time. From 150 euros.

Piazza di Spagna area

Via della Croce 57	**06-679 8660**
00187 Rome	Mon 3:30-7:30
	Tues-Sat 9:30-1, 3:30-7:30

Malo

Imagine you've travelled to Cashmeria, and not on a package tour: Malo is where you've landed. The cashmere is so soft and creamy, it looks like it could melt in your mouth: thick, foamy sweaters look as if grandma knitted them, shawls are so light they could fly like kites, and socks so soft you'll wish they were your second skin. There is also a casual-chic collection of clothes, shoes and bags that seem designed for a weekend in Portofino: sporty and luxurious leather jackets, pale suede loafers, leather and cashmere woven bags in coral and gold. Just as stylish is the quietly elegant shop itself, fitted with black stone, leather and resin, but with the faintest of hi-tech touches.

Piazza di Spagna area

Via Borgognona 5 **06-679 1331**
00187 Rome Mon-Sat 10-7:30, Sun 12-7

Mandarina Duck

Prepare for a real trip upon entering this psychedelic megastore dreamed up by Marcel Vander. The floors and ceilings are made with pebbles encased in colored silicon (gray on the ground floor, yellow on the first floor, light blue on the second), creating the perfect backdrop for the hyper-functional techno-bags of this Italian brand whose name is revered in Germany, Japan and France. Styles include the funny Toys bag, designed like a saddle to fit on top of the backs of chairs, or the delightful Saké evening pouch that can be expanded to three sizes to become an ultra-light city bag or a beach bag. There is also leisurewear, made for comfort from hi-tech materials such as the Faber Duck, a paper-like water-resistant fabric, and some equally practical watches and jewelry. The shop assistants are top quality too, a big bonus.

Piazza di Spagna area

Via Borgognona 42b **06-6920 0837**
00187 Rome Mon 1-7:30, Tues-Sat 10-7:30, Sun 2-7

Marco Polo

Enter this space overflowing with merchandise and you'll feel like you've travelled back in time and space to the glorious Seventies and the streets of Goa or Kathmandu. As the theme is hippy, so is the gear collected on his trips by owner Marco Paoletti, nicknamed Marco Polo, a self-confessed member of the beat generation. Now that hippy is chic, this is a good place to shop freely and cheaply, in the spirit of peace and love. Stock up on printed tees (portraying anything from Ganesh the elephant god to Che Guevara or Impressionist paintings), thick wool jackets from Nepal, Indian embroidered dresses or Moroccan leather sandals. And you'll also get a break from the icy atmosphere of some designer boutiques.

Campo de' Fiori area

Via dei Chiavari 31 **06-687 7653**
00186 Rome Mon-Sat 10-8

Mariella Burani

From a town near Reggio Emilia, the area full of garment manufacturers, Mariella Burani has found her place in Italian fashion with her namesake line as well as with Amuleti, a bridge line for younger customers. The style ranges from sporty to elegant, and there is a wide range of accessories from belts to handbags, foulards to watches. Burani likes colorful flower prints as well as more unusual touches such as fabrics with specks of metal.

Piazza di Spagna area

Via Bocca di Leone 28   **06-679 0630**
00187 Rome   Mon 3:30-7:30, Tues-Sat 10:30-7:30

☆ Marina Rinaldi

You're a MaxMara fan but can't fit into all their clothes? Help is here in the guise of Marina Rinaldi, the plus-size branch of that name we all know and love. Two floors of simple modern decor hold a treasure of goodies to make any fashionista with too many curves happy. You'll find the classic MaxMara coats that fit and look like a dream, pants, tops, dresses, jackets, day and evening wear, all in fine fabrics and tailoring. Size 10s will also find accessories including shoes not available in the other MaxMara stores. If necessary, they will do hems and alterations.

Piazza di Spagna area

Largo Goldoni 43   **06-6920 0487**
00187 Rome   Mon-Sat 10-7:30

Marisa Padovan

Signora Padovan has resolved figure problems for many Roman matrons with her made-to-measure bathing suits and coverups. She also carries a large variety of ready-made bathing suits, including some of the best-known brands.

Piazza di Spagna area

Via del Carozze 81   **06-679 3946**
00186 Rome   Mon 3:30-7:30, Tues-Sat 9:30-7:30

Marlboro

Ah, the charms of country and western interpreted in a sophisticated key by the Italians! The line was originally created by racing driver Andrea de Adamich who convinced the venerable textile and clothes manufacturer Marzotto to buy the license from Philip Morris. The decor is suitably rustic and you'll find jeans, cargo pants, shirts, bermudas, knitwear and T-shirts as well as dressier trousers, jackets and blazers in classic shapes. Most of the clothes will look familiar to Americans but the discerning eye will notice the more European cut and finishings, and Marzotto is known for good quality for money. Jeans and pants run around 80 euros, shirts from 57 up to 140 for a number with gold top-stitching. Ask for Rolando.

Campo de' Fiori area

Via dei Giubbonari 61   **06-686 4062**
00186 Rome   Mon 4-8, Tues-Sat 9:30-1:30, 4-8

Maska

Feeling unadventurous? Take refuge in Maska's simple styles, made for women who like to play it safe. Printed silk and draped jersey dresses, or shirt dresses (one of their trademarks), come in soft shapes and shades; wool suits and coats are in classic lean cuts and neutral tones. The store's appearance mirrors its sober philosophy, and service is usually friendly and smiley. A selection of chill-out and lounge music (think Buddha Bar) is for sale at the cashier's desk.

Piazza di Spagna area

Via Frattina 44-45   **06-6992 5800**
00187 Rome   Mon 3:30-7:30, Tues-Sat 10-2, 3:30-7:30

Max & Co

This roomy store, down the road from its main sibling, hosts MaxMara's younger and more affordable line, made to straighten up that big social injustice all of us have been subjected to: clothes mama wore but that we could never aspire to. Teenagers, twentysomethings and beyond can let themselves loose here on adorable tees and sweat shirts, cute sweaters, frilly feminine dresses, leather or denim jackets that are trendy but very well cut. Accessories are just as desirable, and within the reach of most pockets.

Piazza di Spagna area

Via Condotti 46   **06-678 7946**
00187 Rome   Daily 10-7:30

☆ MaxMara

Dazed and confused by too much fashion extravaganza? Take refuge in this temple of understated, clean modern elegance. MaxMara has become a lifeline for chic yet practical women: think clothes that fit, don't squeeze, and are easy on the eye and on the touch. Their camel, navy blue or black classic wool coats are a must in every winter wardrobe. Their linen suits make you comfy and chic in summer. Lose yourself in this enormous store and get friendly with the variety of their lines, such as Weekend (a casual collection), Sportmax (younger and trendier) and Pianoforte, their eveningwear line. Must-have accessories include classic knee-high boots in suede or leather, and classy bags, gloves, belt and sunglasses.

Piazza di Spagna area

Via Condotti 17-19a   **06-6992 2104/5**
00187 Rome   Mon-Sat 10-7:30, Sun 11-7
Via Frattina 28   **06-679 3638**
00187 Rome   (opening times as above)

Via Nazionale area

Via Nazionale 28-31   **06-488 5870**
00184 Rome   (opening times as above)

Merola

Imagine a shop's walls lined with 330 wooden cases of gloves, arranged by model, color and size. The leather may be kid, pigskin, napa or Merino (which is baby lamb, soft on the outside with its fur on the inside). The gloves may be unlined, or lined in silk, cashmere or fur. Merola has the classic driving glove of cotton and leather (for men and women), a few types of women's evening glove, and some that are trimmed or embroidered.

Piazza di Spagna area

Via del Corso 143   **06-679 1961**
00187 Rome   Mon 3-7, Tues-Sat 10-2, 3-7

Missoni

The Missoni saga is a fascinating tale. Ottavio, the tracksuit maker from Dalmatia, meets Rosita from Varese whose family own a bedding company. They fall in love and with a few knitting machines start producing knitwear for different companies. A golden couple of Italian fashion is born. Their colorful, striped, patterned knits, redolent of the Sixties and Seventies and endlessly copied, become so popular they soon open their own business. Today Missoni means carefree and dynamic luxury: the styles, designed by daughter Angela, have evolved from the original long cardigans and sweaters to include shorts, bikinis, low-waisted pants, long skirts, off-the-shoulder blouses and minidresses that embody the current hippy-chic mood.   www.missoni.com

Piazza di Spagna area

Piazza di Spagna 78   **06-679 2555**
00187 Rome   Mon 3-7, Tues-Sat 10-7

Miss Sixty

Since their comeback the glorious Sixties seem here to stay, and this Italian brand is riding that long, long wave. And they're doing it brilliantly: velour trenchcoats or miniskirts, ribbed turtlenecks, corduroy shirts, all hip and cheeky. But their trump card is the sexy flared hipsters, which come in floral velvet, distressed faux leather, stretch corduroy and natural denim and seem to make even the chubbiest of legs model-thin. The Via del Corso shop, their first in town, resembles an airport lounge of the era, with orange oval faux leather chairs beside white round plastic tables on optical print carpets.

Piazza di Spagna area

Via del Corso 510   **06-321 9374**
00187 Rome   Mon-Sat 10-8

Via Cola di Rienzo area

Via Cola di Rienzo 235   **06-320 0918**
00192 Rome   Mon-Sat 10:30-8, Sun 3-8

Modi di Campagna

Italians (especially among the higher social classes) have always been Anglophiles, and they love nothing better than the typical British country look, as the name of this shop (Country Fashions) suggests. It's country chic for men and women, including hunting jackets…Beretta revisited but not as expensive. There are beautiful shirts, tweed jackets and sweaters…all those easy casual clothes known and loved by generations. They also carry hunting and fishing gear. Barbour, Grisalis, Filson, Husky, La Martina (Argentine polo shirts) and Car Shoes are some of the brands you'll find here.

Piazza di Spagna area

Via dei Prefetti 42   **06-679 4027**
00186 Rome   Mon 3:30-7:30
                    Tues-Fri 10-1:30, 3:30-7:30, Sat 10-7

Molly Bloom

Fashion purists rejoice in this little boutique favored by intellectual types, actresses and journalists alike and packed with the latest by Comme des Garçons, Vivienne Westwood Red Label, Spanish designer Sybilla's young line Yocomomola and Italian designer Lavinia Turra. Co-owner and former fashion model Jeanine Gonzale has also launched her own collection of casuals, mixing Japanese purity with a coquettish French touch. Add shoes by Camper, Stephane Kélian and Sonia Rykiel, and hats by Stephen Jones, and you'll see why this amounts to a must-see.

Campo de' Fiori area

Via dei Giubbonari 27-28   **06-686 9362**
00186 Rome   Mon-Sat 10-8

Moschino

Moschino's unique style is made up of an amusing superimposition of ironic and irreverent touches on overstated shapes and materials. Its flagship store in Via Borgognona perfectly reflects this spirit: it is classic and light, with just a few bright red baroqueish pieces of furniture scattered here and there. On the ground floor, marvel at the fresh styles— lots of flower appliqués and fun prints—of the younger Cheap & Chic line (not that cheap). On the first floor, admire the main men's and women's collections, where unusual seaming, ruching and embroidery stand out on impeccable pinstriped or leather suits, slim coats, tailored jackets and simple sweaters. Some handbags even have golden good luck charms attached, in the shape of a chili pepper or the typical fist with two raised fingers. This stuff will make you cringe while they swipe the plastic, but it's guaranteed to make you and everyone else around you smile when you wear it.   www.moschino.it

Piazza di Spagna area

Via Borgognona 32a   **06-678 1144**
00187 Rome   Mon 12-8, Tues-Sat 9:30-8

Moschino Jeans

More Moschino (three floors of it) and at friendlier prices. This store mirrors the main one in color scheme, and the clothes are here to amuse with the same quirky details, like lines of buttons on a sleeve and colors and prints in unusual combinations. Guys and girls are both catered for, and there is even an entire floor for those adorable little brats. Find also bags, belts, ties and sunglasses.

Piazza di Spagna area

Via Belsiana 57   **06-6920 0415**
00187 Rome   Mon 12-8, Tues-Sat 9:30-8, Sun 10:30-8

☆ Narciso Rodriguez

He might have had just a small cult following before the famous wedding dress (the late Carolyn Bessette's), but today Cuban-born and New York-based Rodriguez has become a major fashion player. His city-slick clothes are sober, essential, expertly cut and ultra-feminine in an unostentatious way. Fabrics are ethereal, light and luxurious, and hemlines discreet. His first boutique in Rome, in the fashion stronghold of Via Borgognona, has the arduous task of converting the slightly baroque Roman signore into this essential chic.

Piazza di Spagna area

Via Borgognona 4f/g   **06-6992 3381**
00187 Rome   Mon 12-7:30, Tues-Sat 10-7:30
                                                          Sun 11-7:30

☆ Nia

Career women with a fashion sense choose this airy store full of classy and fun items. Owner Erminia Ferrante, Nia to her pals, used to own a dressmaker's shop, which explains her taste for the sartorial. Some of the brands here, such as Kiton, creator of impeccable cashmere jackets, are Italian tailors she takes under her wing. Others, like Antonio Fusco and his cashmere and silk coats, need no introduction. Find also Issey Miyake clothes, Robert Clergerie shoes, Antik Batik accessories and Indian embroidered coats with cashmere lining.

Piazza di Spagna area

Via Vittoria 48   **06-679 5198**
00187 Rome   Mon 2:30-7, Tues-Fri 10-2, 2:30-7, Sat 10-2

☆ Nia & Co

High-end casuals with a fresh twist are the specialty of Nia's second (and undersized) store. Sporty-chic chicks find here their Joseph pants, Alberto Aspesi nylon windbreakers, Mexica cowboy boots, and Puma or No Name sneakers. Hervé Chapelier's super-practical bi-colored polyamide and nylon handbags are so in demand that the stock needs to be constantly re-ordered.

Piazza di Spagna area

Via Vittoria 30-31   **06-322 7421**
00187 Rome   Mon 3-7, Tues-Fri 10-2, 3-7, Sat 10-6

☆ Nicol Caramel

Designer Nicoletta Neri's shop is small and elegant and dedicated to the mom-to-be who wants to retain her chic. She deals in specific sizes, rather than the drably ubiquitous

Rome Directory

small, medium and large. The fabulous stretch pants and skirts (that never lose their stretch) can be worn after childbirth until you get your figure back, or they will alter them to your regular size. Find also bras, swimwear and even some pretty and flattering eveningwear, often with low necks.   www.nicolcaramel.com

Piazza di Spagna area

Via di Ripetta 261   **06-361 2059**
00187 Rome   Mon 3:30-7:30, Tues-Sat 9-1, 3:30- 7:30

☆ Nuyorica

Brace yourself for real danger when you enter this temple of the shoe cult. No wonder Cameron Diaz, a self-confessed shoe addict, popped in often while filming Scorsese's *Gangs of New York* in town. But you don't need to be a Hollywood star to end up using all your plastic on the glittering merchandise, including wraparound boots by Rodolphe Menudier, Sigerson Morrison's soft suede ones, Bruno Frisoni girly flats and Pierre Hardy stilettos. Not to mention the capsule compilation of very now clothes and accessories: Balenciaga's tailored jackets or Chloé's butter-soft suede bags, for instance, are simply beyond human resistance. The minds behind the concept? Owners Cristiano Giovagnoli and Emanuele Frumenti, trendsetters to the style set and this year mad for ancient Roman footwear.

Campo de' Fiori area

Piazza Pollarola 36-37   **06-6889 1243**
00186 Rome   Daily 10-8

Officine

Hidden in one of the historic center's narrow cobblestone streets, this store only opened last year but at once became heaven for ethnic accessory lovers. Riding on the ethnomania wave that has hit the Eternal City, Roman girls Federica Pandolfi and Annamaria Cacchio have collected artefacts during their leisure trips in exotic lands. Expect embroidered and fringed Moroccan leather bags, babouches and poufs; Masai jewellery from Kenya; Thai silk purses, and mother-of-pearl Filipino ones; Indian cotton mirror sarongs; and Afghan and Indian antique silver earrings and bracelets. You can choose a model, and have your necklace made from the beautiful selection of beads from Africa, India or Murano in Italy.

Piazza Navona area

Vicolo del Governo Vecchio 60   **06-687 5804**
00186 Rome   Mon-Sat 10:30-7:30

☆ Omero & Cecilia-Vestiti Usati

Make sure you fall into the good graces of charismatic owner Omero Dafano (a good idea is to pet his dog, Nanda)…he might show you priceless pieces hidden in the back or hung out of sight on the ceiling of what he calls his "bazaar of vintage". And a real bazaar it is: you'll come across Sixties Italian dresses, Seventies velvet coats, British tweed jackets, snakeskin purses, Adidas sneakers, old military shirts and jackets, as well as outrageous styles from the Eighties, Omero's decade of choice at the moment. Ah, and Jean Paul Gaultier shops here.

Piazza Navona area

Via del Governo Vecchio 110   **06-683 3506**
00186 Rome   Mon-Sat 10-8

Only Hearts

It is ironic that this boudoir-like shop, home of Helena Stuart's sexy pieces, is located just in front of one of the most imposing churches, the Chiesa Nuova. The featherweight ensembles, frilly G-strings and camisoles, girly see-through slips and lacy French knickers have given local babes a lighter alternative to the more classic (and maybe classy) Italian styles, like those at La Perla. Stuart's day collection of hyper-feminine jersey tops, tulle T-shirts, romantic skirts and slip dresses, worn overseas by everyone from Britney to Liz Hurley, have conquered Italy's trendy female population, including the veline or letterine: young dancer-cum-assistant-TV-presenters, real celebrities in the country and role models for every teenager.   www.onlyhearts.com

Piazza Navona area

Piazza della Chiesa Nuova 21   **06-686 4647**
00186 Rome   Sun-Mon 12-8, Tues-Sat 10-8

Via Vittoria 76   **06-679 3446**
00187 Rome   (opening times as above)

Onyx Fashion Store

Exasperated parents park their grumpy teenagers here for hours at a time, knowing they'll be entertained without too much damage to their credit cards. Mothers, incognito, sometimes pop in too. This megastore, stretching from one shopping street to another and resounding with pumping music spilling from endless TV screens, is the temple of streetwear the Italian way, which means with reasonable quality and style. From jeans and T-shirts to minidresses, coats or sweats, everything comes in the latest models and in an outstanding array of fabrics and colors. Shoes, accessories and even trendy school bags and exercise books are also available, but the ubiquitous Onyx logo can be a bit off-putting.

Piazza di Spagna area

Via del Corso 132   **06-699 321**
or Via Belsiana 75-77   (double entrance)
00187 Rome   Mon-Sat 10-8, Sun 3-8

Via Frattina 92   **06-679 1509**
00187 Rome   Mon 10-8, Tues-Sat 10-7:30

Via Cola di Rienzo area

Via Cola di Rienzo 225-229   **06-3600 6073**
00192 Rome   (opening times as above)

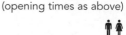

Rome Directory

Pandemonium

Trend-crazed teens and thirtysomethings alike favor this sparkling new store where un-casual casuals have glamorous labels. An immaculate decor dotted by Seventies objects is a suitable setting for upscale streetwear. Looking for jeans? They come with faux holes and suede inserts by D&G, in distressed denim by John Richmond, classic by Calvin Klein or multicolored by Cavalli. Or sneakers: the signature Adidas stripes adorn many of the shelves, while the latest Pumas are classic black and white. And if you are after something a little more daring, you can count on witty items like Jaisalmer's ruffled tops or Nolita's bustier dresses. Guys can also rely on Mason's basic cotton shirts and pants, Lost Sheep T-Shirts and RRD bermudas. The chunky silver rings and bracelets are unisex.

Campo de' Fiori area

Via dei Giubbonari 104   **06-686 8061**
00186 Rome   Mon 3:30-7:30, Tues-Sat 10-7:30
Parioli

Piazza Euclide 7-8   **06-807 7538**
00197 Rome   (opening times as above)

☆ Passion

Wanna feel the heat? Plunge into this den of Latin passion where the clothes are hot, hot, hot. And enjoy the show curvy Italian actresses put on while trying on sizzling styles such as Plein Sud sequined strechy minidresses or ultra-tight jeans, Helene Zoubedia crepe and lace see-through dresses, or VDP Collection's sassy bustiers with tulle appliqués. And don't miss young designer Green Morgan's cheeky little things…not for nothing is she designer Mila Schon's daughter.

Piazza di Spagna area

Via delle Carrozze 39   **06-678 1527**
00187 Rome   Mon 3-7:30, Tues-Sat 10-1:30, 3-7:30

Patrizia Pepe

Modern and feminine, Florentine designer Patrizia Pepe's versatile creations are like manna from heaven for the stylish city girl. Her only store in town, strategically placed on the corner of the gorgeous Piazza di Spagna, is, like her styles, simple with eye-catching details like the olive tree sprouting from a table and a shocking pink paneled wall. You'll find slim body-skirting coats and jackets, pretty chiffon dresses, frilly feminine blouses and pieces with subtle sexy hints, like her lace-up hipster jeans. And don't worry, price tags won't send you into the ER.   www.patriziapepe.com

Piazza di Spagna area

Via Frattina 1   **06-678 4698**
00187 Rome   Daily 10-8 (Sun 10:30-8)

People

Retro-chic chicks dig this cute little shop that reads like a celebration of the glorious Sixties and Seventies. From round mirrors to murals and plastic furniture, everything is an ode to the Beatles era. Twentysomething Roman designers Germana Panunzi and Sara Sorge create optical-print miniskirts, tennis-style dresses, bright hipsters and skimpy tops using original fabrics. They also collect vintage pieces, such as suede and leather jackets and coats, printed T-shirts and shirts, belts, purses and Jackie O glasses, all strictly from their favorite period. Prices are so convenient, you might become a convert too.

Campo de' Fiori area

Piazza Teatro di Pompeo 4a   **338-807 5529**
00186 Rome   Mon 3:30-8, Tues-Sat 10:30-2:30, 3:30-8

Petit Bateau   👩 👨

It might look like any other kids' store, but savvy models and even Hollywood stars (like Cameron Diaz) also shop here. This tiny shop has a small section for grown-ups, storing the French-made T-shirts appreciated by cognoscenti the world over…and they're much cheaper here than in the States. Flirty French styles include the square-neck tee with three-quarter sleeves, the sleeveless turtleneck and the long-sleeved double-faced T-shirt in neutral colors. Same styles, super-cute in small sizes, apply also for children aged from newborn to eight. A kid's favorite? The thick cotton overalls, warm in winter and cool in summer.

Piazza di Spagna area

Via della Croce 45   **06-6920 2154**
00187 Rome   Mon 1-7:30, Tues-Sat 9:30-7:30

Pantheon area

Via Campo Marzio 10b   **06-679 2348**
00186 Rome   Mon-Sat 9:30-7:30

Via Cola di Rienzo area

Via Cola di Rienzo 311   **06-3972 2928**
00192 Rome   Mon 3:30-7:30, Tues-Sat 9:30-7:30

Piccadilly   👨

This unpretentious and slightly old-fashioned shop is for the mom and grandmother who would like to see the children in the classic smocked dress in Liberty fabrics or Scottish tartans. Hence the British-style tweed coat with the velvet collar, the dark blue blazer worn with short grey flannel pants, and the tiny cache-coeur sweaters to wear over the smocked dresses with a deep U neckline so you can still admire the smocking. Christening dresses are made to measure and the owners are very helpful, especially at guessing sizes and making suggestions.

Piazza di Spagna area

Via Sistina 92   **06-679 3697**
00187 Rome   Mon-Fri 9:30-1, 4-7:30, Sat 9:30-1

Pinko   👩

New Romantic? Neo-Gothic? Punk-chic? Trends mix and don't always match with this brand's clothes. Just one thing is for sure, they're desperately seeking cool…and only occasionally succeeding. Like with their satin cargo pants, seen on more that one truly hip chick. Other current styles include Peruvian princess sweaters, cropped baseball sweat shirts, sequined T-shirts, pinstriped dungarees and camouflage pants. Worth checking out, though: something might fit your current fashion mood and the prices won't give your bank balance a jolt.

Campo de' Fiori area

Via dei Giubbonari 76-77   **06-6830 9446**
00186 Rome   Mon 3-8, Tues-Sat 10-8, Sun 12-8

Pantheon area

Via della Scrofa 24   **06-683 3136**
00186 Rome   Mon 12-7:30, Tues-Sat 10-7:30

Planet   ♟♟

Hip-hop types, boys and girls, drop their skateboards and pop into this chilled-out store to check out gear that is a passport to cool, trying to ignore the fact that they're not on an LA street but around Renaissance and baroque palazzos and churches. The brands here are musts for this type of culture. Take the American roadwork clothing label Carharrt: their work pants, T-shirts and baggy sweats are the uniform for teens into this vibe. Cult name Stüssy provides tees, parkas and hooded jackets, while down jackets and walking boots are strictly by The North Face and sneakers by Nike or Globe.

Campo de' Fiori area

Via dei Baullari 132   **06-6880 1396**
00186 Rome   Mon 3:30-8, Tues-Sat 10-1:30, 3:30-8

Pollini   ♟♟

Heighten your senses and prepare to enjoy the performance of an art few nowadays master: effortless, genuine, efficient and extremely polite service...which makes it a pleasure to shop here. Not that the goods need much promotion. Shoes by this 60-year-old family-run company, all still made in Italy, are amazingly well crafted: leathers are top quality, seams impeccable. And take a look at the perfection and beauty of the soles: you'll want to wear these shoes upside down. Styles of footwear come with a matching bag: like the daring leather stiletto boots that only partially cover the leg. A classic? The fabric and leather line of shoulder bags, wallets and travel bags, all with a simple "P" logo, an original alternative to the ultra-popular Vuitton competitors.

Piazza di Spagna area

Via Frattina 22-24   **06-679 8360**
00187 Rome   Mon 2:30-7:30, Tues-Sat 10-7:30

☆ Prada   ♟

Unless you've just landed from Mars and haven't spoken to a soul all the way from the spaceship, you'll know what this name means: 100% modern chic, undiluted. Miuccia Prada reinvents contemporary cool season after season, surprising her dedicated following with unpredictable intuitions. This two-story space, a prime location facing the Spanish Steps, will satiate every Prada fan's cravings. The ground floor is devoted to handbags, sunglasses and a stylish display of the cosmetic line that also comes packaged in mini doses. The first floor has all the gear you could dream of: a vast selection of shoes, including the cult silvery sneakers or the buckled mules; handbags in mind-boggling variety, wallets, make-up bags and diaries in every type of leather or nylon. Plus the sublime chiffon lingerie. And, of course, the clothes collection, dreamed of by every female inhabitant of Earth and worn with nonchalance by a few privileged creatures like Milla Jovovich.   www.prada.com

Piazza di Spagna area

Via Condotti 92	**06-679 0897**
00187 Rome	Mon 3-7, Tues-Sat 10-7, Sun 1:30-7:30

☆ Prada Sport

Prada's Maurizio Bertelli's passion for sport (and sailing in particular) is reflected in this vast collection of hyper-practical, high-quality and incredibly stylish clothes and accessories. This shop is the first in the capital dedicated entirely to the Prada Sport line. Techno-fabrics, functional yet flattering cuts and the signature red tag are constant elements in these collections. From nylon down jackets with fur-trimmed hoods, to work pants, thick belted cotton jackets, zipped nylon jackets, thick denim miniskirts, fleece tops and stretchy T-shirts, these garments are so cool that to call them sports clothes is just restrictive. Accessories like streamlined sunglasses, padded gloves and versatile nylon bags are just as modish. Service is low-key and discreet, very Pradaesque.

Piazza di Spagna area

Via del Babuino 91	**06-3600 4884**
00187 Rome	(opening times as above)

Prada Uomo

What's that subtle, pleasant aroma assailing you as you enter this store? Leather of course, this being Prada, and for men only. This huge, dark space gives guys the opportunity to browse or shop at their own pace, without nagging girlfriends or wives pulling them (and their credit cards) towards the women's section. And what a playground it is, luring the customer with travel bags, attaché cases, sports bags, toiletry bags, sunglasses, diaries and wallets. A space in the back is devoted to classic boots, funky loafers, ultra-popular sneakers and other shoe styles. The rest of the store hosts the main line (and some of Prada Sport), made up of classic wool or leather coats, thick or ultra-fine knits, crisp cotton shirts and stylish suits.

Piazza di Spagna area

Via Condotti 90	**06-679 0897**
00187 Rome	(opening times as above)

Prenatal

This unprepossessing shop for children will surprise you. If you need to outfit your offspring in an emergency, head straight for Prenatal. It looks small as you enter, but twists and winds from room to room and seems to go on endlessly. Nor will you find just clothes, shoes, underwear, pajamas and outfits for newborns, but everything from a baby rattle or pacifier to cribs and baby furniture. Clothes for the mom-to-be, too. Rome is full of shops with fancy duds for infants and toddlers; at Prenatal you'll get a good idea of what ordinary Italians buy for their kids.

Piazza di Spagna area

Via della Croce 50a   **06-679 7181**
00187 Rome   Mon 2-7:30, Tues-Sat 10-7:30

Via Nationale area

Via Nationale 45   **06-488 1403**
00184 Rome   Mon-Sat 10-8, Sun 11:30-1:30, 3-7:30

Prototype

Do you believe in authentic street style but don't mind a little name-dropping? This is the store for you. T-shirts are by Jean Paul Gaultier or Franklin & Marshall, jeans are Levi's Red, Fornarina or E-Play, and sneakers range from the latest Puma to the classic Converse All Star. Other essentials include fishnet tank tops, frilly shirts, faux-fur jackets and embroidered shearling coats. Boys are also catered for with a small selection of casualwear.

Campo de' Fiori area

Via dei Giubbonari 50   **06-6830 0330**
00186 Rome   Mon 3:30-8, Tues-Sat 10-8, Sun 12-8

Pulp

Japanese store buyers periodically scan the racks of this recently renovated unpretentious vintage shop for that extra special little something. Some items, like printed cotton or floral Seventies shirts or gypsy skirts, are relatively standard, but some are not: see the occasional Aquascutum camel coat, the rare Pucci pants, or the Yves Saint Laurent Fifties purse at I-can't-believe-how-cheap-they-are prices. Curiosities include Seventies lamps, clocks, telephones and fake Barbie dolls.

Via Nazionale area

Via del Boschetto 140   **06-485 511**
00184 Rome   Mon 4-8, Tues-Sat 10-1, 4-8

☆ Puma Store

For some reason, right now Puma casual shoes are the hottest brand of their type in Italy, the shoe of the moment. Men and women alike wear the Monster style with their chic suits. It has a flat heel, Velcro closure in the front, wraparound sole and comes in black, white, and dark brown; kids wear them with their jeans. Pumas are more than sport shoes, they're life-style shoes for those tired of the super-sporty look of Nike and Adidas and loved by males and females of every age and social class. Oh, Puma does also sell casual sportswear.

Piazza di Spagna area

Via del Corso 404   06-6880 8205
00186 Rome   Daily 10-8

Pure Sermoneta

Precocious fashionistas, kicking and screaming, drag their designer nannies to this fashion emporium devoted to kids whose favourite bedtime stories are from *Vogue Bambini*. Label-conscious infants can count on collections by Roberto Cavalli, Dolce & Gabbana or Gianfranco Ferré that faithfully mirror the adults' collections. Cavalli's leopard-printed jeans or shearling coats, for instance, look like mummy's shrunk in the washing machine. Same applies to D&G corduroy pants, Peruvian-inspired sweaters and faux-vintage leather boots. Find also Ralph Lauren mini-sweaters and T-shirts, cute Blumarine skirts and dresses, little down jackets by Aspesi, Tod's brown boots and shoes and revisited Levi's jeans. And all sorts of accessories…gloves, belts, hats and silver jewelry. When it comes to fashion, even kids want to have fun.

Piazza di Spagna area

Via Frattina 111   **06-679 4555**
00187 Rome   Mon 1-7:30, Tues-Sun 10-7:30

Red & Blue

Husky was once a terribly British brand of quilted rainproof nylon jacket with a corduroy collar, beloved by the riding and foxhunting set. But in the Seventies it became so popular in Italy that eventually an Italian company bought the name. Lightweight, for traveling in variable weather, it's a welcome addition to your suitcase. For 150 euros it goes with everything and will last for years. This shop carries a large variety in different colors and styles, as well as everything else to dress the horseman or horsewoman. Brands include Burberry, Hogan, Tod's, Moncler, Brunello Cucinelli cashmeres and linen/cotton sweaters and Jeckerson pants and jeans, the only jeans admitted on smart golf courses.

Piazza di Spagna area

Via dei Due Macelli 57   **06-679 1933**
00187 Rome   Mon 3:30-7:30, Tues-Sat 10-7:30

Replay

Jeansy young things rejoice! This Made in Italy label has great styles, and unlike other brands is not yet on every pert wiggly bottom around the planet. Rages of the moment include Seventies vintage-like flares made of denim that go from the just-faded to the faux-dirty sort-of-disgusting, but other cuts, such as the classic bootleg, are also available. Rock-chick T-shirts, glam-babe logo-tees, rodeo girls' python cowboy boots and biker-chic leather jackets are also available. Don't miss their E-play collection, street-style clothes with quirky details and finishes, ideal for club-hopping with style.

Pantheon area

Via della Rotonda 25   **06-683 3073**
00186 Rome   Mon 10:30-8, Tues-Sat 10-8

Roberto Cavalli ♀

Cavalli is riding high, and his Via Borgognona store is a shrine to his trademark jungle-chic looks that make women resemble sexy beasts on heels. Exotic animal prints like zebra and leopard permeate everything from the marbled floors to the long chiffon dresses, stretch jeans, blouses and tops and double-face down jackets. Feast your eyes on long shearling coats with fox collars, over-the-knee boots made of a patchwork of leather and fabrics, and gold sandals decorated with Swarovski crystals. Not for the black-clad crowd.

Piazza di Spagna area

Via Borgognona 7a   **06-6938 0130**
00187 Rome   Mon 1-7:30, Tues-Sat 10-7:30

Romagnoli ♀

Signora Romagnoli has been here since 1938 and has created hats for the high fashion collections. She does have a selection on hand, and her straw hats smothered with flowers are to die for, but Roman ladies come here to have hats made to match their outfits and shoes (often from Dalco) for special occasions. A hat can be made in three or four days, or they'll ship it to you if it takes longer. Go on, indulge yourself—there aren't many places like this left in the world.

Via Gregoriana 54   **06-679 2133**
00187 Rome   Mon-Fri 10:30-1, 4-7

Rubinacci ♂

Mariano Rubinacci comes from a dynasty of Neopolitan tailors who made their name with jackets and shirts cut with sleeves ample enough to move the arms freely. The "Neopolitan jacket" was favored by King Umberto and film director Vittorio de Sica. Today's well-dressed man can choose from ready-to-wear or have his suits, jackets, pants and shirts made to order in British fabrics. The shop also has a selection of handmade shoes, cufflinks, belts, foulards and pullovers. Sofas and armchairs lend an atmosphere of a salon where clients can linger and chat. Ask for Alessandra Rubinacci, daughter of Mariano.

Piazza di Spagna area

Via Fontanella di Borghese 33   **06-6889 2943**
00186 Rome   Mon 3:30-7:30
              Tues-Sat 10:30-1:30, 3:30-7:30

☆ Saddlers Union ♂ ♀

Here is a glimpse of old-world luxury: a charming leather-scented artisan shop which has made bags, shoes and belts for the cream of Italian aristocracy and for major Hollywood stars since 1950. Thick quality leathers are cut and hand-stitched, in the open-air workshop, by the two owners (they seem to be everlasting, like their products) using ultra-resistant saddle-making techniques. The flat loafers, classic shoulder bags with canvas straps, beautiful riding boots or extra-chic travelling bags, can be custom-made, mono-grammed and sent all over the world...and, like some men, look better with age. Genuine status symbols for those who don't need them.

Piazza di Spagna area

Via Condotti 26	**06-679 8050**
00187 Rome	Mon-Sat 10-1, 3-7

Salvatore Ferragamo

Tradition, in the house of Ferragamo, goes back a long, long way. We're talking the shoemaker to the stars, the leg-endary cobbler who worked for the studios in Hollywood in the Twenties, moved back to Italy in the Thirties and set up a small workshop destined to become a worldwide empire. His innovative designs, like the Roman sandal or the wedge heel, and his original use of unconventional materials like raffia, raw silk, lace or nylon have inspired footwear design-ers right up to the present day. Hollywood glamour oozes from the walls of his Roman shop, where black & white pic-tures show Ferragamo with celebrity clients like Audrey Hepburn and the Duchess of Windsor. His perfect-fit classic shoes, like the cute patent-leather pumps with grosgrain bow or the flat loafers, are on display, together with a col-lection of purses, travel bags, Seventies glasses and print-ed silk scarves. Prêt-à-porter styles include Fifties-inspired suits, somber cashmere coats, ladylike silk shirts and under-stated leather jackets. Not recommended to the chronic fashion victim.   www.salvatoreferragamo.com

Piazza di Spagna area

Via Condotti 73-74	**06-679 1565**
00187 Rome	Mon 3-7, Tues-Sat 10-7

Salvatore Ferragamo Uomo

Men, Ferragamo style, are unflinchingly classic, unadven-turous in fashion, and keen on their gentlemen's sports like sailing or hunting. Expect impeccably cut suits and coats, crisp cotton shirts, casual suede jackets, quality leather coats, lush cashmere sweaters and, of course, a crafty col-lection of shoes in a variety of traditional styles. Check out the dazzling array of their signature micro-patterned silk ties and the limited edition Nautical line featuring elegant blue canvas sailing bags. New this year is the Subtil cologne and, for the kids at heart, there is a small selection of teddy bears made from the same silk they use for the ties.

Piazza di Spagna area

Via Condotti 66	**06-678 1130**
00187 Rome	Mon 3-7, Tues-Sat 10-7

☆ SBU

When brothers Patrizio and Cristiano Perfetti, back in 1988, added a denim line (using only the highest quality ultra-soft hand-finished material) to their collection of basics, even they couldn't foresee their success story. Today SBU jeans, sold at Fred Segal in LA, Bergdorf Goodman in NY and Harvey Nichols in London have been spotted clinging to David Beckham's muscley thighs as well as to the more sinuous ones of Monica Bellucci, Helena Christensen and Britney Spears. Hang out in the recently renovated ethno-chic store, inside a 15th-century palazzo, to observe the customers relaxing on the huge Moroccan sofa and the worn leather chairs and Rome's young playboys trying to chat up the super-cute shop assistants. The brothers have just added a bamboo garden to provide even more tranquillity. Dreamy.

Piazza Navona area

Via S.Pantaleo 68-69
00186 Rome

06-6880 2547
Mon 3:30-7:30
Tues-Sat 10:30-1:30, 3:30-7:30

Scapa

The Roman polo set (and those who pretend they're part of it) get part of their gear from this elegant salotto-like store, situated since 1989 in the tiny Via Vittoria which is fast becoming one of the chicest streets in the capital. Anglo-Belgian brand Scapa, a sort of cross between Ralph Lauren and Banana Republic (designed by Scotsman Brian Redding), heralds a British colonial look of riding breeches, shetland jumpers and Harris tweed jackets (linen in summer), in a color palette that favours white, beige, brown, green and the occasional red. There is also a tiny childrenswear corner.

Piazza di Spagna area

Via Vittoria 58-59
00187 Rome

06-678 9368
Mon 3:30-7:30
Tues-Fri 10:30-2:30, 3:30-7:30, Sat 10:30-7:30

Schostal

Hip Roman guys might like their fashion, but not when it comes to socks. For socks and undies they do as their daddies do and shop at Schostal, a classic store dating from 1870 with branches both in the historic center and in the posh district of Parioli. Once you've tried a Schostal sock, we're told, you'll never change: they're supersoft and light and come in cotton, silk, plain wool and cashmere. The same applies to undershirts and briefs. Other attractions: old-style shirts, jerseys and scarves. Luckily the service is old-style too, as in polite and attentive.

Piazza di Spagna area

Via del Corso 158
00186 Rome

06-679 1240
Mon 3:30-7:30, Tues-Sat 9:30-7:30

Parioli

Piazza Euclide 41-42   **06-808 0165**
00197 Rome   Mon 3:30-7:30, Tues-Sat 9:30-1, 3:30-7:30

Sem Vaccaro

Step into this shop and you'll think you're in a Santa Fe store for cowgirls who like to show off. Walls are light blue, orange and yellow, native American faces stare at you from the walls, and the racks are crammed with essentials to build that rodeo-chic look Madonna resurrected a couple of years ago. Prepare to overdose on assorted cowboy boots, myriads of leather jackets, suede mini and maxi skirts, fringed cowboy shirts and frilly gypsy ones, and little floral tops and dresses. Not to mention the python and croc bags, the thick leather belts with silver and turquoise buckles and the faded denim jeans with lacy inserts. Prices are not that high, so you won't have to rob the saloon.

Pantheon area

Via dei Orfani 91   **06-678 4226**
00186 Rome   Mon 3:30-7:30, Tues-Sat 10-7:30

Sergio Rossi

Glam-babes swear by Rossi's creations that instantly give ordinary feet a subtle veneer of sexiness without being overly bold or brassy. Pointed toes, stiletto heels and streamlined shapes are the basics ingredients of Rossi's magic, which will turn you into a femme fatale without the bonus of blistered feet at the end of a walking day. This season's styles range from punk to modern Venus, with leather tassels and grommets, wooden beads and oyster shells livening up the styles. Make room in your closet…you'll want them all.   www.sergiorossi.com

Piazza di Spagna area

Piazza di Spagna 97-100   **06-678 3245**
00187 Rome   Mon 3-7, Tues-Sat 10-7

Sermoneta

Arnie Schwarzenegger wearing fancy gloves? Possible, according to the picture of the smiling action man beside one of a semi-masked Michael Jackson proudly displayed on the stairs of this shop. Even if somewhat frumpy and unhip, it is certainly a great destination for glove aficionados as it dishes out gloves in a variety that challenges the imagination. Winter styles come in calfskin lined with cashmere, rabbit or silk, and tones that go from jade green to orange to canary yellow and shocking pink. Classy brown or black evening gloves come trimmed with mink. Summer styles feature sherbet-shaded gloves hand-painted in oriental floral patterns, while suede ones in apple-green or pink are lined with sheepskin in a contrasting shade. Yummy enough just to have around.   www.sermonetagloves.com

Piazza di Spagna area

Piazza di Spagna 61   **06-679 1960**
00187 Rome   Daily 9:30-7:30

Sisley

Make sure you rummage well through the shelves of this unpretentious store, packed with youngsters, tourists, and Romans in the know. Some very nice items at very pretty prices are regularly dished out by this brand, a trendier branch of Benetton. Sweaters are tiny, in natural fibers, and come in funky shapes, like off-the-shoulder or wraparound; skirts are mini and flattering; while cotton shirts in fashionable shades are short, fitted and very cute. Particularly loved by Tokyo babes, their holiday burdened by monstrous shopping bags.

Piazza di Spagna area

Via Condotti 59	**06-661 0318**
00186 Rome	Mon-Sat 10-7:30
Via Frattina 19a	**06-6994 1787**
00187 Rome	Mon-Sat 10-8

Via Nazionale area

Via Nazionale 84	**06-4782 3415**
00184 Rome	Mon-Sat 10-8, Sun 10-1, 4-8

Via Cola di Rienzo area

Via Cola di Rienzo 155-157	**06-324 3224**
00192 Rome	Mon-Sat 10-8, Sun 10:30-1:30, 3:30-7:30

Sports Suite

Sports gear can be stylish and Sports Suite is here to prove it. This brand-new shop, strategically placed in the heart of mega-brand kingdom, offers a small but carefully chosen selection of items where design and practicality go hand in hand. Sidi's futuristic black and silver spinning shoes, or The North Face's stylish suede climbing boots, are hip enough to wear at a party or out clubbing. Same applies to the Quiksilver Lycra surfing shirts and Versace Sports T-shirts…they've recently stepped out of the gym or off the beach and onto the street. Worth checking out.

Piazza di Spagna area

Via Mario de' Fiori 53-53a	**06-678 4945**
00187 Rome	Mon-Sat 10-7

Stefanel

Count on this label for separates that are easy, wearable, affordable and of acceptable quality. Garments are designed with an eye to the latest trends, but without overdoing it. Styles run from pretty cropped leather jackets, pencil skirts, corduroy hipsters, pinstriped coats and classic pantsuits to wool jerseys in all shapes and colors, cotton tees and jeans. And you can also accessorize, with leather bags, floppy hats, belts and an array of footwear. Service is laid-back, music pumping, and you'll be left alone to roam around at your leisure.

Piazza di Spagna area

Via del Corso 122-125	**06-6992 5783**
00186 Rome	Daily 10-8

Via Frattina 31-33	**06-679 2667**
00187 Rome	Daily 10-8 (Sun 10-2, 3-7:30)

Via Nazionale area

Via Nazionale 57-58	**06-4782 6432**
00184 Rome	Mon-Sat 10-8

Via Cola di Rienzo area

Via Cola di Rienzo 223	**06-321 1403**
00192 Rome	Mon-Sat 10-7:45, Sun 12-2, 4-7:45

Strenesse

Gabrielle Strehle's no-frills clothes are made for the modern dynamic woman who still wants to be stylish. They are clean-cut in simple lines, and the colors tend to be neutral, never loud. Ladies can find basic jackets in natural fabrics; black, beige and white pantsuits and coats cut close to the body; simple stretch tees and jersey tops; and pretty chiffon dresses and stylish laceless sneakers in black and white. The guys can rely on basic suits, long-sleeved cotton tees, classic coats and leather jackets. There is also a line of footwear in natural leathers, and city-slick handbags and belts.

Piazza di Spagna area

Via del Babuino 146	**06-3600 3542**
00187 Rome	Mon 3-7, Tues-Fri 10-7, Sat 10-2

Sub Dued

Oh-so-trendy but, as the name suggests, subdued. The decor sets the tone: white tiled floor and walls, and a large ventilation duct running the length of the shop making it look like the subway. This is like a combination of Gap and Banana Republic but with an Italian look. The colors tend to be subdued too, black and white, but the clothes are well cut and not expensive. It's a sportivo style, but with the right accessory you can make it dressier. A boyish figure helps.

Parioli

Viale Parioli 35	**06-807 3430**
00197 Rome	Mon 4-8 , Tues-Sat 10:30-1, 4-8

Piazza di Spagna area

Via Tomacelli 154-155	**06-687 8431**
00187 Rome	Mon 4-8, Tues-Sat 10:30-8

Taba

For that Bali-babe look Italian girls do so well, head straight to this mini boutique on super-cool Campo de' Fiori with its colorful fruit and vegetable market. Here you'll get the staples for the look, perfect also for those scorching Roman summer days: tie-dyed cotton tank tops, crocheted dresses, floaty cotton pants and frilly gypsy skirts, plus divine sequined sandals, beaded shell and leather belts, raffia beach bags and every possible kind of sarong on earth. Globe-trotting Argentinian owner Carlos Alberto Allevato picks up the stuff on his frequent tours of Asia and South America, so a variety of styles is guaranteed. Taba also has shops in the popular sea resorts of Ponza Island and San Felice Circeo. www.tabashop.com

Rome Directory

Campo de' Fiori area

Piazza Campo de' Fiori 13　　　　　　　**06-6880 6478**
00187 Rome　　　　　　　　　　　Daily 10-8 (Sun 12-8)

Tablo　　　　　　　　　　　　　　　　　†

Do your kids run around looking like rappers while you dream of seeing them attired like little lords? This unfussy, austere store, here since 1960, will restore your faith in good taste. The rails are sparsely filled with impeccable mini-blazers with gold buttons, crisp white shirts, elegant micro-ties and somber belts. Staples for girls are romantic smocked dresses in cotton or linen. No wonder the private schools in this posh part of town order their uniforms here. Also perfect for that formal party look.

Piazza di Spagna area

Via della Croce 84　　　　　　　　**06-679 4468**
00187 Rome　　　　　Mon 3-7, Tues-Sat 9:30-2, 3-7

☆ Tad　　　　　　　　　　　　　　　♀

Join the hip crowd and duck into this joint to catch the vibe, see or be seen, and also fit in a big chunk of shopping. This is Rome's first and only concept store, a mecca for starved fashionistas. They find, under the same 1,000 square metre roof, Alexander McQueen, Hussein Chalayan, Alberto Biani and Alessandro dell'Acqua for clothes; Marc Jacobs, Sartore and Sigerson Morrison for shoes; Aesop beauty products, international magazines, trip-hop, lounge and ethno CDs; and a vast range of furniture, Indian fabrics and exotic homewares. Plus you can have your locks fixed by their in-store hairdresser and have a bite of fusion food in the stylish bar-restaurant. Chances are you'll bump into some cute local celebrity, an always pleasing-to-the-eye experience.　　　　　　　　　www.taditaly.com

Piazza di Spagna area

Via del Babuino 155a　　　　　　　**06-3269 5122**
00187 Rome　　　　Sun-Mon 12-8, Tues-Sat 10:30-7:30

Tebro　　　　　　　　　　　　　　♂♀†

With the look of a department store like Saks Fifth Avenue or Harvey Nichols, this mecca for an old-money clientele carries a wide assortment for men, women and newborns in an air of refined gentility. They have been around for 140 years and the atmosphere is very soothing…wall-to-wall carpeting and warm boiserie. You'll find underwear, night-wear, socks and ties for men, swimwear for both sexes (including Blumarine, Dolce & Gabanna and Roberto Cavalli) and pareos and coverups. Newborns to 18 months have their own corner, where you can get sheets for baby beds or cribs—they'll make these to measure, if you like, just as they'll make sheets to measure for awkward-sized beds on yachts.

Piazza di Spagna area

Via dei Prefetti 46　　　　　　　　**06-687 3441**
00186 Rome　　　　　Mon 4-8, Tues-Sat 9:30-1, 4-8

Tricots

☆ Thé Verde

Guaranteed to fulfill every ethnomaniac expectation. A simple raw silk jacket comes straight from Vietnam; embroidered babouches and thick wool caftans are made in Morocco. The beautiful minimalist pottery is by a French-Chinese artist, the beaded sandals and belts by a Kenyan girl, and the delicate silk purses by a Lebanese. And keep in mind that exhibitions of paintings by young exotic artists are often held in the back.

Piazza di Spagna area

Via Vittoria 23   **06-3211 0174**
00187 Rome   Mon 3:30-7:30, Tues-Sat 10-2, 3:30-7:30

Timberland

Ah, Timberland. It was in the early Eighties that the dark yellow logger's boot from New Hampshire became a cult object with Roman paninari (would-be yuppies). They would ask friends visiting the US to bring Timberlands back to Italy with them, and today Timberland is an international brand for classic casual clothes, accessories, boots, and shoes for men, women, and children. Why check out an American store in Italy? Well, the cut for men's and women's clothes may vary from those sold in the US, slimmer for European figures. And it is a French company which makes the children's clothes for Timberland—the French have always been brilliant at this.

Piazza di Spagna area

Via del Corso 488   **06-322 7266**
00186 Rome   Daily 10-8

Via delle Convertite 6   **06-6992 4724**
00187 Rome   Daily 10-8 (Sun 11-8)

Tod's

Opened in June in the former Fendissime space on the continuation of Via Condotti across Via del Corso. Tod's is decorated in that Seventies David Hicks style, with patterned parquet, walls covered in padded leather, dark brown display cases, chrome trimmings and white vaulted ceilings. The large airy space has the entire Tod's line, as well as the handbags (D bag, Miky and Moccasin), some soft luggage and the Ferrari collection. The staff are helpful but not pushy; ask for Roberto or Stefania.

Piazza di Spagna area

Via della Fontanella di Borghese 56a-57   **06-6821 0066**
00187 Rome   Mon-Sat 10-7:30

Tricots

This slip of a boutique has embarked on a mission to convert Parioli's flashy girls to the zen of avant-garde aesthetics. Racks are crammed with Martin Margiela's first line, his n.6 collection and his footwear. Denim is strictly Helmut Lang, and so are severe black leather shoes, while jersey pieces are by young Italian designer Stefano Mortari.

Rome Directory

Concessions to frivolity are made with some Whistles items and a few Diane von Furstenberg dresses. The shop's appearance, immaculately white with aluminum touches, reflects its current mood.

Parioli

Via D.Chelini 15	**06-808 5815**
00197 Rome	Mon 4-8, Tues-Sat 9-1, 4-8

Trussardi

It's all about leather, say the calfskin-padded walls of this sparkling new emporium. Trussardi's tradition, revived by young creative director Beatrice Trussardi, continues with a breath of new inventiveness. See their leather coats, always a staple: they come in a hippy-de-luxe patchwork of thin leather stripes, with matching miniskirts. Or their classic shoulder bags: the funky Gaia which is triangular and comes in two sizes, one of which is tiny and always sold out. The mood is young and playful also in the men's collection, where printed new-romantic silk pants definitely make a statement.   www.trussardi.com

Piazza di Spagna area

Via Condotti 49-50	**06-679 2151/678 0280**
00187 Rome	Mon-Sat 10-7
Via del Corso 477	**06-322 6055**
00186 Rome	Mon 11-8, Tues-Sat 10-8

Valentino

Welcome to the main boutique of the unofficial emperor of Roman glamour in the über-chic Via Condotti. His clothes, with their flawless cut, simple and elegant shapes and luscious fabrics will make a swan out of any ugly duckling. Every woman should be allowed, once in her life, to wear one of his dresses. Browse around the ground floor of this grand venue for the accessories collection. Climb the magnificent red-carpeted stairway to the first floor for his prêt-à-porter collection and the younger and sportier line, Valentino Roma.   www.valentino.it

Piazza di Spagna area

Via Condotti 13	**06-673 9420**
00187 Rome	Mon 3-7, Tues-Sat 10-7

☆ Valentino Boutique

In tune with the more informal location, Valentino's second boutique is airy and modern, a gallery-like space ending with a view of the charming Via Margutta. This is an ideal location to show the designer's funkiest (if the term can be applied to the master of elegance) collection to date, Valentino Vintage: a new edition of his legendary shapes from the Sixties and Seventies. Expect Veroushka-print boots, Aztec-inspired dresses, T-shirts and foulards, as well as a small diffusion line and a dynamic array of accessories.

Piazza di Spagna area

Via del Babuino 61	**06-3600 1906**
00187 Rome	Mon 3-7, Tues-Sat 10-2, 3-7

Valentino Uomo

Valentino dudes, take note: this is the only boutique in the world dedicated entirely to his men's collections. One huge room hosts seas of impeccable suits from his first line, as well as the more approachable ones from Valentino Roma. Another humungous space features his accessories collection: shoes, bags, belts and some "fashion items" such as embroidered linen shirts and loud blazers...as well as embroidered pashminas and tulle scarves meant to be unisex, actually. The location is stunning: this used to be the dépendance of the historic Palazzo Torlonia.

Piazza di Spagna area

Via Bocca di Leone 16 **06-678 3656**
00187 Rome Mon 3-7, Tues-Sat 10-7

Valleverde

If Kevin Costner can do a TV ad (shown only in Italy) for these comfy but stylish shoes, then you can wear them with confidence. Sometimes you just need a break from the Manolos, and you'll find an amazing variety of styles for both men and women. Walking shoes, sandals and evening shoes come in sizes 39-45 for men, 34-42 for women. There are also a few bags, and we bought a small fat black nylon bag with two zippered compartments that holds everything and can be worn bandolier-style to discourage thieves on mopeds.

Piazza di Spagna area

Via Frattina 109 **06-6938 0372**
00187 Rome Sun-Mon 12:30-8, Tues-Sat 9:30-8

Versace Jeans Couture

Think Versace and think casual: that's what this store is all about. There are the marble floors, the staircase and the very nice black-clad shop assistants, fixed features in Versace haunts. Plus a cameo appearance by perfumes and accessories on the ground floor. But this is predominantly about jeans, as the main floor testifies: the Versus and Versace Jeans diffusion lines turn out jeans with appliqués, strapless denim minidresses, denim jackets, for both female and male aficionados. But there are also kaleidoscopic colored leather jackets, fur-collared coats and jackets, suits with a sexy cut and tight little sweaters. www.versace.com

Piazza di Spagna area

Via Frattina 116 **06-678 7681**
00187 Rome Mon 3-7:30, Tues-Sat 10-1:30, 3-7:30

Verso Sud

When young retailer Ornella di Falco opened this boutique in 1999 in the villagey area of Trastevere, Roman fashion junkies let out a sigh of relief...finally, a store promoting intellectual looks à la Japanese but with a hip and feminine touch. Imagine a Comme des Garçons coat in boiled wool paired with an Isabel Marant paisley-print chiffon dress over leggings and a long T-shirt. Or Romeo Gigli's ample pinstriped coat over classic black New York Industrie pants and an ultra-soft stretch cashmere jumper by BP Studio. Accessories include Jas M.B. distressed-leather Seventies-inspired bags. Clothes are showcased in two minimal rooms with iron and glass details. Simply sublime.

Trastevere

Via San Francesco a Ripa 168   **06-5833 3668**
00153 Rome   Mon 4-8, Tues-Sat 10-2, 4-8

Vestiti Usati Cinzia

If this gallery of vintage street style, with its racks neatly organized by decade, reminds you of a theatrical fashion house, there's a reason. Owner Cinzia Fabbri, a graduate of Rome's Costume and Fashion Academy, once worked as a costume designer for the theater. Her expertise is evident in the choice of quality pieces like Seventies embroidered shearling coats, Austrian leather jackets, bi-colored ski jackets, Sixties striped knits, snakeskin platform boots, and one-offs such as original Palazzo overalls. Make sure you explore the bottom end of the store where the most precious pieces are kept, such as unused sunglasses by YSL, Mary Quant and Dior from the Sixties and Seventies.

Piazza Navona area

Via del Governo Vecchio 45   **(no telephone)**
00186 Rome   Mon-Sat 10-8

Via degli Zingari 10

This store's credo? Surprise the client. Color schemes change every six months and new merchandise comes in every two weeks. Owner Mauro Gagliardini likes to pick new young talent: like ultra-cool Sophie Vhoore and Federica Torlonia and Sophie Galeras, designers of the Ambas line of hippy-chic hand-dyed gauze tunics flaunted in all Italian resorts. Flat ballerina shoes are handmade by Spanish artisans, while fluffy mohair ensembles or faux-pauvre slouch bags in suede or thick wool are part of the store's own line. Definitely original.

Via Nazionale area

Via degli Zingari 10   **06-4782 3889**
00184 Rome   Mon 4-10, Tues-Sat 10-10

Vicolo della Torretta Baby

Small and ultra-chic, this store behind Piazza in Lucina carries small children's shoes by Christian Dior, and a few clothes from Ralph Lauren Polo for kids up to 12 years old.

Piazza di Spagna area

Vicolo della Torretta 17   **06-689 3224**
00186 Rome   Mon-Sat 10-7

Wolford

A little nip or tuck without surgery? Wolford's items squeeze and push just at the right strategic points. Their ultra-flattering bodies come in a variety of stretch fiber and shape.

One of their classics is the velvety sleeveless turtleneck, in all colors from black to baby blue. For a touch of shapely glamour try instead the gold Lurex long-sleeved body, guaranteed to turn you into a curvy Barbie doll. Other staples? Their stretchy tees, lacy tops, body-contouring bathing suits and clever lingerie.   www.wolford.com

Piazza di Spagna area

Via Mario de' Fiori 67	**06-6992 5531**
00187 Rome	Mon 11:30-7:30, Tues-Sat 10-7:30

Yves Saint Laurent

Take fashion's biggest innovator, add today's hottest designer, stir well. The result? YSL today. With Tom Ford's creativity in full gear, the house is dishing out its own brand of cool, so contemporary. Legendary shapes from Master Yves are of course still here—see the trouser suit, the blazer, the tuxedo jacket—but emboldened by materials such as leather and with unexpected turns, like the inserts of stripes of grosgrain, silk and velvet that decorate a black wool suit. Even the plain leather jackets, lean black jeans or jerseys are extremely modern and sexy. The mood of the store is dark and cinematic, like the color palette of clothes and shop assistants alike. Add the new accessories store at the foot of the Spanish Steps, due to open as we went to press, and you really have a serious contender for Rome's fashion district crown.   www.ysl.com

Piazza di Spagna area

Via Bocca di Leone 35	**06-679 5577**
00187 Rome	Mon-Sat 10-7

Zara

Women of every age love this Spanish chain for its low prices and high style sense and, as in London, Zara is now increasing its presence in Italy. A new store is expected to open downtown, probably in the Piazza di Spagna area (how appropriate!), towards the end of the year. It may well be part of an indoor shopping mall in Galleria Colonna, and with its rapidly changing stock will particularly appeal to the Italian passion for something new.

For those who like outdoor shopping and street markets...

The street market on Viale Parioli—especially on Friday, the locals are always out of town on the weekends—is always full of tables and vendors crowding the sidewalks with everything from uniforms for the maids and cooks to inexpensive shoes to copies of Vuitton, Prada and Tod's handbags. You never know what you're going to find—we saw some very fine linen curtains, perfect for a country house—and several of the shops in this guide are within walking distance. The center of the market is at the corner of Via Nino Oxilia. Check the stand of the Carlini family who bring their stylish but inexpensive shoes direct from their factory in Le Marche.

Rome Stores by District

Piazza Navona

V. Pompeo Magno

PONTE MARGHERITA

Piazza della Libertà

R. Tiber

V. dei Gracchi

V. Cola di Rienzo

V. Valadier

Lungotevere dei Mellini

V. A. Farnese

V. G. Belli

V. Cicerone

V. Tacito

V. P Cossa

V. Cassiodoro

V. M. Dionigl

V. Crescenzio

Piazza Cavour

V. V. Colonna

the Vatican

PARCO ADRIANO

Palazzo di Giustizia

Lgo. Prati

Castel San Angelo

Piazza Adriana

Lungotevere Castello

PONTE UMBERTO

Lgo. Marzio

PONTE S. ANGELO

Tevere

V. dell'Orso

Lgo. Tor di Nona

V. Zanardelli

V. di Panico

V. dei Coronari

Corso Vittorio Emanuele

Piazza dell'Oro

Piazza Navona

V. Tor Millina

V. di Parione

V. del Governo Vecchio

Piazza d. Chiesa Nouva

Museo di Roma

Lungotevere del Sangallo

V. Giulia

V. di Monserrato

V. di S. Pantaleo

V. d. Pellegrino

Piazza S. Pantaleo

PONTE MAZZINI

SCALE in miles

0   1/4

Piazza di Spagna

Piazza del Popolo

PINCIO

V. A. Mickievicz

VILLA MEDICI

V. Angelo Brunetti

V. di Ripetta

V. del Corso

V. del Babuino

V. Margutta

French Academy

V. dei Geci

V. d. Frezza

V. Vittoria

V. della Croce

V. di S. Sebastianello

Piazza di Spagna

Augustus's Mausoleum

V. delle Carrozze

Spanish Steps

S. Carlo Al Corso

V. Condotti

V. Belsiana

Piazza Mignanelli

V. Tomacelli

V. Borgognona

V. dell'Arancio

V. Frattina

V. della Vite

V. Fontanella Borghese

V. d Gambero

Piazza S. Lorenzo in Lucina

Poste

V. della Mercede

V. dei Prefetti

V. d. Campo Marzio

V. d. Lucina

Piazza d. Parlamento

Piazza San Silvestro

V. del Pozzetto

Chamber of Deputies

V. del Tritone

Piazza d. Coppelle

Piazza d. Montecitorio

Piazza Colonna

Piazza di Trevi

V. del Corso

V. d. Muratte

Trevi Fountain

Piazza Capranica

V. D. Pietra

V. d. Giustiniani

V d Pantheon

V. d. Seminario

V. d. Umilta

Central Station

Pantheon

d. Rotonda

V. Torre Argentina

V. Pie d. Marmo

Palazzo Colonna

Lgo. d. Torre Argentina

V. d. Plebiscito

Palazzo Venezia

V. C. Battisti

Piazza M. d. Loretto

Rome Districts

Via Nazionale

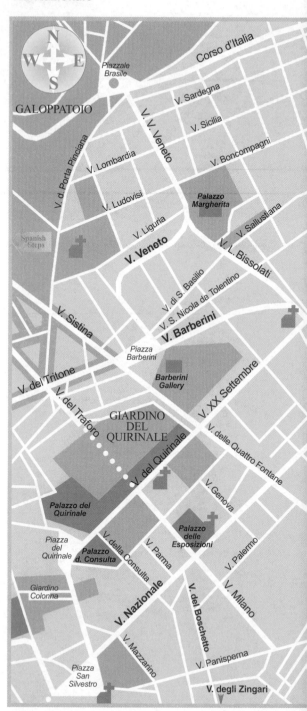

Campo de' Fiori

Museum of Rome

Corso Vittorio Emanuele II

Piazza di S.Pantaleo

Piazza S. Andrea della Valle

Piazza della Pigna

Largo di Torre Argentina

V. del Plebiscito

Piazza Campo dei Fiori

Area Sacra

Piazza San Silvestro

V. dei Giubbonari

V. d. Botteghe Oscure

V. dei Falegnami

Spada Gallery

Piazza B. Cairoli

Piazza Costaguti

V. dei Pettinari

V. d S. Maria

V.S. Maria de' Calderari

V. della Tribuna di Campitelli

Palazzo Cenci

V. Arenula

V. Catalana

Temple of Apollo

Lgo. dei Vallati

Lungotevere de' Cenci

Theater of Marcellus

Piazza San Silvestro

Tiber

PONTE GARIBALDI

L. degli Anguillara

PONTE FABRICIO

Lgo. Raffaello Sanzio

Colosseum

V. della Lungaretta

PONTE PALATINO

Piazza S. Sonnino

V. dei Salumi

S. Gallicano Hospital

V. dei Genovesi

Piazza Mastai

Viale di Trastevere

V. della Luce

V. Aniola

V. S. Michele

Piazza San Silvestro

Porto di Ripa Grande

AVENTINE

Piazza di Porta Portese

Tiber

V. S. Sabina

J. M. Carcani

SCALE in miles

0   1/4

77

Piazza di Spagna area *See map page 75*

Alberta Ferretti	Via Condotti 34
Alexander	Piazza di Spagna 49
Angelo di Nepi	Via Frattina 2
Armani Jeans	Via Tomacelli 137
Armani Jeans	Via del Babuino 70a
AVC by Adriana Campanile	Via Vittoria 18
AVC by Adriana Campanile	Piazza di Spagna 88
Barbara Gregori	Via Vittoria 57a
Bally	Via Condotti 38-40
Banchetti Sport	Via Campo Marzio 38
Barilla	Via del Babuino 33a
Battistoni	Via Condotti 60-61a
BBC Jeans	Via Vittoria 3a
Belsiana 19	Via Belsiana 94
Benetton	Via del Corso 423
Benetton	Piazza di Spagna 67-69
Blunauta	Piazza di Spagna 35
Bonpoint	Piazza San Lorenzo in Lucina 25
Borsalino	Piazza del Popolo 20
Borsalino	Piazza Fontana di Trevi 83
Bottega Veneta	Piazza San Lorenzo in Lucina 7-13
Boutique Versace	Via Bocca di Leone 26-27
Boutique Versace Uomo	Via Borgognona 24-25
Bozart	Via Bocca di Leone 4
Brioni	Via Barberini 79
Brioni	Via Condotti 21a
Brioni	Via Veneto 129
Brugnoli	Via del Babuino 57
Bruno Magli	Via Condotti 6-6a
Camiceria Albertelli	Via dei Prefetti 11
Carla G.	Via del Gambero 24
Carla G.	Via del Babuino 121
Carpisa	Via Belsiana 59
Celine	Via Condotti 20a
Cesare Paciotti	Via Bocca di Leone 92
Chanel	Via del Babuino 98-101
Christian Dior	Piazza di Spagna 73-75
Cisalfa	Via del Corso 475
Corner	Via Belsiana 97
Costume National	Via del Babuino 106
Dalco	Via Vittoria 65
Dancing Duck	Via Belsiana 96b/c
D&G	Piazza di Spagna 93
De Clerq e De Clerq	Via del Carozze 50
Demoiselle	Via Frattina 93
Dolce & Gabbana	Via Condotti 51-52
Diesel	Via del Corso 186

Du.Du.	Via della Croce 78b
Du.Du.	Via delle Carrozze 44a-45
Eddy Monetti	Via Borgognona 35
Eddy Monetti	Via Condotti 63
Eleonora	Via del Babuino 97
Emanuel Ungaro	Via Borgognona 4b-4c
Emporio Armani	Via del Babuino 140
Energie	Via del Corso 486-487
Ethic	Via del Corso 85
Ethic	Via del Carozze 20
Etro	Via del Babuino 102
Expensive	Piazza di Spagna 36
Expensive	Via del Corso 129 & 405
Fendi	Via Borgognona 36-37
Fogal	Via Mario de' Fiori 73
Foot Locker	Via del Corso 39-40
Fratelli Rossetti	Via Borgognona 5a
Fratelli Rossetti	Via del Babuino 59a
Fratelli Vigano	Via Minghetti Marco 8
Furla	Via Condotti 55-56
Furla	Piazza di Spagna 22
Furla	Via del Corso 481
Furla	Via Tomacelli 136
Galassia	Via Frattina 20-21
Galleria Mignanelli	Rampa Mignanelli 10
Gallo	Via Vittoria 63
Gente	Via del Babuino 80-82
Gente	Via Frattina 69
Geox	Via Frattina 3
Giorgio Armani	Via Condotti 77
Giuseppe Messina	Vicolo della Torretta 6
Givenchy	Via Borgognona 21
Gucci	Via Condotti 8
Gucci	Via Borgognona 7b
Gucci	Via Condotti 68a
Hermès	Via Condotti 67
Hogan	Via Borgognona 45
Hugo Boss	Via Frattina 146
Il Baco di Seta	Via Vittoria 65
Il Portone	Via del Carozze 73
Indoroman	Via Gregoriana 36
I Vippini	Via Fontanella di Borghese 65
Intimissimi	Via del Corso 167
Just Cavalli	Piazza di Spagna 82-83
Kristina Ti	Via Mario de' Fiori 40-41
Krizia	Piazza di Spagna 87
La Cicogna	Via Frattina 135
Laltramoda	Via Frattina 113
Laltramoda	Via Borgognona 42b
La Perla	Via Condotti 79

Rome Districts

La Rinascente	Piazza Colonna
Laura Biagiotti	Via Borgognona 43-44
Le 3 C	Via della Croce 40
Leam	Via Bocca di Leone 5
Le Ragazze Gold	Via del Corso 500
Loro Piana	Via Borgognona 31
Louis Vuitton	Piazza San Lorenzo in Lucina 36
Louis Vuitton	Via Condotti 15
Luisa Spagnoli	Via Frattina 84
Luisa Spagnoli	Via del Tritone 30
Luisa Spagnoli	Via Veneto 130
Mada	Via della Croce 57
Malo	Via Borgognona 5
Mandarina Duck	Via Borgognona 42b
Mariella Burani	Via Bocca di Leone 28
Marina Rinaldi	Largo Goldoni 43
Marisa Padovan	Via del Carozze 81
Maska	Via Frattina 44-45
Max & Co	Via Condotti 46-46a
MaxMara	Via Condotti 17-19a
MaxMara	Via Frattina 28
Merola	Via del Corso 143
Missoni	Piazza di Spagna 78
Miss Sixty	Via del Corso 510
Modi di Campagna	Via dei Prefetti 42
Moschino	Via Borgognona 32a
Moschino Jeans	Via Belsiana 57
Narciso Rodriguez	Via Borgognona 4f/g
Nia	Via Vittoria 48
Nia & Co	Via Vittoria 30-31
Nicol Caramel	Via di Ripetta 261
Only Hearts	Via Vittoria 76-76a
Onyx Fashion Store	Via del Corso 132
	or Via Belsiana 75-77 (double entrance)
Onyx Fashion Store	Via Frattina 92
Passion	Via delle Carozze 39
Patrizia Pepe	Via Frattina 1
Petit Bateau	Via della Croce 45
Piccadilly	Via Sistina 92
Pollini	Via Frattina 22-24
Prada	Via Condotti 95
Prada Sport	Via del Babuino 91
Prada Uomo	Via Condotti 92
Prenatal	Via della Croce 50a
Puma Store	Via del Corso 404
Pure Sermoneta	Via Frattina 111
Red & Blue	Via dei Due Macelli 57
Roberto Cavalli	Via Borgognona 7a
Romagnoli	Via Gregoriana 54
Rubinacci	Via Fontanella di Borghese 33

Saddlers Union	Via Condotti 26
Salvatore Ferragamo	Via Condotti 73-74
Salvatore Ferragamo Uomo	Via Condotti 66
Scapa	Via Vittoria 58-59
Schostal	Via del Corso 158
Sergio Rossi	Piazza di Spagna 97-100
Sermoneta	Piazza di Spagna 61
Sisley	Via Condotti 59
Sisley	Via Frattina 19a
Sports Suite	Via Mario de' Fiori 53
Stefanel	Via del Corso 122-125
Stefanel	Via Frattina 31-33
Strenesse	Via del Babuino 146
Sub Dued	Via Tomacelli 154-155
Tablo	Via della Croce 84
Tad	Via del Babuino 155a
Tebro	Via dei Prefetti 46
Thé Verde	Via Vittoria 23
Timberland	Via del Corso 488
Tod's	Via della Fontanella di Borghese 56a-57
Trussardi	Via Condotti 49-50
Trussardi	Via del Corso 477
Valentino	Via Condotti 13
Valentino Boutique	Via del Babuino 61
Valentino Uomo	Via Bocca di Leone 16
Valleverde	Via Frattina 109
Versace Jeans Couture	Via Frattina 116
Vicolo della Torretta Baby	Vicolo della Torretta 17
Wolford	Via Mario de' Fiori 67
Yves Saint Laurent	Via Bocca di Leone 35

Rome Districts

Piazza Navona area *See map page 74*

Abiti Usati	Via del Governo Vecchio 35
Arsenale	Via del Governo Vecchio 64
Fabindia	Via del Banco di Santo Spirito 40
Josephine de Huertas	Via del Governo Vecchio 68
Josephine de Huertas & Co	Via del Parione 19-20
Luna & L'Altra	Via del Governo Vecchio 105
Officine	Vicolo del Governo Vecchio 60
Omero & Cecilia	Via del Governo Vecchio 110
Only Hearts	Piazza della Chiesa Nuova 21
SBU	Via S.Pantaleo 68-69
Vestiti Usati Cinzia	Via del Governo Vecchio 45

Pantheon area *See map page 75*

Borsalino	Via Campo Marzio 72a
Davide Cenci	Via Campo Marzio 1-7
Degli Effetti	Piazza Capranica 75-79 & 93
Ethic	Via del Pantheon 46-47

Petit Bateau	Via Campo Marzio 10b
Pinko	Via della Scrofa 24
Replay	Via della Rotonda 25
Sem Vaccaro	Via dei Orfani 91

Campo de' Fiori area *See map page 77*

Angelo di Nepi	Via dei Giubbonari 28
Benetton	Corso Vittorio Emanuele II 77-79
Borini	Via dei Pettinari 86-87
Cambalache	Via dei Chiavari 30
Edo City	Piazza del Paradiso 18
Ethic	Piazza Cairoli 11-12
Fiore Argento	Vicolo del Malpasso 12
Fonderia	Via dei Balestrari 9
Intimissimi	Via dei Giubbonari 42
Lei	Via dei Giubbonari 103
Loco	Via dei Baullari 22
Marco Polo	Via dei Chiavari 31
Marlboro	Via dei Giubbonari 61
Molly Bloom	Via dei Giubbonari 27-28
Nuyorica	Piazza Pollarola 36-37
Pandemonium	Via dei Giubbonari 104
People	Piazza Teatro di Pompeo 4a
Pinko	Via dei Giubbonari 76-77
Planet	Via dei Baullari 132
Prototype	Via dei Giubbonari 50
Taba	Piazza Campo de' Fiori 13

Via Nazionale area *See map page 76*

Benetton	Via Nazionale 174
De Grillis	Via Campo Carleo 25
Furla	Via Nazionale 54-55
Intimissimi	Via Nazionale 189
Le Gallinelle	Via del Boschetto 76
Lei	Via Nazionale 88
Pulp	Via del Boschetto 140
Sisley	Via Nazionale 84
Stefanel	Via Nazionale 57-59
Via degli Zingari 10	Via degli Zingari 10

Via Cola di Rienzo area *See map page 74*

Angelo di Nepi	Via Cola di Rienzo 267a
Benetton	Via Cola di Rienzo 197-209
Blunauta	Via Cola di Rienzo 303
Carla G.	Via Cola di Rienzo 134
Coin	Via Cola di Rienzo 173
Diesel	Via Cola di Rienzo 245-249
Energie	Via Cola di Rienzo 143
Furla	Via Cola di Rienzo 226

Gente	Via Cola di Rienzo 277-279
Intimissimi	Via Cola di Rienzo 159-161
La Cicogna	Via Cola di Rienzo 268
Laltramoda	Via Cola di Rienzo 54-56
Luisa Spagnoli	Via Cola di Rienzo 191
MaxMara	Via Cola di Rienzo 275
Miss Sixty	Via Cola di Rienzo 235
Onyx Fashion Store	Via Cola di Rienzo 225-229
Petit Bateau	Via Cola di Rienzo 311
Sisley	Via Cola di Rienzo 155-157
Stefanel	Via Cola di Rienzo 223

Parioli

Age d'Or	Via Nino Oxilia 6-8
Age d'Or	Viale Parioli 37
Arli Cashmere	Via Giorgio Vasari 10
Bagheera	Via G.Antonelli 26
Bagheera Accessori	Piazza Euclide 30
BBC	Viale Parioli 122
Brugnoli	Viale Parioli 108
DM	Via Antonelli 10a
Pandemonium	Piazza Euclide 7-8
Schostal	Piazza Euclide 41-42
Sub Dued	Viale Parioli 35
Tricots	Via D.Chelini 15
Viale	Parioli Market

Trastevere

Verso Sud	Via San Francesco a Ripa 168

Rome Districts

Rome Stores by Category

Women's Accessories

AVC by Adriana Campanile
Bally
Battistoni
BBC

Bottega Veneta
Carpisa
Coin
Emporio Armani

Etro
Fendi
Furla
Gucci

Hermès
Hogan
Il Baco di Seta
La Rinascente

Louis Vuitton
Mandarina Duck
Mariella Burani
Marina Rinaldi

MaxMara
Moschino Jeans
Nia
Officine

Prada
Saddlers Union
Salvatore Ferragamo
Sermoneta

Taba
Tad
Thé Verde

Women's Career

Blunauta
Carla G.
Emporio Armani

Giorgio Armani
Luisa Spagnoli
Marina Rinaldi

Maska
MaxMara
Patrizia Pepe

Strenesse
Zara

Women's Cashmere/Knitwear

Arli Cashmere
Battistoni
Davide Cenci
De Clerq e De Clerq

Eddy Monetti
Etro
Gallo

Kristina Ti
Krizia
Laura Biagiotti
Loro Piana

Malo
Prada

Women's Casual

Armani Jeans
Benetton
BBC Jeans
Du.Du.

Marlboro
Max & Co
Nia & Co

Pandemonium
Prada Sport
SBU
Sisley

Stefanel
Timberland
Zara

Women's Classic

Barbara Gregori
Battistoni
Davide Cenci
DM

Eddy Monetti
Marina Rinaldi
Salvatore Ferragamo
Scapa

Women's Contemporary

Alexander
Angelo di Nepi
Arsenale
Bagheera

Costume National
De Grillis
Fiore Argento
Fonderia

Galleria Mignanelli
Gente
Gucci
Il Baco di Seta

Josephine de Huertas
Josephine de Huertas & Co
Kristina Ti
Krizia

Laltramoda
Le Gallinelle
Lei
Luna & L'Altra

Modi di Campagna
Molly Bloom
Moschino Jeans
Nia

Nuyorica
Patrizia Pepe
Prada
Tad

Tricots
Trussardi
Verso Sud
Via degli Zingari 10

Women's Costume Jewelry

Bozart

Women's Custom Tailoring

Battistoni

Women's Dance & Workout Apparel

Banchetti Sport
Cisalfa
Dancing Duck

Foot Locker
Sports Suite

Women's Designer

Alberta Ferretti
Boutique Versace
Celine
Chanel

Christian Dior
Degli Effetti
Dolce & Gabbana

Eleonora
Emanuel Ungaro
Fendi

Galassia
Gianfranco Ferré
Giorgio Armani

Givenchy
Gucci
Laura Biagiotti
Louis Vuitton

Mariella Burani
Moschino
Narciso Rodriguez

Prada
Roberto Cavalli
Valentino

Valentino Boutique
Versace Jeans Couture
Yves Saint Laurent

Rome Categories

Women's Ethnic

Angelo di Nepi
Cambalache
Edo City

Ethic
Fabindia
Galleria Mignanelli

Indoroman
Marco Polo
Officine

Taba
Thé Verde

Women's Eveningwear

Alberta Ferretti
Arsenale
Barbara Gregori

Blunauta
DM
Giorgio Armani

Givenchy
La Perla
Mariella Burani

Valentino
Valentino Boutique

Women's Furs

Christian Dior
Fendi

Women's Gloves

Sermoneta

Women's Handbags

AVC by Adriana Campanile
Bally
Bottega Veneta
Dalco

Eddy Monetti
Fendi
Gucci

Hermès
Prada
Saddlers Union
Salvatore Ferragamo

Tod's
Trussardi

Women's Hats

Borsalino
Coin

La Rinascente
Romagnoli

Women's Hosiery

Coin
Fogal
Gallo

La Rinascente
Wolford

Women's Juniors

Diesel
Energie
Miss Sixty

Onyx Fashion Store
Sub Dued

Women's Leather

Brugnoli
Fendi
Gianfranco Ferré
Gucci
Hermès

Louis Vuitton
Prada
Sem Vaccaro
Trussardi

Women's Lingerie

Coin
D&G
Fogal

Intimissimi
Kristina Ti
La Perla

La Rinascente
Only Hearts
Prada

Tebro
Wolford

Maternity

Nicol Caramel
Prenatal

Women's Shoes

AVC by Adriana Campanile
Bagheera Accessori
Bally
Barilla

Borini
Brugnoli
Bruno Magli
Cesare Paciotti

Coin
Dalco
De Grillis
Fratelli Rossetti

Furla
Geox
Giuseppe Messina

Gucci
Hogan
Le 3 C
Loco

Mada
Nuyorica
Pollini
Prada

Puma Store
Saddlers Union
Salvatore Ferragamo
Sergio Rossi

Tad
Tod's
Valleverde

Women's Sportswear

Red & Blue

Women's Swimwear

Benetton
Coin
D&G

Demoiselle
DM
Gallo

Kristina Ti
La Perla
La Rinascente

Marisa Padovan
Tebro

Rome Categories

Women's Vintage & Retro

Abiti Usati
Arsenale
Le Gallinelle
Omero & Cecilia-
  Vestiti Usati

People
Pulp
Vestiti Usati Cinzia

Women's Young & Trendy

D&G
Diesel
Energie
Expensive

Just Cavalli
Le Ragazze Gold
Only Hearts
Onyx Fashion Store

Miss Sixty
Pandemonium
Pinko
Planet

Prototype
Replay
Sem Vaccaro
Sub Dued

Men's Business Apparel

Battistoni
Belsiana 19
Brioni
Davide Cenci

Eddy Monetti
Salvatore Ferragamo
Valentino Uomo

Men's Casual

BBC
Belsiana 19
Benetton
Corner

Du.Du.
Fratelli Vigano
Marlboro

Modi di Campagna
Pandemonium
SBU
Sisley

Stefanel
Timberland

Men's Cashmere/Knitwear

Arli Cashmere
Battistoni
Belsiana 19
Brioni

Davide Cenci
Gallo
Hermès

Loro Piana
Malo
Modi di Campagna
Prada Uomo

Rubinacci
Schostal

Men's Contemporary

BBC
Belsiana 19
Carpisa
Costume National

Degli Effetti
De Grillis
Emporio Armani
Etro

Fonderia
Gente
Gucci
Leam

Moschino Jeans
Prada Uomo
Strenesse
Trussardi

Men's Custom Tailoring

Battistoni
Brioni

Rubinacci

Men's Designer

Boutique Versace Uomo
Degli Effetti
Dolce & Gabbana
Gianfranco Ferré

Giorgio Armani
Gucci
Hermès
Hugo Boss

Leam
Moschino
Roberto Cavalli
Rubinacci

Valentino Uomo
Versace Jeans Couture
Yves Saint Laurent

Men's Ethnic

Marco Polo

Men's Furs

Fendi

Men's Gloves

Sermoneta

Men's Hats

Borsalino
Fratelli Vigano

Men's Juniors

Benetton
Diesel

Energie
Onyx Fashion Store

Men's Leather

Brugnoli
Bruno Magli
Fendi

Prada Uomo
Trussardi

Men's Leather Goods *(bags, briefcases etc)*

Bally
Fendi
Fratelli Rossetti
Hermès
Mandarina Duck

Prada Uomo
Saddlers Union
Salvatore Ferragamo
Trussardi

Men's Shirts

Belsiana 19
Camiceria Albertelli
Davide Cenci
Il Portone

Prada Uomo
Salvatore Ferragamo
Schostal
Tebro

Men's Shoes

Bally
Brugnoli
Bruno Magli

Hogan
Loco
Pollini

Cesare Paciotti
Davide Cenci
De Grillis

Prada Uomo
Puma Store
Saddlers Union

Fendi
Fratelli Rossetti
Geox

Salvatore Ferragamo
Tod's
Valleverde

Men's Sportswear

Banchetti Sport
Cisalfa
Foot Locker
Fratelli Vigano

Modi di Campagna
Prada Sport
Red & Blue
Sports Suite

Men's Swimwear

Coin
Energie
Gallo
Il Portone

La Rinascente
Pandemonium
Tebro

Men's Ties

Davide Cenci
Fratelli Vigano
Gallo
Hermès

Il Portone
Rubinacci
Salvatore Ferragamo
Tebro

Men's Undergarments

Coin
D&G
Il Portone
Intimissimi

La Rinascente
Schostal
Tebro

Men's Vintage & Retro

Abiti Usati
Le Gallinelle
Omero & Cecilia-
  Vestiti Usati

Pulp
Vestiti Usati Cinzia

Men's Young & Trendy

D&G
Diesel
Energie
Just Cavalli
Onyx Fashion Store

Pandemonium
Planet
Prototype
Replay

Unisex Accessories

Bally
Coin

Gucci
La Rinascente

Unisex Athletic

Banchetti Sport
Cisalfa
Foot Locker
Puma Store

Sports Suite
Tod's
Valleverde

Unisex Department Stores

Coin
La Rinascente

Unisex Ethnic

Cambalache
Marco Polo

Tebro

Unisex Jeans

Armani Jeans
Diesel
Just Cavalli

Pandemonium
Replay
SBU

Unisex Outdoor Sports Equipment & Apparel

Banchetti Sport
Cisalfa
Foot Locker
Fratelli Vigano

Modi di Campagna
Prada Sport
Red & Blue

Unisex Secondhand

Abiti Usati
Le Gallinelle
Omero & Cecilia-
  Vestiti Usati

Pulp
Vestiti Usati Cinzia

Children's Clothing

Age d'Or
Arli Cashmere
Benetton
Bonpoint

La Cicogna
La Rinascente
Moschino Jeans
Petit Bateau

Christian Dior
Coin
Gallo
I Vippini

Prenatal
Tablo
Tebro

Children's Designer

Piccadilly
Pure Sermoneta

Children's Shoes

Age d'Or
AVC by Adriana Campanile
Bonpoint

La Rinascente
Pure Sermoneta
Tablo

Coin
I Vippini
La Cicogna

Timberland
Vicolo della Torretta Baby

Rome Services

Barbers

Haircuts (unisex)

Hair Salons

Hair Extensions

Beauty Treatments

Hair Removal

Manicures/Pedicures

Day Spas (unisex)

Massage Therapists

Make-up Artists

Fitness Studios

Yoga

Dry Cleaners

Mending & Alterations

Custom Embroidery

Custom Tailor

Shoe & Leather Repairs

Trimmings (ribbons, buttons etc)

Personal Shopper

Prescription Glasses

Italian Fashion Website

Barbers

Antica Barbieria Peppino
Via della Vite 62

06-679 8404
Tues-Sat 8:30-7

Arcangelo
Piazza Pasquino 75

06-686 5691
Tues-Sat 8-6

Barber Shop Mario
Piazza del Teatro di Pompeo 44

06-687 9038
Tues-Sat 8:30-7

Fulcinciti
Via del Governo Vecchio 117

06-6880 4258
Tues-Sat 8:30-7

Valentino
Via dei Banchi Vecchi 8

06-6880 1860
Tues-Sat 9-7

Haircuts (unisex)

Aldo Coppola
Via Vittoria 78-79

06-6920 0673
Tues-Sat 9:30-7

Alternativa
Piazza della Cancelleria 70

06-686 9154
Tues-Sat 9:30-7

Jean Louis David
Via dei Baullari 36

06-6813 6672
Tues-Sat 9-7

Jean Louis David
Corso Rinascimento 6

06-6880 3698
(as above)

Jean Louis David
Via Cola di Rienzo 30-32

06-321 4751
Tues-Sat 10-7

Jean Louis David
Via Quattro Fontane 111

06-481 8826
(as above)

Hair Salons

Alternativa
Piazza della Cancelleria 70

06-686 9154
Tues-Sat 9:30-7

Compagnia della Bellezza
Via del Babuino 76

06-361 1003
Tues-Sat 9-6

I Cinque
Via delle Carrozze 29

06-679 4331
Tues-Sat 9:30-6:30

I Sargassi
Via Frattina 48

06-679 0637
Tues-Sat 9-6:30

Liborio
Via di Ripetta 148

06-686 5903/687 4835
Mon-Sat 9:30-7:30

Paride & Marco
Vicolo della Campana 2

06-686 4330
Tues-Sat 9-7

Roberto D'Antonio
Via di Pietra 90-91

06-679 3197
Tues-Sat 9:30-7:30

Sergio Russo
Piazza Mignanelli 25

06-678 1110/678 0457
Tues-Sat 8:30-6

Sergio Valente
Via Condotti 11

06-679 4515/679 1268
Mon-Sat 9:30-7

Hair Extensions

Great Lengths
Via della Vite 14
06-678 1037
Tues-Sat 9:30-7:30

Beauty Treatments

Compagnia della Bellezza
Via del Babuino 76
06-361 1003
Tues-Sat 9-7

Hotel de Russie Spa
Via del Babuino 9
06-3600 6028
Daily 7-9

I Sargassi
Via Frattina 48
06-679 0637
Tues-Sat 9-6:30

Oskarova
Via Savoia 20
06-841 5490
Mon-Fri 9:30-7

Sergio Valente
Via Condotti 11
06-679 4515/679 1268
Mon-Sat 9:30-7

Hair Removal

Compagnia della Bellezza
Via del Babuino 76
06-361 1003
Tues-Sat 9-7

Hotel de Russie Spa
Via del Babuino 9
06-3600 6028
Daily 7-9

I Sargassi
Via Frattina 48
06-679 0637
Tues-Sat 9:30-6

Liborio
Via di Ripetta 148
06-686 5903/687 4835
Mon-Sat 9:30-7:30

Oskarova
Via Savoia 20
06-841 5490
Mon-Fri 9:30-7

Paride & Marco
Vicolo della Campana 2
06-686 4330
Tues-Sat 9-7

Sergio Valente
Via Condotti 11
06-679 4515/679 1268
Mon-Sat 9:30-7

Manicures/Pedicures

Compagnia della Bellezza
Via del Babuino 76
06-361 1003
Tues-Sat 9-6

Hotel de Russie Spa
Via del Babuino 9
06-3600 6028
Daily 7-9

I Sargassi
Via Frattina 48
06-679 0637
Tues-Sat 9:30-6

Le Vespe
Via della Purificazione 13
06-4201 2880
Tues-Sat 9:30-8:30

Liborio
Via di Ripetta 148
06-686 5903
Mon-Sat 9:30-7:30

Paride & Marco
Vicolo della Campana 2
06-686 4330
Tues-Sat 9-7

Sergio Valente
Via Condotti 11
06-679 4515 / 679 1268
Mon-Sat 9:30-7

Day Spas (unisex)

Aveda — **06-6992 4257**
Rampa Mignanelli 9 — Mon 3:30-8, Tues-Sat 10-8

Dabliu — **06-807 5577**
Viale Romania 22 — Mon-Fri 7-10:30, Sat 9-8, Sun 10-2

Hotel Hilton — **06-350 91**
Via Cadlolo 101 — Mon-Fri 7-10, Sat-Sun 9-7

Hotel de Russie Spa — **06-3600 6028**
Via del Babuino 9 — Daily 7-9

Massage Therapists

Hotel de Russie Spa — **06-3600 6028**
Via del Babuino 9 — Daily 7-9

Liborio — **06-686 5903/687 4835**
Via di Ripetta 148 — Mon-Sat 9:30-7:30

Mariuccia — **347 607 9705**
(by appointment)

Patrizia Ricagno (shiatsu massage) — **06-689 6054**
c/o Erboristeria degli Angeli — Mon-Sat 9-8
Piazza della Cancelleria 10

Make-up Artists

I Sargassi — **06-679 0637**
Via Frattina 48 — Tues-Sat 9:30-6

Sergio Valente — **06-679 4515/679 1268**
Via Condotti 11 — Mon-Sat 9:30-7

Fitness Studios

Farnese Fitness — **06-687 6931**
Vicolo delle Grotte 32 — Mon-Sat 9-10

Fight & Fitness (kick-boxing) — **06-8068 7664**
Viale Parioli 162 — Mon-Fri 10-10, Sat 10-8

The Health Club at the Hotel Excelsior — **06-4708 2896**
Via Veneto 12 — Daily 7-10 (Sun 8-10)

La Tua Palestra — **06-689 6104**
Via dei Banchi Nuovi 39 — Mon-Sat 9-9:30

Linea Fitness — **06-679 8356**
Via Bocca di Leone 60 — Mon-Sat 8-9:30

Roman Sports Center — **06-320 1667/321 8096**
Via del Galoppatoio 33 — Mon-Sat 9-10

Spazio Danza Fitness — **06-6880 5454**
Via Monte della Farina 14 — Tues-Fri 9-10

Yoga

Associazione Kundalini Yoga — **06-5730 0550**
Via G.Galvani 40 — Mon-Sat 5-7:30

Daniele Rastelli c/o Ials   **06-323 6396**
Via Fracassini 60   Daily 9-11

Margherita Peruzzo   **347 637 8303**
c/o Centro La Balena   classes Mon 1:30
Via dei Cappellari 127   Tues/Thurs 1:30 & 7:30
(occasional Sat workshops)

Dry Cleaners

(i) Haute Couture & Bridal

Tintoria La Flavia   **06-474 5544**
Via Flavia 85   Mon-Fri 9-3, 5-7:30

(ii) Leather & Suede

Tintoria al Parlamento   **06-687 3609**
Via dei Prefetti 15a/b   Mon-Fri 8-12:30, 3:30-7:30, Sat 9-2

Tintoria La Torretta   **06-687 1325**
Piazza della Torretta 21   Mon-Fri 8:30-7:30, Sat 9:30-12:30

(iii) All-purpose

Tintoria 104 Margutta   **06-323 6474**
Via Margutta 104   Mon-Fri 8:30-8, Sat 10-1

Tintoria al Parlamento   **06-687 3609**
Via dei Prefetti 15a/b   (as before)

Tintoria La Torretta   **06-687 1325**
Piazza della Torretta 21   (as before)

Tintoria Rita   **06-687 9096**
Piazza Campo de' Fiori 38   Mon-Sat 9-2, 3-8

Mending & Alterations

Orlo Jet   **06-687 3663**
Via del Clementino 95b   Mon-Fri 10-1, 3-7:30, Sat 3-7:30

Raniero Sartoria Cretara   **06-487 0657**
Via del Boschetto 75   Mon-Sat 10:30-2:30, 5-7:30

Sartoria Paola e Fabio   **06-6830 7180**
Via dei Banchi Vecchi 19   Mon-Sat 8:30-1, 3-7

Speedy Orlo   **06-683 2086**
Vicolo dei Bovari 8   Sun-Fri 9:30-6

Custom Embroidery

Moltedo   **06-6813 4223**
Via della Rotonda 37   Mon-Sat 10-7:30

Custom Tailor

Franco Cimenti   **06-7720 7288**
Via Faleria 50   Mon-Sat 8-8

Shoe & Leather Repairs

Calzolaio   **(no telephone)**
Via Monserrato 110

Giuseppe Di Iorio (no telephone)
Via Arco della Ciambella 14

Leotta **06-481 9177**
Via del Boschetto 20   Mon 8:30-1, Tues-Fri 8:30-1, 3:30-7

Mario (no telephone)
Vicolo del Lupo 4

Sciuscia (shoe shine only) **06-4201 3733**
Via Emilia 50 Mon-Fri 10-2, 4-7

Trimmings (ribbons, buttons, etc)

Alfis **06-6880 1970**
Largo dei Ginnasi 6 Mon-Fri 9:30-6:15, Sat 9:30-1

Angelo Piperno **06-686 4394**
Via S.Maria del Pianto 56 Mon-Sat 9-1, 4-8

Branciforte **06-686 5271**
Piazza Paganica 12 Mon-Fri 9-7, Sat 9-1

Liguori **06-678 3769**
Via Belsiana 1 Mon 4-7:30, Tues-Sat 10-1, 4-7:30

Passemanerie d'Epoca (no telephone)
Via dei Cappellari 62

Valle al Tritone **06-488 2931**
Via del Tritone 126 Mon-Sat 9:30-7:30

Personal Shopper

Barbara Lessona www.personalshoppersinitaly.com
348 450 3655 / 06-855 1630 / 06-4423 7225

Prescription Glasses (one-hour service)

Grand Optical **06-4201 4565**
Via del Tritone 115 Mon-Sat 9:30-8, Sun 2-8

Italian Fashion Website

Logan Bentley www.made-in-italy.com

Where to Wear Florence 2004

Best Picks

Restaurants

Florence Best Picks

A Piedi Nudi Nel Parco	Gerard Loft
Basic	Gianfranco Lotti
Bonora	Gucci (accessories)
Bottega delle Antiche Terme	La Perla
Bottega Veneta	Loro Piana
BP Studio	Luisa Via Roma
Bruno Magli	Miu Miu
Calvani	Moda Sartoriale
Casadei	Paola del Lungo
Dolce & Gabbana	Patrizia Pepe
Elio Ferraro	Pollini
Emilio Pucci	Prada (women)
Etro	Roberto Cavalli
Fausto Santini	Roberto Ugolini
Fendi	Space
Frette	Valentino
Gerard	Vilebrequin

Florence Restaurants

DUOMO/CENTRAL SHOPPING AREA

Angels   055 239 8762
Via del Proconsolo 29-31
cutting-edge restaurant and wine bar

Astor Caffè   055 239 9000
Piazza Duomo 20
cocktails with complimentary mini plates of pasta

Bar San Firenze   055 211 426
Piazza di San Firenze 1
coffee bar with lots of ice cream

Buca Lapi   055 213 768
Via Trebbio 1
best steaks in town

Caffè Concerto Paszkowski   055 210 236
Piazza della Repubblica 31-35
up-market wine bar

Caffè Gilli   055 214 412
Piazza della Repubblica 39
right on the square, ideal for paninis or a post-meal amaretto

Caffè Rivoire   055 214 412
Via Vaccherecio 4
hot chocolate and delicious club sandwiches

Cantinetta Antinori   055 292 234
Piazza Antinori 3
world-renowned winemaker's bar and restaurant

Cantinetta dei Verrazzano   **055 268 590**
Via dei Tavolini 18-20
enoteca with delicious focaccia

Chiaroscuro   **055 732 1718**
Via delle Torri 55
fantastic coffee and salads

Colle Bereto   **055 283 156**
Piazza Strozzi 5
serious sunglass-clad shoppers' bar

Coquinarius   **055 230 2153**
Via delle Oche 15
traditional Tuscan

Hotel Savoy   **055 27351**
Piazza della Repubblica 7
for the best Martinis in town

J.K. Place   **055 264 5181**
Piazza Santa Maria Novella 7
cocktails on the terrace

Nerbone   **055 219 949**
Mercato Centrale, San Lorenzo
traditional Tuscan with extensive wine list

Oliviero   **055 21242**
Via delle Terme 51
pumpkin ravioli to die for

Paoli   **055 216 215**
Via dei Tavolini 12
old-worldly traditional Tuscan

VIA DEI TORNABUONI / VIA DELLA VIGNA NUOVA AREA

Beccofino   **055 290 076**
Piazza degli Scarlatti 1
inventive Tuscan

Caffè Giacosa   **055 277 6328**
Via della Spada / corner Via dei Tornabuoni
(in Roberto Cavalli)
one of the city's best known cafés and a favorite with the jet set

Latini   **055 210 916**
Via Palchetti 6
atmospheric Tuscan

Roses   **055 287 090**
Via del Parione 26
fashionable sushi bar

Tredici Gobbi   **055 284 015**
Via del Porcellana 9
traditional Tuscan

PONTE VECCHIO / LUNGARNO ACCIAIUOLI (RIVERSIDE)

Capo Caccia   **055 210 751**
Lungarno Corsini 12-14
where to be seen at the cocktail hour

The Fusion Bar (Gallery Hotel Art)   **055 27263**
Vicolo dell'Oro 5
*for tasty snacks (The name "Fusion" is no accident. This is a
uniquely Florentine fusion of fashion and hotels. The Gallery
Hotel Art is owned by the Ferragamo group, which also owns
Lungarno Suites at Lungarno Acciaiuoli 4. For information,
call 055 2726 8000 or visit www.lungarnohotels.com)*

PIAZZA OGNISSANTI AREA

Harry's Bar   **055 239 6700**
Lungarno Vespucci 22
*Needs no introduction. It's for the stars, of course,
but why shouldn't that include you?*

SANTA CROCE AREA

Baldovino   **055 241 773/7220**
Via San Giuseppe 18-22
enoteca and lively restaurant

Cibreo   **055 234 1100**
Via Andrea del Verrocchio 5
a clear favorite of Americans in Florence

La Baraonda   **055 234 1171**
Via Ghibellina 67
basic trattoria (pasta, risotto etc)

Osteria dei Benci   **055 2344 923**
Via dei Benci 13
hip Tuscan with a twist

Osteria del Caffè Italiano   **055 289 368**
Via Isola delle Stinche 11-13
best puddings on the planet

SOUTH OF THE ARNO

Caffè Pitti   **055 239 9863**
Piazza Pitti 9
for candle-lit evenings

Cammillo   **055 212 427**
Borgo San Jacopo 57
noisy, but a popular tourist hang-out

Hemingway Bar   **055 284 781**
Piazza Piattellina 9
for the best hot chocolate in town

La Dolce Vita   **055 284 595**
Piazza del Carmine 6
for twentysomethings

Osteria del Cinghiale Bianco   **055 215 706**
Borgo San Jacopo 43
genuine rustic, wooden tables, and wild boar is the specialty

Quattro Leoni   **055 218 562**
Via dei Vellutini 1
where the A-list dines

Trattoria Angiolino   **055 239 8976**
Via S.Spirito 36
for the best bistecca fiorentina (T-bone) with fagioli

Trattoria del Carmine   **055 218 601**
Piazza del Carmine 18
Tuscan cucina

Florence Store Directory

Newcomers to Italy's proudest cities may be amazed to discover that many stores close during the lunch hour, and in some cases the "hour" is in practice two or two and a half hours. Don't despair, they will re-open! It's just that having invented one of the world's greatest cuisines, they see no reason why they shouldn't enjoy it. Our advice is to join them, and for each of the cities in this book we have provided a select list of restaurants, sidewalk cafés, salad bars, pizzerias etcetera, ideal for your shopping excursions.

We have also listed the opening hours for each store, though these may vary considerably; to avoid frustration, we recommend checking by telephone if in doubt. And finally, while Italian fashion and Italian clothing stores are among the most stylish in the world, you may be disappointed if you plan your shopping in August. The Italians have a special relationship with August (which is often fiendishly hot), and are happy to forsake retail in favor of the beach. To the regular astonishment of workaholic Protestant-ethic northern Europeans and Americans, many Italian stores happily close for weeks—yes, weeks!—at a time. It's a Mediterranean thing…

Agnona

Need a fix of pure self-indulgence? Then the Agnona cashmere label is sure to hit the right spot. Sweaters, scarves, waterproof cashmere coats and a slouchy homewear collection are just a few of the cozy treats in store for the hedonist. The super-soft luxury brand is now owned and produced by Ermenegildo Zegna, Italy's largest producer of wool, cashmere fabrics and clothing. Each piece is spun from only the finest yarns; silk angora, wool and alpaca, and fine cashmere. You won't want to take it off.

Via dei Tornabuoni   **055 268 226**
50123 Florence   Mon 3-7, Tues-Sat 10-2, 3-7

Anichini   🛉

Worried that the good old days when children only spoke when spoken to, girls only wore pink and all boys looked like Little Lord Fauntleroy have long gone? Not here. This is one of Florence's oldest family-run stores and it devotes itself entirely to handmade, beautifully crafted, traditional children's clothing. Sailor suits, smock dresses, bonnets, knitted booties—they are all here and Assunta Anichi, the proprietor, will even make items to order for that very special occasion. There is also a delightful collection of old-fashioned teddies to keep the little darlings occupied while you get carried away. Now all you need is the perambulator.   www.anichini.net

Via del Parione 59   **055 284 977**
50123 Florence   Mon 3:30-7:30, Tues-Sat 9-1, 3:30-7:30

☆ A Piedi Nudi Nel Parco

"Barefoot in the park" is the idiomatic translation of this quirky little clothing and accessories boutique well worth getting lost to find. The owner Stella Falautano is *not* barefoot, but that's what makes her happy and happiness the inspiration behind her collections. She is a big fan of the unusual but practical, and stocks many Italian ready-to-wear labels with that little edge. On our most recent visit, Rose e Sassi's boldly patterned handsewn dresses were causing great excitement along with Fornarina's tops in an array of different colors. Unusual swimwear is also one of her passions, with the tops on current lines studded with metal. And if handbags are your thing, you just won't be able to leave without picking up one of Bagamunda's funky little numbers. Perfect to spice up any occasion.

Via Borgo degli Albizi 46   **055 234 0768**
50122 Florence   Mon 3-8, Tues-Sat 10-8

Athletes World

This sports shop offers an Olympic range of clothes and accessories, both for serious enthusiasts and for those more interested in dressing in edgy, street-style looks. There is an ample selection of urban clothing from Italian streetwear brand Gas Jeans—denim jeans and jean skirts as well as cargo pants and cotton sweatshirts. If you want to look like Madonna, the Puma range for women includes stylish tops and shorts. The footwear department has trainers from Nike, Converse, Adidas and New Balance to name but a few.

Via dei Cerretani 26-28	**055 288 094**
50123 Florence	Daily 9:30-7:30

Bally

Fashion houses and their stores can always do with a good spring cleaning, and Bally, Switzerland's finest, is the latest to benefit. With the introduction of ready-to-wear several seasons ago, the label once synonymous with sensible leather shoes has turned itself into an ultrachic luxury brand. Its signature stripes and the interlocking B pattern which started out on canvas luggage and leather handbags are continued each season in new color combinations. And should you wish to take the Swiss look to hip new heights, Bally's trainers with a cross stitched on the heel are perfect for walking the St Bernard. www.bally.com

Via Calimala 11	**055 230 2857**
50123 Florence	Mon-Sat 10-7

Baroni

Whatever your kids might need can be found here, from clothes to towels to blankets and even made-to-measure cots and beds. Everything in the Baroni line is hand-finished and made from natural fabrics…silk, cotton, wool and linen. The clothing line is extensive and includes little tops, skirts and pea coats from France's Petit Bateau and denims from Oshkosh. Baroni's own line of dresses made from Liberty print fabrics and its classic wool duffle coats for children aged 5-12 are seriously cute. The Tornabuoni store is a bit disorganised but does offer a small range of beautifully made nightwear and delicate lingerie, definitely not for the children.

Via dei Tornabuoni 9	**055 210 562**
50123 Florence	Mon 3:30-7:30
	Tues-Sat 9-1, 3:30-7:30

Via Porta Rossa 56	**055 280 953**
50121 Florence	Mon 3:30-7:30, Tues-Sat 10-7:30

☆ Basic

For some—usually those of the long-legged variety—the cut of a Joseph trouser is like that of no other. They will be pleased to know that there is one store in Florence which carries their favorite label as well as a handpicked selection of international ready-to-wear brands. Basic is a good all-round women's ready-to-wear store which includes Alberta Ferretti and her sporty diffusion line Philosophy, as well as finely spun cashmere sweaters and scarves in a range of subtle colors from the Italian knitwear company Faliero Sarti. The staff are extremely helpful and you can browse at your leisure without being stalked. As we went to press, a new store was underway, although exactly where was a closely guarded secret.

Florence Directory

Via Por Rossa 109-115   **055 212 995**
50123 Florence   Mon 3-7:30, Tues-Sat 10-7:30

Benetton

OK, so there are Benetton stores the world over, but there has to be something said for shopping in a Benetton store in its country of origin. For a start, you can find different collections, more accessories and the chance to get hold of its latest jeans before anyone else. This is the biggest and newest of all the Benetton stores in Florence. Inside the blinding white interior you'll find an extensive collection of kids', teenagers', men's and women's clothing and accessories. Just remember to keep your shades on.   www.benetton.com

Via Borgo San Lorenzo 15   **055 264 5643**
50100 Florence   Mon 3:30-7:30, Tues-Sat 10-7:30
            Sun 12-7:30

Benetton 0-12

Luciano Benetton's trendy line of clothing for 0-12 year-olds is a hit with Italian mamas in search of value for money. The sprawling store is easy to navigate, with each area clearly marked according to age group. Downstairs, as well as tiny terrycloth romper suits, bibs, booties and useful baby accessories, Benetton's latest range of maternity wear for mums-to-be—think Benetton women's collection, only bigger—includes trousers, shirts and skirts made from extra-comfortable fabrics. The staff are happy to help and pram-friendly too.

Via dei Cerretani 60-62   **055 214 639**
50123 Florence   Mon 3:30-7:30, Tues-Sat 10-7:30

Bonora

One hundred and thirty phases of manual work go into every made-to-measure shoe produced here, but all you have to do is pick a leather while your feet are being measured. Bonora's own artisans will then construct wooden prototypes of each foot and build the shoes around them. It takes up to six months for custom-made shoes to be finished. For a faster option pick from Bonora's ready-made line which includes driving shoes, English style brogues and suede moccasins for men and women. And should you wish to travel in style, Bonora sells a sturdy leather shoe case specially designed to carry up to three pairs, plus brushes and polish.

Via del Parione 11-15   **055 283 280**
50123 Florence   Mon 3:30-7:30, Tues-Sat 10-7:30

Bottega delle Antiche Terme

Simone Abbarchi makes shirts to measure in a busy atelier that was once an ancient spa. With over 500 fabrics to choose from in cotton, silk and linen, and 20 different collar designs, it's no wonder customers who shop here don't want too many people to know about it. But try as they may, word travels and those lucky enough to hear about Abbarchi are quick to place their orders for one-off pieces which no one else will have. Abbarchi makes trousers too...just try not to tell everyone.

Borgo Santissimi Apostoli 16   **055 210 552**
50123 Florence   Mon 3:30-7:30, Tues-Sat 10-1, 3-7:30

Bottega Veneta

In some style capitals, getting your hands on Bottega's latest woven leather bag means putting your name on a long waiting list even before the goods themselves have left the runway. Here, however, there are plenty of bags to choose from and very beautiful they are too. Since its acquisition by Gucci, the Bottega Veneta label has been given a brand new look, making every fashion editor's "must have" list season after season. The Florence store, housed in the historic Palazzo Gianfigliazzi, also carries the latest ready-to-wear line of leather jackets, tailored skirts, trousers and chunky sweaters and some of the most sought-after shades this side of the Atlantic. And the best thing is, you got them here first!   www.bottegaveneta.com

Via dei Tornabuoni 7   **055 284 735**
50123 Florence   Mon 2:30-7, Tues-Sat 10-7

☆ BP Studio

These Italian knitwear specialists certainly spin a mean weave. Stripy nautical sweaters, V-neck tops and even floor-length coats are made from the best wool, cashmere and cotton. The architects-turned-fashion-designers behind the label take their inspiration from faraway lands: India, Nepal and Morocco are just a few of the places which influence colors and styles. The winter collection, for example, includes chunky natural yarn cardis which evoke Peruvian costume. The store also stocks a range of colorful jewelry and a small homeware collection.

Via della Vigna Nuova 15   **055 213 243**
50123 Florence   Mon 3-7:30, Tues-Sat 10-7:30

Brioni

You too can look like James Bond. Well, almost. Brioni, Pierce Brosnan's favorite tailor, cuts killer suits from the pick of English and Italian fabrics. Pinstripes, herringbone, tweed, cashmere and lightweight wools are just a few of the luxury fabrics to choose from. The Calimala store, which has a frescoed ceiling dating back to 1359, showcases the company's most exclusive collections, from suits and shirts to sportswear, shoes, ties and cashmere socks. If you seek the classic, custom-made elegance that has made Brioni famous the world over, remember to allow one month until the last button is stitched on.

Via Calimala 22   **055 210 646**
50123 Florence   Mon 3:30-7:30
     Tues-Sat 9:45-1, 3:30-7:30

Florence Directory

Via Rondinelli 7   **055 210 646**
50123 Florence   (opening times as above)

☆ Bruno Magli

Since its acquisition by Opera, this undisputed king of the hide has been going from strength to strength and this beautifully designed store is adequate testament. The sumptuous brown and rich orange interior envelops you in a state of pure luxury and it is impossible to resist the expertly crafted leather shoes and accessories displayed like jewels in glass cases. The women's collection of butter-soft leather jackets, shoes and handbags can be found towards the front of the shop, while the men can indulge themselves in jackets, shoes, ties and bags towards the rear. If your budget is more little league that major league, don't despair because there are also a number of smaller items to be had, packaged just as beautifully. Irresistible. Even the shop assistants are in awe.   www.brunomagli.com

Via Roma 26-28   **055 239 9497**
50123 Florence   Mon 3-7, Tues-Sat 10-7

Cabo

If you must have a little Missoni magic in Florence then this rather chaotic boutique is your best bet. Cabo boasts a huge collection of the label's luxurious knitwear with its famously attention-grabbing swirls and stripes, and delights in those items that push the knitwear boundary just that little bit further. Currently the collection spans from sweeping cardigans to suits and further still to bikinis and dressing-gowns. You won't disappear into the crowd wearing Missoni, but you will be the envy of others dying for a little of the razzmatazz. One word of warning. Don't go anywhere near this shop if you are feeling fragile. If the colors and patterns don't send you over the edge, the swirly whirly flooring definitely will. It's a disaster.

Via Porta Rossa 77-79   **055 215 774**
50121 Florence   Mon-Sat 10-1, 2-7:30

☆ Calvani

Are you the kind of person who strives to be different? If so, this is the shoe store you've been waiting for. Calvani's owner has a magpie eye for finding new footwear talent in and around Italy. Her latest picks include Dove Nuotano Gli Squali (which means Where the Sharks Swim) and Trans Parent, a company obsessed with the notion of making a mockery of all that is considered good and proper. Their open-toed sandals, for example, are both open and "toed", for the big toe anyway. Roberto Del Carlo is another new name to watch for, but as well as such upcoming designers Calvani also stocks familiar brands such as Converse, Dries Van Noten and Camper.

Via degli Speziali 7   **055 265 4043**
50123 Florence   Mon 2-7:30, Tues-Sat 10-7:30
                                                 Sun 3:30-7:30

Camper

Camper, the sunny shoe company from Majorca, fits right in here on Florence's central shopping strip. It is best known for its unconventional designs—some pairs have completely different shoes for each foot—so you're sure to find something totally new. In this two-story boutique the shoes are displayed on a green Astroturf platform. All the Camper favorites are here, such as the Pelotas, a sort of sneaker-cum-lace-up hybrid. The soles of these signature shoes are covered in dozens of small bubbles, while the leather uppers are updated each season in new colors. The big excitement this year is the new Mistol, weighing just 250 grams and perfect for pounding those pavements.   www.camper.com

Via Por Santa Maria 47   **055 267 0342**
50120 Florence   Daily 10-7:30 (Sun 11-7:30)

☆ Casadei

These are the kind of shoes that look perfect on Hollywood stars teetering down the red carpet at the Oscars. Gold boots, mules covered in Swarovski crystals, daringly high stiletto heels and slingbacks topped with feather plumes are just a few of the glamorous shoes Casadei creates for an international clientele. So, if you're looking for a basic brown leather lace-up this is not the store for you—head-to-toe glamour is what it's all about, and the staff aren't afraid to tell you so.

Via dei Tornabuoni 33   **055 287 240**
50123 Florence   Mon 3-7, Tues-Sat 10-7

Castellani

Not feeling particularly adventurous but really need that practical little something? Pop in here and your panic will subside. Italian designer Flavio Castellani specialises in beautifully cut, infinitely wearable trousers, shirts, tops and dresses and shies away from fancy fabric experimentation. Expect a multitude of cottons, linens and other natural fabrics, punctuated by the occasional Lycra or nylon mix. At the time of writing, they were supremely confident in their retailing philosophy and were only selling items in white, red and black. Slightly arrogant, maybe, but their devotees aren't complaining; the prices are fairly reasonable too. Our advice would be to stock up, ship out and head to somewhere outrageous. There is nothing like an overload of oh-so-useful-but-really-quite-boring items to get you back on the fashion wagon.

Via Calimala 19   **055 265 8073**
50123 Florence   Mon 3-8, Tues-Sat 10-8, Sun 3-8

Cesare Paciotti

Despite the cream, padded leather walls, this is a relatively sane environment for a wild and wacky shoe collection. Paciotti's style is seriously sexy—pink satin and ostrich-

Florence Directory

feather boots and black sneakers embroidered with Swarovski crystals are just a few of his designs guaranteed to get your feet tapping. The men's line is equally extravagant—eel-skin loafers in pale blue, and pointed cowboy boots sprinkled with golden studs. And don't be shy about strutting your stuff around the store...the staff seem to get a real kick out of it.   www.cesare-paciotti.com

Via della Vigna Nuova 14   **055 215 471**
50123 Florence   Mon 3-7, Tues-Sat 10-7

Champion

This American sportswear label packs a powerful punch among Florence's predominantly Italian sports stores. Expect a whole range of casual styles for just hanging out or for getting down to a serious workout. Hooded sweat tops, T-shirts, tracksuits, footwear and socks are all splashed with the Champion logo, and only the finest American cotton and breathable synthetics are used. You'll have to be small to move around the cramped childrenswear department in the basement, but the racks are overspilling with mini trainers, T-shirts and vests for budding young Olympians.

Via Por Santa Maria 52-54   **055 280 120**
50100 Florence   Mon 3-7:30, Tues-Sat 10-7:30

Christian Dior

Dior has only recently arrived on Via Tournabuoni but you wouldn't think it. John Galliano's brash, edgy style fits in beautifully here and the racy Florentines and globe-trotting fashionistas just can't get enough of it. In the current collection, corset dresses in dirty pink suede sit alongside in-your-face fluorescent yellow bikinis, while for fall a distinctively gothic-punk mood is forecast. Expect brawls in the street for the rich red and black leather combos. Shoes, jewelry and accessories can also be found here, along with a small children's selection. Swarovski-crystal nappy pins may, however, be pushing things too far but we're not complaining. Go on, take a walk on the wild side. Just don't expect to leave with much change.   www.dior.com

Via Tornabuoni 57-59   **055 266 9101**
50123 Florence   Daily 10-7:30

Coccinelle

Tote bags, baguettes, travel cases, shoppers, make-up bags and purses...you name it, Coccinelle has it in just about every shape, size and color. Like Furla, Italy's other affordable accessories brand, Coccinelle's bags, small leather goods and accessories are great value for money. Made from quality materials such as leather, suede, crocodile and calfskin, and topped with metallic rims, suede fringing and costume jewelry fastenings, these super snazzy bags can be seen swinging from the most stylish shoulders in town.

Via Por Santa Maria 49   **055 239 8782**
50122 Florence   Daily 10-8 (Sun 11-8)

Coin

Now here's an Italian department store with a difference. Not content with the usual modern edifice, this family-owned group has a penchant for acquiring and renovating historic buildings in city centers. In Florence it has done just that with a 16th-century palazzo, which it has topped with a glass roof and all the mod cons that make for today's shopping. There's a MAC make-up corner in the ground-floor entrance and an impressive range of sportswear from Fred Perry, Esprit and Trussardi once inside. Upstairs in the kids' department, you'll wish the dusty pink pea coats came in grown-up sizes.   www.coin.it

Via Calzaiuoli 56   **055 280 531**
50122 Florence   Daily 10-8 (Sun 11-8)

Del Moro Cappelli

Del Moro's heady creations are perfect for all occasions. Each one is handmade, or can be tailored to your own design. This tiny store-cum-atelier which opened five years ago carries a wide range. There are handwoven raffia sun hats and a large selection of panamas for spring/summer, while for the winter season the fabrics appropriately change to include felt, fur (real and fake) and waterproof nylon. The store also stocks a selection of famous brands such as Stetson, Barbisio and Olney, all neatly displayed on hat stands. Most of the styles are traditional, but if you want something a little more modern it's best to ask for the bespoke service.

Via S.Elisabetta 15   **055 213 805**
50122 Florence   Mon 3:30-7:30
                    Tues-Sat 10-1, 3:30-7:30

Desmo

You never knew just what else they could do to a handbag until you saw Desmo's latest eclectic designs. Desmo will sew strips of ponyskin and python together in small clutch bags, or sprinkle satin evening bags with glittering threads and precious stones. Woven raffia shoppers are topped with hand-finished handles, and silk clutch bags snap shut with silver claps. And that's just for starters! With an exotic shoe collection to boot, you'll find it hard leaving this store without one last gaze at the burnt orange sandals and matching tote bag, festooned with leather roses.

Piazza Rucellai 10   **055 292 395**
50123 Florence   Mon 3-7, Tues-Sat 10-7

Diesel

Renzo Rosso's cult fashion label needs no introduction. Only the coolest of the cool are found shopping at this store in search of Diesel's 14-ounce denims, cropped jean jackets and aviator-style shades. New Yorker Andre Halyard runs the place with a passion. You want the low-cut jeans with special rust-look finish from Diesel's latest collection?

Florence Directory

No problemo, Halyard will rush to your aid. With an over-whelming range of engineered denims on the ground floor and the complete womenswear and accessories collections on the first, the store has a spacious feel and a seriously hip groove to it. www.diesel.com

Via dei Lamberti 13 055 239 9963
50123 Florence Sun-Mon 2-7:30, Tues-Sat 10:30-7:30

☆ Dolce & Gabbana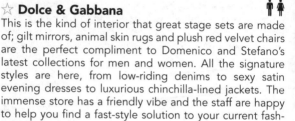

This is the kind of interior that great stage sets are made of; gilt mirrors, animal skin rugs and plush red velvet chairs are the perfect compliment to Domenico and Stefano's latest collections for men and women. All the signature styles are here, from low-riding denims to sexy satin evening dresses to luxurious chinchilla-lined jackets. The immense store has a friendly vibe and the staff are happy to help you find a fast-style solution to your current fash-ion dilemma. Just remember to go easy on the leopard print and mind you don't trip over the zebra rug on your way out. www.dolcegabbana.it

Via della Vigna Nuova 27 055 281 003
50123 Florence Mon 3-7, Tues-Sat 10-7

E-Play

Replay's edgy, adolescent brother likes to push street style just that little bit further, and in most cases succeeds. Jeans are too cheeky for words (and for the vast majority of pub-lic places), sweaters are slashed and torn, tops are sexy, sparkly and boldly printed, and dresses have a distinctive gypsy-chic feel. Hems this season are either skyscraper-high or swooping, exposing just a touch of the knee, and trousers are predominantly denims or cropped. Boys will find jeans with just that little unusual something, for exam-ple a gorilla printed on the reverse, and shirts with pockets that dive down the body. They say the devil is in the detail and that sure is true of the E-Play collection. Be a little hot and naughty.

Via Tosinghi 14 055 293 440
50123 Florence Mon 3:30-7:30, Tues-Sat 10-7:30

☆ Elio Ferraro

Anyone who can relate to a longing for a little treasure trove with all your favorite things will know exactly where Ferraro is coming from with his vintage men and women's clothes-shop-cum-gallery-cum-accessories playground. Contemporary-vintage pieces like Evisu's Eighties jeans sit perfectly alongside vintage vintage items like Pucci's Fifties expandable shopping bag and Pierre Cardin's original velour tracksuit tops. Juicy Couture, eat your heart out. Ferraro also has a collection of his own pieces, including bags and evening dresses, each of which is unique but per-haps not quite as desirable. It's perfectly possible to lose yourself in this shop for hours and stumble across some real gems. Just don't think it's going to be bargain. Nothing really wonderful ever is.

Via del Parione 47
50123 Florence

055 290 425
Mon 3-8, Tues-Sat 10-8

☆ Emilio Pucci

The pre-psychedelic prints Emilio Pucci so memorably created in the Sixties keep coming back to life in vibrant new ways. With Christian Lacroix now firmly ensconced as artistic director of this iconic fashion house things are getting better and better. Like Pucci's sunny, Mediterranean personality, Lacroix collections spin hot new color combinations and a pop-influenced print that's guaranteed to warm up even the most miserable of summers. Swirls of Pucci prints are splashed across the walls of this white space-pod interior, and lounge music is pumped from the speakers to put you in real retro Pucci mood.   www.emiliopucci.com

Via dei Tornabuoni 20-22
50123 Florence

055 265 8082
Mon-Sat 10-7:30

Emporio Armani

Giorgio Armani's innovative diffusion line offers sportier, younger styles with the high-quality fabrics and tailoring you expect from the maestro. The vast collection includes eyewear, perfume, men's and women's apparel and a full range of unassuming accessories. Emporio moved into this clean-cut store less than a year ago and the fittings and minimal decor follow the same restrained lines as Armani's megastores across the globe. Like the grown-up Armani brand, expect some seriously streamlined jackets, trouser suits, evening dresses and jackets cut as only Giorgio knows how.   www. emporioarmani.it

Piazza Strozzi 16
50123 Florence

055 284 315
Mon 3:30-7:30, Tues-Sat 10-7:30

Enrico Coveri

Shades are strongly advised when entering this store. Designer Enrico Coveri loves color and boy, does he want you to know it. Hot pink, lime-green, tangerine orange and sunshine yellow are just a few of the shades he works into sweaters, jeans, T-shirts and jackets. Coveri's funky You Young diffusion line is also available here. Like the main line, there is plenty of color and some great basic pieces such as sweaters and jeans which cling rather tightly to the leg. Oh, just in case your retinas can't take all that color, they sell sunglasses too.

Via dei Tornabuoni 81
50123 Florence

055 211 263
Mon 3:30-7:30, Tues-Sat 10-7:30

Ermanno Scervino

Take a deep breath when you enter this store because if the clothes don't wind you, the prices certainly will. Ermanno Scervino is very, very expensive but if you are after the glamorous fairy princess look it has few rivals. Delicate chiffon and silk dresses whisper to you as you pass and the dainty strappy sandals just can't be ignored. This season there is also a collection of beautifully embroidered tops, from powder-pink to charcoal-gray, and flower-petal-inspired handbags that collapse oh so elegantly when you put them down. Hunt around the ground floor for croc belts in every conceivable color and some beautifully cut fitted shirts and trousers. Some items are laughably expensive, like the silver nylon raincoat at 600 euros, but we can't all be perfect.   www.ermannoscervino.com

Piazza Antinori 10   **055 260 8714**
50123 Florence   Mon 3-7:30, Tues-Sat 10-7:30

Ermenegildo Zegna

Zegna is a fourth-generation family-run enterprise with a tradition of designing and producing the finest formalwear and accessories from its own eclectic fabrics. With the trend toward more comfortable suits the race is on to produce new blends. For the second season Zegna's finely tuned suits are spun from "15MilMil 15", a lightweight fabric made of superfine merino wool fibers, and Zoltex, a summer silk and wool blend. Heritage, the jacket line made from traditional textiles like tweed, wool cloth and herringbone is still winging its way out of the store. The staff are happy to help with alterations, which take up to four weeks to complete. Last year the former Zegna Sport shop was integrated into this one, so you can now find that line's casual weekend styles here. Jackets are made from Zegna's exclusive Microtene fabric which is engineered to be wind and waterproof. And there are ultralight fleeces and stretch jackets which could defy a tough day's shopping just as easily as the strongest storm.   www.zegna.com

Piazza Rucellai 4-7   **055 283 011**
50123 Florence   Mon-Sat 10-7:30

Escada

Swoosh, whoosh, ooohhh will ring in your ears when you try on these luxurious, elegant and oh-so-glam evening gowns. Escada's prêt-à-porter has come a long way from its humble beginnings in the late Seventies and is now a firm favorite on the red carpet of many an opening night...quite a feat for a fashion house originally named after an Irish racehorse. But if those premiere invitations have failed to reach you yet again, don't worry. This store also has a large selection of those classically styled, seasonless shirts, skirts and suits and a few items from the more relaxed Escada Sport line.

Via degli Strozzi 32   **055 290 404**
50123 Florence   Mon 3-7, Tues-Sat 10-9

☆ Etro

This luxury house is mostly noted for its paisley print cashmere scarves and "got to have it" ready-to-wear for both men and women. The Florence store is one of the largest in Italy, housed in what were once the frescoed stables of the affluent Rucellai family. As well as elegant hand-embroidered evening dresses, tailored men's suits and a vast range of suede and leather shoes, belts and handbags, the store carries Etro's latest homeline. Along with the sweet-scented candles and fragrant room sprays there are shaving creams and aftershaves as well as an entire women's fragrance collection.   www.etro.it

Via della Vigna Nuova 50   **055 267 0086**
50123 Florence   Mon 3-7, Tues-Sat 10-2, 3-7

Expensive

Well no, not really. But if you are after that "so this season" item then this could be just the cheap ticket. Pumping tunes draw you in off the street and are at a volume which either gets you in the spending groove or sends you running. All the staples are here, from jeans, sweaters and funky tees to Lycra tops and figure-hugging dresses, but there is also a large selection from their Athletic line for those sportier ones among you. The average age of the customer may be pre-secondary school but don't let that put you off. They are only here because they can afford it, whereas you are working on your disposable wardrobe. Show them how it's done.

Via dei Calzaiuoli 78   **055 265 4608**
50122 Florence   Mon 11-8, Tues-Thurs 10-7, Fri-Sat 10-8

☆ Fausto Santini

Fausto Santini is one of Rome's most celebrated shoe and handbag designers. His unique designs, for both men and women, with their soft round toes and ultra-flat heels are more like sculptured objects than shoes. His color wheel is equally delicate, ranging from powdery blue to darker tones of slate-gray and plum. This is a tiny shoe box of a store and, unlike Santini's bigger flagship stores in Milan and Rome, the Florence space also works as a discount outlet selling Santini's shoes from past and present collections at around 20-40% less than usual.   www.faustosantini.it

Via Calzaiuoli 95   **055 239 8536**
50122 Florence   Mon 3:30-7:30, Tues-Sat 10-7:30
                                                          Sun 12-7:30

☆ Fendi

Prepare yourself to step into a better world, a masterly combination of fabric and design. Women's and men's luxurious ready-to-wear hangs invitingly beside the most enticing display of shoes, scarves, sunglasses and watches and those handbags that year after year are the height of desirability. Silvia Venturini's famous baguettes again take center stage, this season reincarnated in powder-blue python form. There is something of a Ken Adam's James Bond set feel to this brand new store, with its rich, dark interior and shiny black tiling and a futuristic fur room at the back just begging you to play baddie. Envelop yourself in chinchilla, fox and mink and experience just for a second how lucky those Contessas are. Just don't look at the price tags—they put most countries' national debt to shame.   www.fendi.com

Via degli Strozzi 21   **055 212 305**
50123 Florence   Mon-Sat 9-7:30, Sun 2-9

Foot Locker

As the sneaker culture continues to boom, US sportswear and athletic shoe specialist Foot Locker is a must for all sneaker heads. At the Florence flagship store you'll find all the big names such as Nike, Puma, Adidas and Converse. The shoes, together with some of the coolest urban and specialist Italian sportswear from the likes of Fila, Lotto and Umbro, are displayed on one rather cramped ground-floor space. Fans are currently hotfooting it here for Nike's new Airmax Plus sneakers as well as Foot Locker's exclusive re-released Nike Tuned line and, just in case you've overdone it on the pasta, skipping ropes and arm weights are also on hand.

Via Borgo San Lorenzo 19   **055 291 400**
50121 Florence   Mon-Sat 10-7:30
                    Sun 11:30-1:30, 3:30-7:30

Via Calzaiuoli 27-35   **055 214 030**
50100 Florence   (opening times as above)

Francesco Biasia

This little slip of a shop that opened last October is a real find for great quality, practical but fashionable women's shoes, handbags, accessories and watches. Sliding wooden shelves expose other small leather delights, such as belts and wallets, and the best bit is they are really not expensive. They have gone crazy for Francesco Biasia in the US, especially for the distressed leather white, beige or black Ciclamino bags. You may get a sense that you have seen some of these bags before and you are probably right. Vincenza-based Biasia keeps a close-eye on the handbag heavyweights and delights in sailing just a little close to the wind. The three-color brown, tan and cream Fifties-style Anemone bag, for example, is by no means a Biasia original but we're not complaining. And at the prices, we guarantee you won't be either.   www.biasia.com

Via della Vigna Nuova 16   **055 282 961**
50123 Florence   Mon 3-7:30, Tues-Sat 10-7:30

Fratelli Rossetti

When Fratelli Rossetti produced a pair of brown leather moccasins in the Fifties it caused a stir among the more traditional lace-up brigade. Always one for innovation, Rossetti's design content is diverse, the details rich and the technique and materials perfect. Towering lacquered heels, flat sporty soles and high slim-cut boots are updated each season in Rossetti's signature colors: cardinal red, octane blue and toffee yellow. The Flexa line of comfort shoes, made from waterproof suedes and leathers and built on an anti-slip sole, gets the stamp of approval from Rossetti fans from film stars to Prince Charles.   www.rossetti.it

Piazza della Repubblica 43-45   **055 216 656**
50123 Florence   Mon-Sat 10-7:30, Sun 2-7

☆ Frette

This is the ultimate store for luxury linens and homewear. You'll be hard pressed not to want to wallow in every cashmere blanket and silk duvet cover stacked neatly in the wooden display cabinets. Indeed, you may not even wish to leave once you see the goods. Apart from the 20 different prints in the men's silk pajama collection, Frette's women's collection includes floaty silk robes, organza dresses and suede slippers with a silk trim. The collection is so elaborate it would be a shame not to be seen out of the house in it.

Via Cavour 2   **055 211 369**
50126 Florence   Mon 3:30-7:30, Tues-Sat 9:30-7:30

Furla

Like most Italian leather goods and accessories labels, Furla is steeped in history. Founded in 1927 by the Furlanetto family, the Bologna-based brand is now run by a third generation of savvy siblings. Furla launched its first footwear collection only two years ago, part of a project to widen its range and strengthen its international presence as a lifestyle brand. The goods are 100% handcrafted by the best Italian artisans, with elaborate finishes and intricate details throughout the entire collection. You will also find watches, scarves and jewelry at great prices.

Via della Vigna Nuova 28   **055 282 779**
50123 Florence   Daily 10-7:30 (Sun 11:30-7:30)

Via Calzaiuoli 47   **055 238 2883**
50123 Florence   Daily 9:30-7:30 (Sun 10:30-7:30)

☆ Gerard

The Pecchiolis are considered *the* fashion family by many of those in Florence's inner fashion circle, and quite right too. This store is a dream. See by Chloé, Luna Bi knitwear and girly tops, and Marc Jacobs shoes all rest elegantly beside Balenciaga's silky-soft leather bags and Helmut Lang's stylish denims. Tiny productions of more experimental lines also find a place here and add to the store's kudos. This season they are mad for Alexandra Jane's unusual silk vintage dresses that die on the hanger but spring into life when worn, and Wushu classic feather-light sneakers that you would have thought defied gravity. Also look out for their own line of well-made tees, trousers and sweaters—all very popular with the boys. It may all get too much but not to worry. Stagger upstairs to collapse into the vintage Louis Vuitton sofa and immerse yourself in acres of the distinctive monogram. Now that really is worth seeing.

Via Vaccherreccia 18   **055 215 942**
50123 Florence   Sun-Mon 2:30-7:30, Tues-Sat 10-7:30

☆ Gerard Loft

This is Gerard's younger sibling. Rebellious and experimental, it's the height of Florence cool and a vintage haven, perfect if you are in need of a quick fix. Levi's Red label, Evisu

Florence Directory

Delux and Diesel Style Lab are all regulars and funky lines like Flu's Ear and Parosh make occasional appearances. For the guys, there is an extensive collection of Stone Island's chunky knits, and Gola and Swear sneakers to really get you in the groove. There is also a small area devoted to the trendiest kids' clothes on the planet, with Inge van den Broeck's feisty little trousers being the pick of the bunch. Just be careful not to fall over the bits of loft dotted around the store or pay at the DJ station when you leave.

Via dei Pecori 36   **055 282 491**
50123 Florence   Mon 2:30-7:30, Tues-Sat 10-7:30

☆ Gianfranco Lotti

Brace yourself. This is handbag heaven. When this boutique, Lotti's only one, opened last January the entire Vigna Nuova was closed to traffic and a section of it was draped in a red carpet to lead the hungry press and the chosen few of Florence's elite through the doors. They weren't disappointed. Beautifully designed to be modern but respectful of the palace's 18th-century roots, the store seduces you, tempting you not only with bags but also with small leather items, scarves, stoles, gloves, hats, eyewear and fashion jewelry. Lotti insists on using only the very best leathers and sophisticated fabrics, and his designs range from the classic to the downright racy. The tiny Sexy bags, for example, the butt-cheek inspired blood-red satin number, are hotter than hot at the moment and the alligator line such a tribute to the leather that Mother Nature herself couldn't object. Men are not forgotten either. Head to the back of the store and you will find the sail-canvas bag series, durable enough to withstand the most severe battering. This is leatherwork at its best.

Via della Vigna Nuova 45   **055 211 301**
50123 Florence   Mon 3-7:30, Tues-Sat 10-7:30

Gilardini

Despite the large entrance hall and the bright, glitzy display cases, the store's interior lacks any kind of modern aesthetic. But there are two reasons why you would consider stopping here: the Bruno Magli and Santoni collections. Magli's exotic materials (crocodile, snake and pony, for example) together with his eclectic style make his shoes second to none; Santoni is famous for hand-finished brogues and comfortable leather moccasins. Gilardini has its own line too, but once you have seen Magli and Santoni it looks rather average in comparison.

Via dei Cerretani 8 & 20   **055 212 412**
50123 Florence   Daily 9:30-7:30 (Sun-Mon 3:30-7:30)

Giorgio Armani

With Armani's new ranges of cosmetics, eyewear and watches now in full swing and Armani Mania floating through perfume halls the world over, you would have thought that the designer with the distinctive silver hair and all-year tan would be hanging up his scissors. Not a bit of it. This store contains the latest of his much copied but never beaten classic signature items and. The store, like his clothes, has a no-fuss interior, although the sandstone walls giving way to new rooms create an almost maze-like feel. www.giorgioarmani.com

Via dei Tornabuoni 48 **055 219 041**
50123 Florence Mon 3-7, Tues-Sun 10-7

Giotti

This is a large-scale outlet for the Bottega Veneta range of canvas and leather travel cases and bags and leather jackets. The store's own brand, Giotti, is a slick mix of Prada meets Gucci. Choose from the selection of colored leathers and the Florentine artisans who work with Giotti will make up jackets, trousers and skirts to suit your style requirements. It's well worth the wait while they fashion your order, as the quality is excellent. Other great picks include the chocolate-colored leather rain hats which look like fluted flowerpots. www.giotti.com

Piazza Ognissanti 3-4 **055 294 265**
50123 Florence Mon-Sat 9-1, 3:30-7:30

Golden Point

If you believe all good things come in small packages, this store will be right up your street. Hugging a prominent corner, it beckons sun worshippers constantly on the lookout for that next flattering costume and also anyone on the search for good value, if somewhat unimaginative, lingerie. All the goods are laboriously stuffed into little plastic envelopes just begging to be unwrapped, which thankfully the staff don't seem to object to. Flying off the shelves this season are the classic, black, front-tied Atene bikinis and the Hue Beachwear surf-trunks. There is also a small selection of stretchy tees and Lycra tops, and woolen socks for when it gets a little cooler. A word of warning: don't accept any of the free gifts they try to fob you off with. They really are too small, even for your children. www.goldenpointonline.com

Via degli Speziali 1 **055 277 6224**
50122 Florence Sun-Mon 11:30-7:30, Tues-Sat 10-7:30

☆ Gucci (accessories)

Is your pooch turning heads in Gucci's latest leather dog-collar and lead? Are you all set for an equestrian weekend in the country but still haven't got the Gucci calfskin saddle and matching riding-whip? And what about that hand-finished silver cigarette case with the GG logo print? Or the foldable yoga mat in printed GG rubber for that matter? Relax. These and other Gucci treats, including small leather goods, bags, watches, jewelry and sunglasses, can all be found in this sleek, three-story boutique, designed specifically to house Tom Ford's latest accessories collections. www.gucci.com

Via Roma 32 **055 759 221**
50123 Florence Mon 3-7, Tues-Sat 10-7, Sun 2-7

Gucci (ready-to-wear)

Right, so you've already got the leather skipping-rope and silver Gucci scissors from the accessories store next to the Duomo, but now it's time to get the complete Gucci look from the latest men's and women's ready-to-wear lines. Creative director Tom Ford shows no signs of slowing his fast and furious design ethic. That is to say, minimal lines, great fabrics and a whole lot of va-va-vroom. This is a real lair of a shop and it is quite easy to get lost in the winding corridors which bring you, eventually, to the various collections.

Via dei Tornabuoni 73   **055 264 011**
50123 Florence   Mon 3-7, Tues-Sat 10-7, Sun 2-7

Guess?

The American jeans and womenswear label is a big hit in Florence. On entering the ground floor, don't be alarmed by the piles of jeans that look as if they just got run over by a truck. They are supposed to look that way. It's fashion, darling. Head downstairs to the basement for more elegant pieces from the womenswear collection. As well as sexy backless evening dresses you will find a classy range of strappy shoes and sandals to match. The red cube-shaped seats in the shoe department are a welcome relief from the overpowering white interior.   www.guess.com

Via degli Speziali 9-11   **055 213 035**
50123 Florence   Daily 10-7:30 (Sun 3-7:30)

Guya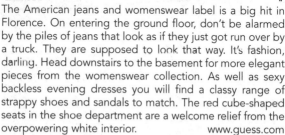

Ask anyone who knows anything about serious shopping in Florence and they will come up with the same name: Guya. This is a true family affair, with each of the shops run by one parent and one daughter who all share a passion for items verging on the avant-garde. Vivienne Westwood Gold label, Comme des Garçons, Martin Margiela and A.F. Vandervorst all feature heavily in Via Calimala, with their diffusion lines taking pride of place in Via Por Santa Maria. This season they are also experimenting with Preen's bohemian chic, Bernard Willhelm's trashy romantic and Yoshi Ogawa's lively linen and cotton mixes. Definitely worth a look but don't expect fancy shop fittings or gushing assistants. It's all about the clothes, shoes and accessories —well, what else is there?

Via Calimala 29   **055 219 163**
50123 Florence   Mon 2:30-7:30, Tues-Sat 10:30-7:30

Via Por Santa Maria 76   **055 282 764**
50123 Florence   (opening times as above)

Hermès

In spite of expansion around the world, the credo of founder Thierry Hermès is still present in every product. Silk scarves, porcelain plates, jewelry, shoes and ready-to-wear from the French house are displayed in dark wooden cabinets from the days when the store was an 18th-century pharmacy. There's a strong equestrian theme throughout the entire collection. Saddles, horse blankets, riding hats and boots are displayed on walls and tables. And for smaller four-legged friends, Hermès have a complete range of dog-collars and leads.   www.hermes.com

Piazza Antinori 6   **055 238 1004**
50123 Florence   Mon 3-7, Tues-Sat 10-7

Florence Directory

Hogan
The interior of this store is quite something. Back in 1843 it was an English pharmacy and many of the original features are still here, including the large wooden and glass display cases and the dreamy frescoed ceilings. It is a great background for Diego Della Valle's Hogan footwear and accessory collections. His signature canvas and leather lace-ups are a regular sight on VIP feet, from Sharon Stone's to Tom Cruise's. In addition to the current Hogan collection for men, women and children, the store carries a range of sleek leather handbags.

Via dei Tornabuoni 97   **055 274 1013**
50123 Florence   Mon-Sat 10-7

Hugo Boss
Hugo Boss, Germany's biggest clothing maker, may have shown both men's and womenswear together on the New York runway last year, but to date the Florence flagship store carries only the various menswear lines. These include Boss, the company's core brand with its clear-cut contemporary design and high-quality detail, and the sportier Black, Orange and Red labels. Best picks include soft leather car coats, streamlined suits, cotton shirts and a vast collection of colorful silk ties for every occasion. Five glass display cases hold the watch collection.

Piazza della Repubblica 46   **055 239 9176**
50123 Florence   Mon 3:30-7:30, Tues-Sat 10-7:30

Iceberg
Paolo Gerani's fusion of all that is lively and vibrant may not be to everyone's taste but if you are after something a little unusual, this might be the place. In the ingeniously designed, Perspex-enclosed loggia, rows and rows of brightly colored and boldly patterned shirts, dresses, trousers and tops fight for your attention. There is the occasional more subdued piece buried deep within the piles but you would not really come here for those. We have a particular piece of advice: at prices rendering the clothes not quite disposable, think carefully before you buy. That fuchsia-pink shirt splattered with Spanish motifs that works so beautifully in the Florence sunshine might not be quite the thing back home.

Piazza Rucellai 1   **055 265 4648**
50123 Florence   Mon 3-7:30, Tues-Sat 10-1:30, 2:30-7:30

Il Giglio

This store is slightly off the beaten track but packs enough designer discount labels to make you walk just that little bit further. They include Moschino, Yves Saint Laurent, Versace, Dolce & Gabbana and Prada. Most of the pieces are from last season's collections but hey, who cares when you can get a 60% discount. The store itself is not much to look at, in fact it's a bit of a mess. Just divert your eyes to the shoe section, where on a good day you can find snakeskin Miu Miu pumps and sparkling Casadei slingbacks.

Via Borgo Ognissanti 64   **055 217 596**
50100 Florence   Mon-Sat 9:30-1:30, 3:30-7:30

Il Rifugio Sport

This is a good all-round sports store housing leading labels on two floors. All the big names are here…Nike, Adidas, Puma, New Balance and Arena. There's a good children's department too which carries mini football shirts and T-shirts as well as tiny sneakers from all the major brands. And should you feel a sun salute coming on, you'll find Puma's latest yoga collection with its stretch leggings and stylish sweat tops. With a hefty range of weights and sports equipment as well, you have no excuse not to get in shape.

Piazza Ottaviani 3   **055 294 736**
50123 Florence   Mon 3-7:30, Tues-Sat 9-7:30

Via dei Fossi 67   **055 238 1326**
50123 Florence   (opening times as above)

Intimissimi

Ever fancied a whole draw of really sexy lingerie but not felt bold or frivolous enough? This store may be the answer. Intimissimi delights in combining colors that could never be worn on the outside but work perfectly hidden away. Hunt out the lacy sorbet yellow and aquamarine ensembles and the very now honeycomb-knit military-green bras. You won't want to keep them forever, but they don't break the bank and are great little pieces of harmless fun. They also sell more classic monotone pieces and a line of infinitely useful stretchy tees and cotton nightwear. The boys get a look in too, with a range of cotton underwear in colors just as lively.   www.intimissimi.it

Via dei Calzaiouli 99   **055 230 2609**
50122 Florence   Mon 10-8, Tues-Fri 9:30-8, Sat-Sun 10-8

Via dei Cerretani 17   **055 260 8806**
50123 Florence   (opening times as above)

Italobalestri

This is a real gem of a store that sits in relative calm just off the incredibly noisy Via dei Cerretani. The owners have kept the frescoed wall panels, dark teak fittings and original chandelier from what was once an eyeglass store. It's in this rather unusual setting that Italobalestri's hand-finished shoes come to life. There are plenty of exotic, couture styles to choose from as well as a more serious collection of polished leather lace-ups for men. Take a walk on the wild side with the latest animal prints...the zebra-print mules, for example, are pure Versace.

Piazza Santa Maria Maggiore 7   **055 211 230**
50123 Florence   Mon 3-7:30, Tues-Sat 9:30-7:30
                              Sun 10-1, 3-7:30

Lacoste
The Lacoste label is instantly recognisable for its snappy crocodile logo. Its best-selling polo tops are synonymous with tennis players and sportswear enthusiasts the world over. Indecisive shoppers may find this store a bit of a nightmare as the famous polos come in over 30 different colors and are stacked according to shade. If you want to keep the staff happy, ask before you start to pull their painstakingly perfect displays apart. The store also carries Lacoste's complete range of men's and women's sportswear as well as accessories and the men's underwear line.

Via della Vigna Nuova 33   **055 216 693**
50123 Florence   Mon 3-7:30, Tues-Sat 9:30-7:30

☆ La Perla
Lingerie so decadent it's a shame to cover it up. La Perla uses delicate fabrics and intricate lace for its popular line, which ranges from the sweet and demure to bold-colored and racy. The basic Logo collection (featuring embroidery with the La Perla logo) is consistently the most popular style, while the lower priced Malizia collection includes Lycra and cotton basics. Icelandic designer Steinum Sigurd has joined the label, introducing delicate sweaters and knit dresses into the La Perla studios. Friendly staff are on hand to help you find the perfect bra.   www.laperla.com

Via della Vigna Nuova 17-19   **055 217 070**
50123 Florence   Mon 3-7, Tues-Fri 10-1:30, 2:30-7
                              Sat 10-7

La Rinascente
There are only three reasons for visiting Italy's premier department store (sorry, make that four if you need to use the bathroom). They are: the La Perla studio (the only undies worth buying in the lingerie department); Alessi home gadgets on the fourth floor; and La Prairie's cellular anti-ageing creams and make-up on the ground floor. As department stores go, this one looks great on entering but as soon as you start to ascend the escalators things go downhill. But if you do manage to make sense of the misleading floor divisions, you'll find Trussardi Sport, Versace Classic and Kenzo as well.   www.rinascente.it

Piazza della Repubblica 1   **055 219 113**
50123 Florence   Mon-Sat 9-9, Sun 10:30-8

Le Silla
If you are not immediately repelled by the pink plastic splats dripping down the windows and have a penchant for

Florence Directory

ridiculous footwear, Le Silla is for you. Part of the bizarrely named C-Cup fashion group, these shoes are not for the faint-hearted but they really are addictive. The ground floor acts as a teaser and the real fun happens upstairs. Imagine dusty-pink stiletto boots, festooned with an array of sequins and shiny metal stars, or hand-painted kitten-heeled mules, so colorful and lively you would think even they were embarrassed. LS-NYE-93 is the big collection this year—think totter, totter, sparkle, sparkle and your shoes being the only thing talked about for weeks. They are not for everyone, but they do have some fans out there. Honest. www.lesilla.com

Via Roma 23   **055 265 8969**
50123 Florence   Mon 3-7:30, Tues-Sat 10-7:30

Les Copains   👨👩

Knits! Knits! Knits! More then 75% of the Les Copains collection is spun from precious natural yarns like cashmere, pure wool, and wool and silk blends. Ribs, bouclés and sweater looks with intricate stitching and monochromatic color combinations make these knits instantly recognisable. The latest collection includes a variety of lengths for skirts and dresses, from miniskirts to maxi coats, as well as knitted trousers and trouser suits. Jackets, trousers and long coats have sculptured cuts, while some silhouettes have an egg or tulip shape that's a bit larger, inspired by haute couture.

Piazza Antinori 2-3   **055 292 985**
50123 Florence   Mon 3-7, Tues-Sat 10-7

Liverano & Liverano   👨

This family-run tailor has seen its fair share of styles over the years. These days, however, most customers ask for two-piece jackets and narrow trousers made from the finest wools that Ermenegildo Zegna, Loro Piana and Marzotto have to offer. There's also a good selection of English wools and tweeds. The historic atelier has a work room at the back where master tailors stitch away after closing hours, and you can be sure that the shirts, suits and accessories are all made according to old-school tailoring traditions. The staff are rather gruff, but just tell yourself it's all part of its charm.

Via dei Fossi 37-39   **055 239 6436**
50123 Florence   Mon-Sat 9-1, 3:30-7:30

☆ Loro Piana   👨👩

Europe's leading cashmere clothing and fabric producer, Loro Piana puts a super-smooth spin on cashmere ready-to-wear for men and women as well as homewares and sumptuous accessories. Piana is the ultimate in cashmere softness. Sweaters, slippers, blankets and (the best invention of all) cashmere pashminas come in a gamut of spicy tones as well as a lightweight gauge (for the cashmeres). Also, this all-beechwood store has an extensive collection of Piana's handbags and other smaller leather delights.

Via della Vigna Nuova 37   **055 239 8688**
50123 Florence   Mon-Sat 10-7

Florence Directory

Louis Vuitton

All the Louis Vuitton accessories you could ever dream of—travel cases, briefcases, belts, scarves—are here in this brand-new, beautifully designed, zen-like store. Following the huge success of Marc Jacobs and Takashi Murakami's magically colorful and playful totes, there are plenty more treats in store. Next season's wish list will undoubtedly include those same bags again (but this time in black) and the most lavishly embellished beaded dresses just dying to be taken dancing. Start saving now.　　www.vuitton.com

Piazza Strozzi 1　　　　　　　　　　**055 266 981**
50123 Florence　　　　　　　　　Daily 10-7 (Sun 2-7)

☆ Luisa Via Roma

If there was ever such a thing as staff training day here, several employees must have been off sick. But despite the rather frosty sales attitude, Luisa Via Roma is a magnet for the Florentine fashion set. John Galliano for Dior, Balenciaga, Yves Saint Laurent, Bottega Veneta and Ermenegildo Zegna are just a few examples of what's in store for both men and women. Watch out for hot new British designer Rick Owens and Luisa's shoe island, impossible to circumnavigate without snatching a few treasures from the likes of Marc Jacobs and Privée. Meanwhile, both J.Lo and Madonna will be pleased to know that terrycloth tops and hot pants by their favorite leisure label, Juicy Couture, are also stocked here, along with Yohji Yamamoto's Y3 line.　　www.luisaviaroma.com

Via Roma 19-21　　　　　　　　**055 217 826/7**
50123 Florence　　　　　　　　　Daily 10-7 (Sun 11-7)

Madova

There are numerous glove stores in Florence but this is one of the best. The family-run business has been making hand-finished gloves since 1919 and there are plenty of styles to choose from in this tiny store. Each glove is lined in a luxurious choice of silk, wool or cashmere. Best picks include leather gloves with fancy, colored cuffs, colored finger inserts and contrasting top stitches. For winter, this is the place to find the ultimate classic sheepskin mittens in shades of mustard, yellow and rust. The friendly owners are happy to mail gloves directly to you anywhere in the world.
www.madova.com

Via Guicciardini 1　　　　　　　　**055 239 6526**
50125 Florence　　　　　　　　　Mon-Sat 9:30-7:30

Mandarina Duck

With terrestrial names like Urban and Frog, Mandarina Duck's latest range of travel bags and cases, briefcases, purses and daytime shopping bags have a strong tactile edge and multi-functional appeal. The ingenious new accessories collection (architects and industrial designers are used as consultants) is clearly different from any other travelwear label. Curvilinear sack bags close with magnetic fasteners, trolley cases are hard as a nut and only the most resilient water and scratch-proof materials are used. The store on Via dei Cerretani is a bit of a squeeze, so Via Por Santa Maria may be a better bet. www.mandarinaduck.com

Via dei Cerretani 64-66	**055 219 210**
50123 Florence	Mon-Sat 9-7:30

Via Por Santa Maria 23	**055 210 380**
50122 Florence	(opening times as above)

Massimo Rebecchi

Tuscan designer Massimo Rebecchi creates men's and womenswear with an urban twist. In the womenswear store, leather, nylon and wool blends, linen and cashmere are just a few of the fabrics which this canny designer likes to snip and double stitch into ground-breaking new shapes. The store is compact and sleek, just like Rebecchi's streamlined style. In addition to the designer's latest asymmetrical skirts, drainpipe trousers and finely tuned jackets the store packs a jazzy range of accessories and shoes to suit even the simplest of tastes.

Via della Vigna Nuova 26 (women)	**055 268 053**
50123 Florence	Mon 3:30-7:30, Tues-Sat 10-7:30

Via della Vigna Nuova 18-20 (men)	**055 268 053**
50123 Florence	(opening times as above)

Matucci

Don't expect to be charmed by either of these stores but if you think of them purely in terms of clothing supermarkets you won't be disappointed. The men's store is hideously designed and impossible to navigate, but if you invest the time you will eventually stumble across Hugo Boss, Armani, Diesel and D&G underwear. The women's store is marginally less of a chore, with all the Miss Sixty, Kookaï, DKNY and Diesel staples. It won't be enjoyable but you might get lucky, and that's reason enough for us.

Via del Corso 44-46 (women)	**055 212 018**
50142 Florence	Mon 3:30-7:30, Tues-Sat 10-7:30

Via del Corso 71-73 (men)	**055 239 6420**
50142 Florence	(opening times as above)

Max & Co

Nifty pinstripe suits, casual trousers, denim skirts and groovy accessories all with a trendy twist. As MaxMara's youngest label, Max & Co is aimed at sassy girls about town. Like most fashion stores, the boutique has a brilliant white interior, light wood fittings and piercing spotlights. As well as the extensive clothing line-up which comes in a good range of sizes, you will also find Max & Co's sleek new travel bag collection. This includes multi-functional black nylon bags on wheels and sleek leather carry-ons. Staff at this store have all graduated from smile school.

Via Calzaiuoli 89	**055 288 656**
50122 Florence	Mon-Sat 10:30-7:30, Sun 11-7

MaxMara

The camel hair coat is an icon for MaxMara, the foundation upon which one of Italy's most successful family fashion empires was built; the challenge each fall is to find a new context in which to frame that timeless piece. The minimally furnished store also carries MaxMara's family of brands: Sportmax, Sportmax Code as well as Weekend and MaxMara Basic. There is a good range of accessories from shoes to handbags and that all-important silk scarf. At the time of writing, a new store was eagerly awaited on Via Tornabuoni.

Via dei Pecori 23   **055 287 761**
50123 Florence   Daily 10-7:30 (Sun 10:30-7:30)

Miss Sixty

This is a very clean store. The staff seem to be buffing, hoovering or spraying surfaces any chance they can get. It's quite small too, and fills to spilling point easily. That said, if you're prepared to fight your way through the dust busters and crowds, a feast of groovy denims await you. Displayed in a bright, pop-art interior, Miss Sixty's trademark denim jackets and boot-leg jeans are sprayed, embroidered and pinched with studs. With a colorful selection of equally funky bags, belts and sunglasses you'll be glad you stayed.   www.misssixty.com

Via Roma 20   **055 239 9549**
50123 Florence   Mon-Sat 10-7:30, Sun 11-1:30, 2:30-7:30

☆ Miu Miu

Prada's quirky little sister Miu Miu comes up with colorful surprises every season. Founded as an experimental collection in 1992 by Miuccia Prada, Miu Miu is always on the cutting edge of fashion. Here men's and women's clothes as well as bags, belts and other accessories are all on one spacious floor. The clothes are colorful enough for interior distractions which explains the white, no-frills decor jazzed up with the odd strip of red Perspex. Check out Miu Miu's latest collection with bold, Hawaiian prints splashed vibrantly over cropped trousers to bikinis.   www.miumiu.it

Via Roma 8   **055 260 8931**
50123 Florence   Daily 10-7

☆ Moda Sartoriale

Franco Cisternino has been putting chalk to cloth along with his brothers for as long as he can remember. There are plenty of tailors in Florence but this is where the insiders like to shop. Cisternino has a swish line-up of VIP clients, including Sting (who has a large estate and vineyard in Tuscany) and members of the British and Italian governments. Following an initial measuring and one subsequent fitting, Cisternino and his small team will have the perfect suit, shirt or trench coat sent to your door anywhere in the world.

Via del Purgatorio 22   **055 280 118**
50123 Florence   Mon-Sat 9-1, 3-8

Montgomery

It's impossible not to be charmed by Massimo Facchini and Patrizio Bonciolini who take such delight in bringing up-to-the-minute street style to Italian youth. Designer jeans, funky tees and cutting-edge sweaters take up most of the shelves in this trendy club-like store and quite a lot of it is British. Fake Genius and Fake London battle it out with Katharine Hamnett and Walsh, but Dick Bikkembergs gets a look in too with his eclectic Belgian style. The collections are small but carefully chosen, so thankfully there's not a lot of sifting through needed. This year, the boys are especially proud of their Mihara Yasuhiros, pumas so exclusive that only one or two styles are produced each year. Just don't ask to try them on—you will be put through an almost religious ritual.

Via Pellicceria 22   **055 216 283**
50123 Florence   Mon 3:30-7:30, Tues-Sat 9:30-1, 3-7:30

Murphy & Nye

In 1933 Jim Murphy and Harry Nye Jr established Murphy & Nye in Chicago as specialist sailmakers for pleasure craft. Today, the company has expanded its knowledge of sturdy waterproof fabrics into a range of fashionable clothing for men, women and children. The new line includes denim jackets with seriously nautical names like Oar and Rig. Elsewhere in the collection there are argyle sweaters, fleece jackets and canvas boat shoes in a gamut of funky colors, and a new line, Jr, for kids. The best thing about this store is the silver sales counter which is shaped, you guessed it, like a sail-boat.

Via Calimala 16-18   **055 265 8035**
50122 Florence   Daily 10-7:30 (Sun 2-7:30)

Nannini

The Nannini family is famous in these parts. Their shoe-making company is steeped in the history of Florentine craftsmanship and can be traced back for centuries. Their collections for men and women are made from the softest leathers and suedes. This season, dusty-pink suede sneakers nestling on beds of rose petals and pillar-box red handbags are taking pride of place in their new store on Via dei Calzaiuoli. The house also cuts a cool collection of fringed leather bags, travel cases and shades for that all-important weekend at the beach.

Via Porta Rossa 64   **055 213 888**
50121 Florence   Mon 3:30-7:30, Tues-Sat 10-7:30

Via dei Calzaiuoli 8   **055 238 2763**
50122 Florence   (opening times as above)

Nara Camicie

Shirts, shirts, shirts and more shirts. Sleeved, sleeveless, patterned, plain, buttoned, zipped, daring, classic…they are all here in this tiny shoebox of a shop. If you can negotiate your way past the hordes, men's shirts line one side of the shop and women's the other. Pick your style, suggest your size and you will be whisked away into the back of the store to try them on. This is efficient shopping at its best. The more adventurous women this season are tackling the Adam Ant inspired ruffled-collar, drawstring-waisted chiffon styles and the boys are experimenting with cotton caftans. Some details may be a little off-putting but the label is heading for world domination with its franchising policy and those Greeks do like their over-the-top embroidery.   www.naracamicie.it

Via Porta Rossa 25   **055 264 5721**
50121 Florence   Sun-Mon 2-7:30, Tues-Sat 10-7:30

☆ Paola del Lungo

Paola del Lungo puts a brand new spin on men's and women's shoes and accessories with unusual fabrics and some seriously quirky heel shapes. Not one for making conventional leather lace-ups, Paola prefers to let her imagination run wild. As a result, denim slingbacks are sprinkled with sequins, silk mules are printed with butterflies and heels on strappy wooden clogs are topped with a suede fringe. She gets just as carried away on a range of leather and suede handbags covered in studs and rivets. And the Via de Bardi location has just become an outlet store with some almost criminal discounts. Definitely worth a trip over the river.

Via Porta Rossa 7   **055 284 881**
50121 Florence   Daily 9-7:30 (Sun 11:30-7:30)

Via dei Cerretani 72   **055 280 642**
50123 Florence   (opening times as above)

Via de Bardi 69   **055 212 356**
50120 Florence   Mon-Sat 10-7

Parody

Well, it's just not. But this little gem of a store is a refreshing change from the might of the fashion heavyweights on Via Tornabuoni just spitting distance away. Owner Cristina Lunarde wanted to inject the Florentine fashion scene with a little *je ne sais quoi* and her latest collections for men and women prove that she's doing just that. Marithé et Francois Girbaud's classy French street style (think the zippiest, most high-tech microfiber cargo pants and you are just about there) nudges shoulders with Paul Smith, Katharine Hamnett and those moreish Petit Bateau stretch-cotton tops in every conceivable color. Our picks: for the boys, the super-soft Girbaud jeans; and for the girls, we just could not keep our hands off French designer Paco Chicano's Bohemienne tees. Printed with Hawaiian beach themes and just a twist of Moulin Rouge, they make you want to hoola hoola and cha cha cha all day.

Via della Spada 18-20   **055 214 583**
50123 Florence   Mon 2:30-7:30, Tues-Sat 10-7:30

☆ Patrizia Pepe ⚹

Launched in 1993 by Patrizia Bambi and Claudio Orrea, two entrepreneurs from Tuscany, this hip womenswear label is loved by Italian girls across the land. As well as the minimal styles and slinky fabrics—silk jersey, cashmere, linen and lightweight microfibers, to name but a few—they cut a desirable range of snug-fitting tailored suits, crisp white shirts and floaty evening dresses. There are also plenty of accessories, from silver baseball boots to soft leather bags and funky costume jewelry. It's well worth taking the stairs to the second floor for more goodies and a tourist-free view of the Duomo.   www.patriziapepe.it

Piazza San Giovanni 12   **055 264 5056**
50129 Florence   Mon 3:30-7:30, Tues-Sat 10-7:30

Peruzzi ⚹⚹⚹

Dare we say it? This is one of those imposingly vast, characterless leather warehouses which you should try to avoid at all costs but if you must go to one, this is considered the best. The lights dazzle you, the shop assistants either harass or ignore you and the layout resembles a Jackson Pollock painting but if brands are what you are after, look no further. Burberry, Gucci, Zegna, Dunhill, Coccinelle, Celine, Etro, Dior, Bruno Magli, Versace, Moschino, YSL…they are all here and in quantities sufficient to stuff the 2,000 square metre space. As well as the obligatory shoes, handbags, wallets and belts, you will also find sunglasses and even a new cosmetics counter. The philosophy appears to be: if you can get it in, sell it. Unsurprisingly, this does not lead to an enjoyable shopping experience, but you might come away with a little gem—just try and forget where you bought it.   www.peruzzispa.com

Via Anguillara 5-23 (odd nos)   **055 289 039**
50122 Florence   Daily 9-7

Piazza Pitti ⚹

Located directly opposite the historic Pitti Palace, this designer discount outlet is still a relatively well kept secret among Florence's fashion pundits. It's the only place in town where you can get discounts of up to 60% on same-season collections from Roberto Cavalli, Prada, Blumarine and Paul Smith amongst others. And if that weren't reason enough to head away from the central shopping area on the other side of the Ponte Vecchio, then perhaps the latest funky top from the exclusive Voyage Passion label at a snip of the original price is.   www.piazzapitti.it

Piazza Pitti 32-33   **055 260 8730**
50125 Florence   Mon-Sat 10-7:30, Sun 11-7

Piero Guidi ⚹⚹

Just like the Prada stores all over Italy, Piero Guidi's flagship store in Florence is usually brimming with Japanese tourists in search of a good deal on leather goods and clothing.

Guidi is a colorful designer with a penchant for experimenting with leather in his distinctly unconventional collections. Colored strips of hide are woven into bags, sandals and belts. Leather biker-style jackets come in shades of hot red and vibrant yellow. Shoes are pointy and very high, verging on the kinky. Best to leave your inhibitions outside.

Via della Vigna Nuova 46-48   **055 264 5503**
50123 Florence   Mon 3:30-7, Tues-Sat 9:30-1, 3:30-7

☆ Pollini

The flavor at Pollini is distinctly stylish and new. And let's face it, whose little pinkies wouldn't be dancing in a pair of Pollini strappy pumps which tie around the ankle or butter-soft leather slingbacks with a sassy kitten heel for that matter? Quality is a key component at Pollini, which explains why ready-to-wear designers such as Alberta Ferretti, Jean Paul Gaultier and Moschino have their shoe collections produced by this Italian footwear specialist. The L-shaped store on Via Calimala may not be as big as that in Milan, but the staff are well used to customers pawing at the collections. A second store has been opened on Via Por Santa Maria housing all the latest handbags and accessories.   www.pollini.com

Via Calimala 12   **055 214 738**
50123 Florence   Mon-Sat 10-7

Via Por Santa Maria 42   **055 288 672**
50123 Florence   (opening times as above)

Prada (men)

Just a couple of doors up from the Prada womenswear store on the bustling Via dei Tornabuoni, sits the men's. Miuccia Prada splashes many of the same elements she uses in womenswear into the men's collection. Those offbeat color schemes, plush fabrics and unusual cuts form the basis of the collection; sharp black suits, silk shirts and buffed leather shoes are amongst the best sellers. This is also a great store for travel bags and small leather goods such as wallets and belts to complete your oh-so-stylish Prada look.   www.prada.com

Via dei Tornabuoni 67   **055 283 439**
50123 Florence   Mon 3-7, Tues-Sat 10-7

☆ Prada (women)

There are probably not many stores around the world that can boast a 15th-century frescoed ceiling but this one can. All the Prada favorites are here, from wedge-heeled mules to pleated wool skirts, sharp tailored jackets and long cashmere coats. The staff are friendly and helpful and should all that shopping have left you feeling a little, well, wiped out, then stop for a minute in the cubby-hole near the front door which is filled with Prada's latest age-combating moisturisers. Here you can sample Prada's extensive make-up and beauty lines before you head out.

Via dei Tornabuoni 53   **055 267 471**
50123 Florence   Mon 3-7, Tues-Sat 10-7

Florence Directory

Prenatal

Prenatal, the Italian baby and childrenswear company, is good news for busy mums and those soon to be. You'll find just about everything the little ones could ever need here: terrycloth romper suits, bibs, bottles, prams and a huge selection of toys, games and books. For mums, there is a good range of pregnancy clothes which includes trousers, skirts, shirts and jeans, all with stretchy waistbands. Prenatal also stocks a wide selection of cots and baby carriers made from natural materials. And for those mamas carrying an extra load, the store has big soft sofas to take the weight off your feet.

Via Brunelleschi 22   **055 213 006**
50100 Florence   Mon 3:30-7:30, Tues-Sat 10-7:30
Sun 3:30-7:30

Raspini

There are several Raspinis scattered around the center of Florence but the store on Via Por Santa Maria is the original flagship. Don't expect to find many international labels here, as Raspini carries only the best names in Italian ready-to-wear for both men and women. Miu Miu, Armani, Blumarine, Prada Sport and Roberto Cavalli are some of the labels swinging from the racks. Raspini's own footwear line is well worth taking a look at, as is Venice-based Incotex who make great trousers that miraculously make your waist look smaller and your legs longer. Now isn't that good news?

Via Por Santa Maria 72   **055 215 796**
50122 Florence   Mon 3:30-7:30, Tues-Sat 9:30-7:30
Via Martelli 5-7   **055 239 8336**
50129 Florence   Mon 3:30-7:30
Tues-Sat 9:30-1, 3:30-7:30

Via Roma 25   **055 213 077**
50100 Florence   (opening times as above)

Replay

Too cool for school? This is your place. Jeans hang from meat hooks in a variety of different cuts, ranging from funky hipsters to flattering leg-huggers, and hyper-trendy tees, battered into one inch of their life with right-on graphics, stack up the shelves. Canvas and leather biker jackets have been added to the mix this year, along with military-style shirts and jackets and rumpled denim shirts, an ironing dream. There is an unmistakably industrial feel to the stores and a kicking vibe with just a hint of the apocalypse. Replay appears to be taking on Diesel head-on, so let the battle of the logos commence. Just keep the kids away from their Alien-inspired pod changing-rooms—they're enough to frighten even the hardest little 'un.

Via dei Pecori 7   **055 293 041**
50123 Florence   Mon 3-7:30, Tues-Sat 10-7:30
Sun 2:30-7:30

Via Por Santa Maria 27   **055 287 950**
50123 Florence   (opening times as above)

Piazza C. Goldoni 6 **055 239 8833**
50123 Florence (opening times as above)

Roberto Biagini

This shop might look a bit fusty from the outside, but once inside you'll forget about the aesthetics when faced with some of the finest menswear this side of the Arno. Biagini caters to a gentleman's stylish requirements—pure cotton shirts, three-button overcoats and classic Italian suits, all made to measure from the pick of Italian and British fabrics. And in addition to the choice selection of menswear staples and the exquisite artisan cut which goes into each piece, Biagini's beautiful, handmade leather shoes are among some of the finest in town.

Via Roma 2-4 **055 294 253**
50123 Florence Mon-Sat 10-7:30, Sun 10-1, 3:30-7:30

☆ Roberto Cavalli

Italy's wild man of fashion has a list of celebrity fans ranging from J.Lo to Lenny Kravitz. It's his rock-star chic style that makes him one of Italy's most exciting designers and one who never ceases to amaze, season after season. Who else makes jeans like this man? Each pair is treated like a canvas on which Cavalli works his magic with a splash of rhinestones, embroidery and raw-edge finishes. After all those distinctive animal prints and high hems you might need a stiff drink in the Caffè Giacosa. It's part of the Cavalli store, open weekdays from 7:30am to 8:30pm, and you'll find the entrance around the corner on the Via della Spada. www.robertocavalli.it

Via dei Tornabuoni 83 **055 239 6226**
50123 Florence Mon 3-7:30, Tues-Sat 10-7:30, Sun 3-7:30

☆ Roberto Ugolini

Stepping into Roberto Ugolini's artisan workshop is like taking a time machine into the past. The walls are covered in black and white photos of the city and of its craftsmen sewing leather hides and hammering pins into shoes. Antique wall-brackets are lined with wooden prototypes of feet from past and present. Roberto and his two-man team are relatively young as far as artisan shoemakers go. Part of Florence's savvy thirtysomething generation, they know exactly what's hot on the footwear scene and will make the latest styles according to the traditions which have been passed down to them.

Via Michelozzi 17 **055 216 246**
50125 Florence Mon 3:30-8, Tues-Sat 9:30-1:30, 3:30-8

Salvatore Ferragamo

The store is on the ground floor of the historic Palazzo Spini, which also houses Ferragamo's famous shoe museum as well as the company offices. Men's, women's and children's clothing and accessories are divided by category in this sprawling, open-plan interior. The ceilings are covered

in frescoes and the walls are filled with huge black and white photos of Hollywood stars in their Ferragamo shoes. There's a relaxed atmosphere and even a husband-friendly zone, where he can watch television and read the papers while you get carried away by Ferragamo's tapered skirts and soft cashmere pullovers. (Even though there are two addresses, it's the same building.)   www.ferragamo.com

Via dei Tornabuoni 14 (women)   **055 292 123**
50123 Florence   Mon 3:30-7:30, Tues-Sat 10-7:30

Piazza S.Trinita (men)   **055 268 776**
50123 Florence   (opening times as above)

San Lorenzo Market

Located between the Medici-Riccardi Palace, the Basilica of San Lorenzo and the Medici chapel, the sprawling San Lorenzo market is an obligatory stop for those in search of a cheap and cheerful thrill. Stalls are cram-packed with clothes and accessories and the quality is surprisingly high. Of particular note are the cozy sheepskin gloves, soft leather jackets and superb knock-off handbags after the likes of Botttega Veneta, Tod's and Prada—they're so well made no one will spot the difference. You'll also find a small selection of trendy seasonal clothing as well as the usual ethnic tat and Florentine memorabilia. Go early to avoid the crowds.

Piazza del Mercato Centrale and around San Lorenzo
Mon-Sat 9-6

Sarah Pacini

Floaty, flared linen trousers, flattering knitwear and practical, everyday tops are all here but just don't expect patterns or bright colors. These don't exist in Pacini's world. She is a natural fiber and neutral color devotee but likes to have a little fun with them. Metal threads are sewn into linen and cotton trousers to help them keep her signature scrunchy look, and skirts are weighted down to avoid those embarrassing Marilyn moments. Lines are kept clean so that the clothes can be worn by every shape and all the knitwear is of the one-size-fits-all variety. And amazingly enough, it really does. Our favorite is the off-the-shoulder wraparound cardi that needs a degree in physics to tie up but makes you feel like a cross between Darcy Bussel and Scarlett O'Hara.

Via del Corso 43   **055 268 461**
50142 Florence   Mon-Sat 10-7:30

Sergio Rossi

Where better to get a fabulous shoe fix than at Sergio Rossi? After all, when it comes to making seriously sexy shoes one of Italy's leading shoe designers surely knows what women want. Since selling a 70% stake in the business to Gucci, Rossi (which until now had never deviated from its core product) has added a men's footwear collection as well as a bags and leather goods line. Everything is made from eclectic fabrics such as crocodile, suede and butter-soft leathers. Heel heights for women vary from the kitten to

Rossi's signature five-inch stiletto pumps. Just let your feet
do the walking. www.sergiorossi.com

Via Roma 15 **055 294 873**
50123 Florence Mon 3-7, Tues-Sat 10-7

Sisley

The trendy Parisian fashion label, whose raunchy bill-
board campaigns are the cause of many a traffic jam, has
a knack of anticipating future trends in extremely up-to-
date collections. The high-tech store with its minimalist
white interior houses sport clothes and casualwear as well
as formal and elegant dresses. Though Sisley is constantly classed with Stefanel and Benetton, its various collections, notably the menswear range, have a slightly cooler
edge. www.sisley.com

Via dei Cerretani 57 **055 210 683**
50123 Florence Daily 9:30-7:30 (Sun 3:30-7:30)
Via Roma 16 **055 286 669**
50123 Florence Daily 10-7:30 (Sun 11-7:30)

☆ Space

This store was once just an alley running between two large
palazzos before Paolo Vasi covered it over in glass and put
a hip designer line-up on the racks. Costume National,
Dries Van Noten, Paul Smith and Helmut Lang are a few of
the names which make Space what it is today. And there are
some hot new labels to look out for too: Danish jeweler
Monies makes avant-garde necklaces from uneven pearls,
and Italian designer Mario Matteo cuts a mean range of
trousers and shirts for men and women.

Via dei Tornabuoni 17 **055 216 943**
50123 Florence Mon 3-7:30, Tues-Sat 10-7:30

Stefanel

Come rain or shine, you are guaranteed to find all your
basic wardrobe essentials here. T-shirts, sweaters, jeans and
a full range of accessories are displayed on two easy to navigate floors. Following its recent style injection, Stefanel's
men's and women's ranges look decidedly cool and prices
are well within most budgets. The staff are a little over-
friendly—they won't stop saying hello—but the store is so
big you can usually shake them off. Each collection is well
stocked for sizes but for certain colors it's best to ask.
www.stefanel.it

Via dei Cerretani 46-48 **055 215 526**
50123 Florence Mon-Sat 10-8, Sun 11-1, 3:30-7:30
Via dei Calzaiuoli 44 **055 212 418**
50122 Florence (opening times as above)

Strenesse

Strenesse, the German maker of upscale womenswear,
does exceptionally well in Italy. Gabriele Strehle's sleek
designs and beautiful fabrics seem to suit the tastes of

those stylish Florentine women who also shop at Armani. Trouser suits, long shearling coats, elegant cocktail dresses and a full range of accessories are made from the finest materials, wool, silk, cashmere and linen. Strenesse did launch its first menswear collection at Milan Fashion Week back in March 2002, but for the time being the Florence store with its bright white interior continues to house only the womenswear collection.

Via Porta Rossa 81-85 **055 287 987**
50125 Florence   Mon 3:30-7:30, Tues-Sat 10-1, 3-7:30

Tanino Crisci

Remember the last time you were called into your father's study? This mahogany-walled store may invoke those same feelings of trepidation but the beautifully crafted handmade leather goods will soon put you at ease. Sophisticated tanning techniques transform only the very best Italian leather into classic shoes, belts, bags and jackets. You will struggle to find a stiletto here but check out the blue-denim nubuck lizard loafers and the orange napa leather sandals. In shoe terms, they are about as wild as it gets here, although the names of some of the handbags (e.g. the "spank" bag) may make you think differently. Tanino Crisci may be a little conservative for some (although not for Michael Portillo, whose business card we spotted on the desk) but it has been under the watchful eye of the same family for four generations and looks set to continue for another four. So sit back, relax and let the softly spoken sales assistants do all the work.   www.taninocrisci.com

Via dei Tornabuoni 43-45 **055 214 692**
50123 Florence   Mon 3-7, Tues-Sat 10-7

Tod's

Diego Della Valle, the designer behind the Hogan footwear label, likes to put a comfy spin on his other shoe collection, Tod's. The label, launched 23 years ago, is known mostly for its stylish leather car shoes with little plastic spheres on the soles. The moccasin designs are not just restricted to the car, of course; nowadays they are far more likely to be seen treading the boards in St Tropez. But here you will also find Della Valle's latest creation, the Dado bag, inspired by the boxy shape of dice.   www.tods.com

Via dei Tornabuoni 103 **055 219 423**
50123 Florence   Mon-Sat 10-7

Trussardi

It's not every designer store where the staff are genuinely happy to see you, but here you really are made to feel right at home. As well as the women's and men's ready-to-wear lines, Trussardi carries new children's and babywear collections and a range of scooter accessories, the coolest things to be seen zipping around town in. There's even a gleaming silver scooter standing on the shop floor, from a limited edition collection. The store itself was once the stables of a rich Florentine family and the frescoed walls have been kept intact. www.trussardi.com

Via dei Tornabuoni 34-36   **055 219 903**
50123 Florence   Mon 3-7, Tues-Sat 10-7, 3-7

Universo Sport

Two floors of sportswear, accessories and equipment within easy reach of the Duomo. The ground-floor shoe department carries plenty of leading brands, but it's the clothing department upstairs where the real goodies lie. These include the Prada Sport line for both men and women as well as denims from Levi's, skatewear from Carhartt and hot American surf brands Helly Hansen and Sundek. The children's department shrinks the same brands down to size. Energetic tiny tots will love the mini treadmill which is free for use on the second floor.

Piazza Duomo 6   **055 284 412**
50100 Florence   Daily 9:30-7:30

☆ Valentino

Prepare to gasp out loud over the fairytale dresses, hand-finished shoes and dreamy wedding gowns that fill the racks here. The pick of ready-to-wear and couture from the Valentino collections is topped by the Garavani accessories collection. The plush line-up includes hand-beaded evening bags, dazzling slingbacks, embroidered belts and kitten-heeled boots. Fur coats, tweed suits and silk shawls are brought to the fore by the store's dazzling ceiling lights which are designed to look like tiny stars. Even the shoes are lit to twinkle. www.valentino.it

Via della Vigna Nuova 47   **055 293 142**
50100 Florence   Mon 3-7, Tues-Sat 10-2

Versace

Ever felt as though you had just walked into a store wearing a big pink wig on your head? Well, that's the kind of feeling you get when you walk in here. But if you can ignore the looks of some of the snootiest sales staff in town, then Versace's collections for men and women, as well as its home line, are well worth a look. Elton John's favorite sequined jackets can be found in the basement menswear department, along with skimpy underwear, shirts, coats and ties, while the women's collection on the first floor has a section of evening dresses which can be made to order.

Via dei Tornabuoni 13   **055 239 6167**
50123 Florence   Mon-Sat 10-7

Versus

Fashion's sassiest designer Donatella Versace shows no signs of holding back on the glitz in the jeans, zebra-print shirts and rock-chick dresses with the Versus label. The boutique, with its signature Medusa heads painted on the walls and floors, houses the men's and women's collections as well as those must-have rock-star accessories on two floors. Fringed leather bags and spiky stiletto heels are just what you need for a fiery post-punk look. With its spray-on jeans and body-hugging T-shirts you might want to hold off on the tiramisu.

Via della Vigna Nuova 38   **055 217 619**
50123 Florence   Mon 3:30-7:30, Tues-Sat 10-7:30

☆ Vilebrequin

Dragged to Florence when you would rather be at the beach? Don't despair, head straight to this new store and step into the Med. This is the latest in Vilebrequin's brilliantly planned expansion in which locations and fittings are chosen just as carefully as the fabrics. Nestling among sun-baked tiles and exotic plants are rows and rows of swimming trunks in every conceivable pattern. You can swim with dolphins, prance around with big pink flowers or go a little citrussy—nothing is too much for these stylish trunks. And whether you are after something short or long (not too short though—this is not Speedo slinky territory), bold or quiet, the perma-tanned assistant will happily oblige. It has taken them a long time to leave St Tropez and bring quality swimwear to the masses, but let's be grateful they did. Only one question remains: "What about the ladies?" www.vilebrequin.com

Via Roma 12   **055 291 008**
50123 Florence   Mon 3-7, Tues-Sat 10-7

Wolford

Wolford, the upmarket Austrian lingerie and hosiery makers, have a thing for legs. Their latest stockings and hose come in an endless range of colors, textures and shapes. Whether they're sheer, matte, high-sheen or fishnet, your legs, so Wolford say, will be radically transformed for the better. In addition to the sexy hosiery, the Wolford collection now includes slips, bodies, nightwear and a great selection of microfiber bras and vests. According to the smiley store manager, this season is all about sheer/transparency. Go on, give those pins a treat.

Via della Vigna Nuova 93-95   **055 213 651**
50125 Florence   Mon 3:30-7:30, Tues-Sat 10-7:30

Yves Saint Laurent

Yves Saint Laurent handed over the reins of his ready-to-wear collection to Gucci's Tom Ford in late 1999, and ever since then Ford's creative direction has given a strong impetus to the Yves Saint Laurent and Rive Gauche lines. Ford makes his own unique mark on the womenswear line in the shape of sexy, leopard-print chiffon shirts, figure-hugging tuxedo jackets and suede skirts cut with a jagged hem. The store also houses leather goods and handmade bags in a black-lacquered wood interior and is set to expand next door at some point this year.

Via dei Tornabuoni 29　　　　　**055 284 040**
50123 Florence　　　　　　　　　　Mon-Sat 9-7

The Last Good Buy   *(not to be missed by serious shoppers)*
Rotating around the mother ship of Florence are discreet
towns and suburbs with outlets offering massive discounts on
top-brand clothes and accessories. Here are five of the best.

Celine and Loewe
Relative newcomers to the Florence outlet scene, Celine
and Loewe have quickly made their mark as another must
on the trail for that jaw-dropping, tear-inducing designer
bargain. The space is equally divided between the two
fashion houses and the clothes, accessories and shoes are
displayed with a little more thought than at some of the
other units. If your timing is spot on, you may just find one
of Celine's Boogie bags or a pair of Loewe's chocolate
brown leather trousers, but sharpen your elbows and be
prepared to run…the really sought-after pieces aren't
around for long.

Via Pian Dell'Isola　　　　　　　**055 834 7155**
50067 Rignano sull'Arno　　　Mon-Sat 10-7, Sun 3-7

Dolce & Gabbana Industria S.P.A.
Shhh! Not many people know about Dolce & Gabbana's
factory outlet, which is why you can still pick through the
endless racks of goodies in relative calm. With discounts of
30-60% on the main line as well as on its D&G diffusion line,
even the most frugal of shoppers will find it hard to resist
the sparkly evening dresses, tailored suits and funky denims
on offer. And if it's accessories you're after, this is the place
to be. The outlet stocks sunglasses, silk ties and luxurious
leather goods, all perfect for the dolce vita.

S.Maria Maddalena 49　　　　　**055 833 1300**
Via Pian Dell'Isola　　　　　　　Daily 9-7 (Sun 3-7)
50064 Incisa in Val d'Arno

Fendi
The Fendi outlet is on the same street as Dolce &
Gabbana's discount warehouse, despite the different
ways of describing the location. Here in the stark white
Fendi space, leather bags, scarves, ready-to-wear and
shoes from previous seasons can be snapped up at a snip
of the original price. So if you haven't yet purchased that
chic suede skirt or one of those much sought-after
baguette bags designed by Silvia Venturini, now's the
time to whip out your credit card. But before you do, it's
worth calling ahead to check opening hours as they are
subject to sudden changes.

Via Pian Dell'Isola 66　　　　　**055 834 981**
50067 Rignano sull'Arno　　　　Daily 10-7 (Sun 3-7)

Florence Directory

I Pellettieri d'Italia

In this low-lying building which doubles as Prada's factory outlet the fashion house sells directly to the public, wiping out mark-ups which can account for half the price. With kitten heels, loafers, clutch bags and ready-to-wear by Prada and Miu Miu as well as Helmut Lang and Jil Sander, you had best book yourself a wake-up call. Otherwise be prepared to enter a scrum with the Japanese coach parties who get here at dawn and are just not interested in the new minimalist, so-very-Prada café next door.

Localita Levanella 69   **055 91961**
52025 Montevarchi   Daily 9:30-7 (Sun 2-7)

The Mall

If you thought a mall was something synonymous with fast food and cheap sneakers, think again. Italy puts a brand new spin on the cheesy mall concept with a deluxe ever-expanding shopping center packed to capacity with high-end luxury labels. With Bottega Veneta, Emanuel Ungaro, Giorgio Armani, Gucci, Loro Piana, Salvatore Ferragamo, Sergio Rossi, Valentino, Yves Saint Laurent etcetera all in separate spaces under one roof, it's no wonder fashionistas feel dizzy. And with discounts of up to 70%, remember to pack the smelling salts.

Via Europa 8   **055 865 7775**
50060 Leccio Reggello   Daily 10-7 (Sun 3-7)

Florence Stores by District

Florence

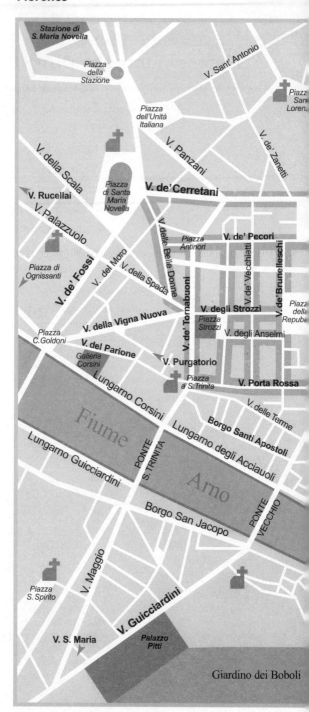

Stazione di
S. Maria Novella

Piazza
della
Stazione

V. Sant' Antonio

Piazza
San
Loren.

Piazza
dell'Unità
Italiana

V. Panzani

V. della Scala

V. de Zanetti

V. de'Cerretani

V. Rucellai

Piazza
di Santa
Maria
Novella

V. Palazzuolo

V. delle Belle Donne

Piazza
Antinori

V. de' Pecori

Piazza di
Ognissanti

V. de' Fossi

V. del Moro

V. della Spada

V. de' Vecchietti

V. de' Brunelleschi

Piazza
della
Repub

V. della Vigna Nuova

V. de' Tornabuoni

V. degli Strozzi

Piazza
Strozzi

Piazza
C. Goldoni

V. del Parione

V. degli Anselmi

Galleria
Corsini

V. Purgatorio

Piazza
a S. Trinita

V. Porta Rossa

Lungarno Corsini

V. delle Terme

Fiume

Borgo Santi Apostoli

Lungarno degli Acciauoli

Lungarno Guicciardini

PONTE S. TRINITA

Armo

PONTE VECCHIO

Borgo San Jacopo

V. Maggio

Piazza
S. Spirito

V. Guicciardini

V. S. Maria

Palazzo
Pitti

Giardino dei Boboli

Piazza di
S.Giovanni

S. Maria
d.Fiore

Museo
dell'Opera
del Duomo

Museo
di Firenze

V. Camillo Cavour

V. Ricasoli

V. dei Servi

V. de' Pucci

V. de' Martelli

V. M.Bufalini

V. dell'Oriuolo

V. dell' Oche

V. dei Calzaiuoli

V. dello Studio

V. del Proconsolo

V. Sant' Elisabetta

V. Dante Alighieri

Borgo degli Albizi

V. Cimatori

V. Ghibellina

V. della Vigna Vecchia

V. dell'Anguillara

Piazza
della
Signoria

V. dei Leoni

Borgo de' Greci

V. de Benci

Piazza
della
Repubblica

Galleria
degli Uffizi

Lungarno Generale Diaz

Lungarno delle Grazie

Lungarno Torrigiani

PONTE
ALLE GRAZIE

Lungarno Serristori

SCALE in metres

0   100   200   300

Central Shopping Zone *See map pages 146-147*

Athletes World	Via dei Cerretani 26-28
Bally	Via Calimala 11
Baroni	Via Porta Rossa 56
Basic	Via Por Rossa 109-115
Benetton 0-12	Via dei Cerretani 60-62
Brioni	Via Calimala 22
Bruno Magli	Via Roma 26-28
Cabo	Via Porta Rossa 77-79
Calvani	Via degli Speziali 7
Castellani	Via Calimala 19
Coin	Via dei Calzaiuoli 56
Del Moro Capelli	Via S.Elisabetta 15
Diesel	Via dei Lamberti 13
E-Play	Via Tosinghi 14
Expensive	Via dei Calzaiuoli 78
Fausto Santini	Via dei Calzaiuoli 95
Foot Locker	Via dei Calzaiuoli 27-35
Fratelli Rossetti	Piazza Repubblica 43-45
Gerard Loft	Via dei Pecori 36
Gilardini	Via dei Cerretani 8
Golden Point	Via degli Speziali 1
Gucci (accessories)	Via Roma 32
Guess?	Via degli Speziali 9-11
Guya	Via Calimala 29
Hugo Boss	Piazza della Repubblica 46
Intimissimi	Via dei Calzaiuoli 99
Intimissimi	Via dei Cerretani 17
La Rinascente	Piazza della Repubblica 1
Le Silla	Via Roma 23
Luisa Via Roma	Via Roma 19-21
Mandarina Duck	Via dei Cerretani 64-66
Max & Co	Via dei Calzaiuoli 89
MaxMara	Via dei Pecori 23
Miss Sixty	Via Roma 20
Miu Miu	Via Roma 8
Montgomery	Via Pellicceria 22
Murphy & Nye	Via Calimala 16-18
Nannini	Via Porta Rossa 64
Nannini	Via dei Calzaiuoli 8
Nara Camicie	Via Porta Rossa 25
Paola del Lungo	Via Porta Rossa 7
Paola del Lungo	Via dei Cerretani 72
Pollini	Via Calimala 12
Prenatal	Via Brunelleschi 22
Raspini	Via Roma 25
Replay	Via dei Pecori 7
Roberto Biagini	Via Roma 2-4
Sergio Rossi	Via Roma 15

Sisley	Via dei Cerretani 57
Sisley	Via Roma 16
Stefanel	Via dei Calzaiuoli 44
Stefanel	Via dei Cerretani 46-48
Strenesse	Via Porta Rossa 81-85
Vilebrequin	Via Roma 12

Duomo area *See map pages 146-147*

Patrizia Pepe	Piazza San Giovanni 12
Sisley	Via Dogana 4
Universo Sport	Piazza Duomo 6

North of Duomo

Benetton	Via Borgo San Lorenzo 15
Foot Locker	Via Borgo San Lorenzo 19
Frette	Via Cavour 2
Raspini	Via Martelli 5-7

South of Duomo

A Piedi Nudi Nel Parco	Via Borgo degli Albizi 46
Sarah Pacini	Via del Corso 43
Matucci	Via del Corso 44 & 71

Piazza Ognissanti area *See map page 146*

Giotti	Piazza Ognissanti 3-4
Il Giglio	Via Borgo Ognissanti 64
Il Rifugio Sport	Piazza Ottaviani 3
Il Rifugio Sport	Via dei Fossi 67
Liverano & Liverano	Via dei Fossi 37-43

Ponte Vecchio/Lungarno area *See map page 146*

Bottega delle Antiche Terme	Borgo Santissimi Apostoli 16
Camper	Via Por Santa Maria 47
Champion	Via Por Santa Maria 52-54
Coccinelle	Via Por Santa Maria 49
Gerard	Via Vaccherreccia 18
Guya	Via Por Santa Maria 76
Mandarina Duck	Via Por Santa Maria 23
Pollini	Via Por Santa Maria 42
Raspini	Via Por Santa Maria 72
Replay	Via Por Santa Maria 27

South of the Arno *See map pages 146-147*

Madova	Via Guicciardini 1
Piazza Pitti	Piazza Pitti 32-33
Paola del Lungo	Via de Bardi 69
Roberto Ugolini	Via Michelozzi 17

Santa Croce area

| Peruzzi | Via Anguillara 5-23 |

Florence Districts

Via dei Tornabuoni area *See map page 146*

Agnona	Via dei Tornabuoni 3
Baroni	Via dei Tornabuoni 9
Bottega Veneta	Via dei Tornabuoni 7
Brioni	Via Rondinelli 7
Casadei	Via dei Tornabuoni 33
Christian Dior	Via dei Tornabuoni 57-59
Emilio Pucci	Via dei Tornabuoni 20-22
Emporio Armani	Piazza Strozzi 16
Enrico Coveri	Via dei Tornabuoni 81
Ermanno Scervino	Piazza Antinori 10
Escada	Via degli Strozzi 32
Fendi	Via degli Strozzi 21
Giorgio Armani	Via dei Tornabuoni 48
Gucci	Via dei Tornabuoni 73
Hermès	Piazza Antinori 6
Hogan	Via dei Tornabuoni 97
Les Copains	Piazza Antinori 2-3
Louis Vuitton	Via dei Tornabuoni 26
Parody	Via della Spada 18-20
Prada (women)	Via dei Tornabuoni 53
Prada (men)	Via dei Tornabuoni 67
Roberto Cavalli	Via dei Tornabuoni 83
Salvatore Ferragamo	Via dei Tornabuoni 14
Space	Via dei Tornabuoni 17
Tanino Crisci	Via dei Tornabuoni 43-45
Tod's	Via dei Tornabuoni 103
Trussardi	Via dei Tornabuoni 34
Versace	Via dei Tornabuoni 13
Yves Saint Laurent	Via dei Tornabuoni 29

Via della Vigna Nuova area *See map page 146*

Anichini	Via del Parione 59
Bonora	Via del Parione 11-15
BP Studio	Via della Vigna Nuova 15
Cesare Paciotti	Via della Vigna Nuova 14
Desmo	Piazza Rucellai 10
Dolce & Gabbana	Via della Vigna Nuova 27
Elio Ferraro	Via del Parione 47
Ermenegildo Zegna	Piazza Rucellai 4-7
Etro	Via della Vigna Nuova 50
Francesco Biasia	Via della Vigna Nuova 16
Furla	Via della Vigna Nuova 28
Gianfranco Lotti	Via della Vigna Nuova 45
Iceberg	Piazza Rucellai 1
Lacoste	Via della Vigna Nuova 33
La Perla	Via della Vigna Nuova 17-19
Loro Piana	Via della Vigna Nuova 37

Massimo Rebecchi	Via della Vigna Nuova 18-20 & 26
Moda Sartoriale	Via del Purgatorio 22
Piero Guidi	Via della Vigna Nuova 46-48
Replay	Piazza C. Goldoni 6
Valentino	Via della Vigna Nuova 47
Versus	Via della Vigna Nuova 38
Wolford	Via della Vigna Nuova 93-95

West of Via dei Cerretani

Italobalestri	Piazza Santa Maria Maggiore 7

Florence Districts

Florence Stores by Category

Women's

Men's

Children's

Women's Accessories

A Piedi Nudi Nel Parco
Bally
Benetton
Bonora

Bottega Veneta
Christian Dior
Coccinelle
Coin

Del Moro Cappelli
Desmo
Elio Ferraro
Ermanno Scervino

Escada
Fendi
Francesco Biasia

Furla
Gerard
Gerard Loft

Gianfranco Lotti
Giotti
Gucci
Guya

Hermès
Il Giglio
La Rinascente
Loro Piana

Louis Vuitton
Mandarina Duck
Nannini
Peruzzi

Patrizia Pepe
Raspini
Sisley

Stefanel
Tanino Crisci

Women's Activewear

Athletes World
Benetton
Champion

Coin
Expensive
Foot Locker

Golden Point
Il Rifugio Sport
Lacoste

La Rinascente
Murphy & Nye
Universo Sport

Women's Bridal

Valentino

Women's Cashmere/Knitwear

Agnona
BP Studio
Cabo
Escada

Fendi
Guya
Les Copains
Loro Piana

Women's Casual

Benetton
Coin
Diesel
E-Play

Expensive
Gerard Loft
Guess?
Iceberg

La Rinascente
Matucci
Max & Co

MaxMara
Miss Sixty
Montgomery
Parody

Patrizia Pepe
Raspini
Replay
Sisley

Stefanel
Universo Sport

Women's Classic

Castellani
Coin
Escada
Etro

Giorgio Armani
Hermès
La Rinascente

Loro Piana
Luisa Via Roma

MaxMara
Nara Camicie
Piazza Pitti
Sarah Pacini

Strenesse
Trussardi
Valentino

Versace
Yves Saint Laurent

Women's Contemporary

A Piedi Nudi Nel Parco
Basic
BP Studio

Diesel
Gerard
Guess?

Guya
Luisa Via Roma
Massimo Rebecchi

Matucci
Max & Co
Parody

Patrizia Pepe
Piazza Pitti
Raspini

Space
Strenesse

Women's Department Store & High Street Chains

Athletes World
Benetton
Camper
Champion

Coin
Diesel
Expensive

Foot Locker
Furla

Golden Point
Iceberg
Intimissimi
La Rinascente

Nara Camicie
Replay
Sisley

Stefanel
Universo Sport

Women's Designer

Bally
Bottega Veneta
Bruno Magli
Cabo

Christian Dior
Dolce & Gabbana
Emilio Pucci
Emporio Armani

Enrico Coveri
Ermanno Scervino
Escada
Etro

Fendi
Gerard
Giorgio Armani

Gucci
Hermès
Les Copains

Louis Vuitton
Luisa Via Roma
Massimo Rebecchi
MaxMara

Miu Miu
Piazza Pitti
Piero Guidi
Prada

Raspini
Roberto Cavalli
Sergio Rossi
Space

Strenesse
Trussardi
Valentino

Versus
Yves Saint Laurent

Florence Categories

Women's Formalwear, Eveningwear & Special Occasions

Casadei
Christian Dior
Del Moro Cappelli
Dolce & Gabbana

Enrico Coveri
Ermanno Scervino
Escada

Etro
Fendi
Gerard

Giorgio Armani
Gucci
Luisa Via Roma
Piazza Pitti

Raspini
Strenesse
Trussardi

Valentino
Versace
Yves Saint Laurent

Women's Handbags

A Piedi Nudi Nel Parco
Bally
Bottega Veneta
Bruno Magli

Christian Dior
Coccinelle
Coin
Desmo

Elio Ferraro
Ermanno Scervino
Escada
Etro

Fausto Santini
Fendi
Francesco Biasia
Furla

Gerard
Gianfranco Lotti
Giotti
Gucci

Guya
Hermès
Le Silla
Louis Vuitton

Mandarina Duck
Peruzzi
Piero Guidi
Prada

Tanino Crisci
Valentino
Yves Saint Laurent

Women's Hats (and gloves*)

Coin
Del Moro Cappelli
*Madova

Women's Leather Goods

Bally
Bonora
Bottega Veneta
Bruno Magli

Christian Dior
Coccinelle
Coin
Desmo

Etro
Fendi
Francesco Biasia
Furla
Gianfranco Lotti

Giorgio Armani
Giotti
Gucci
Hermès

Louis Vuitton
Madova
Peruzzi
Piero Guidi

Prada
Tanino Crisci
Trussardi
Yves Saint Laurent

Women's Lingerie & Nightwear

Coin
Frette
Golden Point
Intimissimi

La Perla
La Rinascente
Wolford

Maternity

Baroni
Benetton 0-12

Coin
Prenatal

Women's Shoes

Bally
Bottega Veneta
Bruno Magli
Calvani

Camper
Casadei
Cesare Paciotti
Christian Dior

Coin
Desmo
Ermanno Scervino
Escada

Fausto Santini
Fendi
Foot Locker
Francesco Biasia

Fratelli Rossetti
Gerard
Gerard Loft
Gianfranco Lotti
Gilardini

Gucci
Guya
Hermès
Hogan

Il Giglio
Italobalestri
Le Silla
Luisa Via Roma

Miu Miu
Nannini
Paola del Lungo
Peruzzi

Piero Guidi
Pollini
Prada
Raspini

Sergio Rossi
Tanino Crisci
Tod's
Valentino

Women's Trend & Streetwear

Athletes World
Benetton
Champion
Coin

Diesel
E-Play
Expensive

Foot Locker
Gerard Loft
Iceberg

Il Rifugio Sport
Lacoste
Miss Sixty
Montgomery

Murphy & Nye
Parody
Replay

Sisley
Stefanel
Universo Sport

Florence Categories

Women's Vintage

Elio Ferraro
Gerard Loft

Men's Accessories

Athletes World
Bally
Benetton
Bonora

Brioni
Bruno Magli
Coin
Diesel

Dolce & Gabbana
Elio Ferraro
Ermenegildo Zegna
Etro

Fendi
Fratelli Rossetti
Gerard
Gerard Loft

Gianfranco Lotti
Giorgio Armani
Giotti
Gucci

Guya
Hermès
Hugo Boss

Il Giglio
Liverano & Liverano
Loro Piana
Louis Vuitton

Mandarina Duck
Matucci
Miu Miu
Montgomery

Murphy & Nye
Peruzzi
Piero Guidi
Prada

Roberto Biagini
Roberto Ugolini
Salvatore Ferragamo
Sisley

Stefanel
Tanino Crisci
Trussardi
Versace

Vilebrequin
Yves Saint Laurent

Men's Activewear

Athletes World
Benetton
Champion
Coin

Foot Locker
Golden Point
Il Rifugio Sport

La Rinascente
Lacoste
Murphy & Nye
Replay

Universo Sport
Vilebrequin

Men's Cashmere/Knitwear

Agnona
Dolce & Gabbana
Fendi
Gerard

Giorgio Armani
Guya
Hugo Boss

Les Copains
Loro Piana
Luisa Via Roma
Prada

Roberto Biagini
Stefanel

Men's Casual

Athletes World
Benetton
Coin
Diesel

E-Play
Elio Ferraro
Gerard Loft

Iceberg
Il Rifugio Sport
Montgomery

Murphy & Nye
Parody
Raspini
Replay

Roberto Biagini
Sisley
Space

Stefanel
Universo Sport

Men's Classic

Agnona
Bottega delle Antiche
  Terme
Brioni

Ermenegildo Zegna
Fendi
Gerard

Giorgio Armani
Gucci
Hugo Boss

Liverano & Liverano
Loro Piana
Luisa Via Roma
Massimo Rebecchi

Moda Sartoriale
Prada
Roberto Biagini

Salvatore Ferragamo
Trussardi
Yves Saint Laurent

Men's Contemporary

Coin
Dolce & Gabbana
E-Play
Emporio Armani

Ermenegildo Zegna
Gerard
Gerard Loft

Giorgio Armani
Guya
Hugo Boss

Luisa Via Roma
Murphy & Nye
Parody
Raspini

Replay
Sisley
Space

Stefanel
Universo Sport

Men's Department Store & High Street Chains

Athletes World
Benetton
Coin

E-Play
Golden Point

Il Rifugio Sport
La Rinascente
Sisley

Stefanel
Universo Sport

Florence Categories

Florence Stores by Category

Men's Designer

Brioni
Bruno Magli
Diesel
Dolce & Gabbana

Emporio Armani
Ermenegildo Zegna
Etro

Fendi
Gerard
Giorgio Armani

Gucci
Hermès
Hugo Boss

Loro Piana
Luisa Via Roma
Miu Miu
Prada

Raspini
Space
Tod's

Trussardi
Universo Sport
Versace

Versus
Yves Saint Laurent

Men's Formalwear & Special Occasions

Bottega delle Antiche
  Terme
Brioni
Dolce & Gabbana

Ermenegildo Zegna
Etro
Fendi
Giorgio Armani

Gucci
Hermès
Hugo Boss
Liverano & Liverano

Loro Piana
Luisa Via Roma
Massimo Rebecchi
Moda Sartoriale

Prada
Raspini
Roberto Biagini
Trussardi

Versace
Versus
Yves Saint Laurent

Men's Hats (and gloves*)

Coin
Giotti
*Madova

Men's Leather Goods

Bally
Bonora
Bruno Magli
Coin

Ermenegildo Zegna
Etro
Fendi
Fratelli Rossetti

Gianfranco Lotti
Giotti
Gucci
Hermès

Hugo Boss
Louis Vuitton
Madova

Mandarina Duck
Peruzzi
Piero Guidi
Pollini

Prada
Raspini
Roberto Biagini
Salvatore Ferragamo

Space
Tanino Crisci
Trussardi
Versace

Versus
Yves Saint Laurent

Men's Shirts

Bottega delle Antiche Terme
Brioni
Coin
Dolce & Gabbana

Emporio Armani
Ermenegildo Zegna
Etro
Fendi

Gerard
Gerard Loft
Giorgio Armani
Gucci
Guya

Hugo Boss
La Rinascente
Liverano & Liverano
Luisa Via Roma

Massimo Rebecchi
Moda Sartoriale
Nara Camicie
Prada

Raspini
Roberto Biagini
Space
Trussardi
Versace

Men's Shoes

Athletes World
Bally
Bonora
Brioni

Bruno Magli
Calvani
Camper
Casadei

Cesare Paciotti
Champion
Coin
Dolce & Gabbana

Emporio Armani
Ermenegildo Zegna
Etro
Fausto Santini

Fendi
Foot Locker
Fratelli Rossetti

Gianfranco Lotti
Gilardini
Giorgio Armani

Gucci
Hogan
Il Giglio
Il Rifugio Sport

Italobalestri
Luisa Via Roma
Montgomery
Nannini

Paola del Lungo
Peruzzi
Piero Guidi
Pollini

Prada
Raspini
Roberto Biagini
Roberto Ugolini

Salvatore Ferragamo
Tanino Crisci
Tod's

Trussardi
Universo Sport

Men's Tailors

Bottega delle Antiche
  Terme

Liverano & Liverano
Moda Sartoriale

Men's Trend & Streetwear

Athletes World
Benetton
Diesel
E-Play

Foot Locker
Gerard
Gerard Loft
Hugo Boss

Lacoste
Montgomery
Murphy & Nye
Replay

Sisley
Stefanel
Universo Sport

Men's Vintage

Elio Ferraro
Gerard Loft

Children's Clothes

Anichini
Athletes World
Baroni
Benetton 0-12

Champion
Coin
Foot Locker

Hogan
Il Rifugio Sport
La Rinascente

Murphy & Nye
Prenatal
Replay
Salvatore Ferragamo

Sisley
Stefanel
Trussardi

Universo Sport
Vilebrequin

Florence Services

Hairdressers (unisex)

Barbers

Beauty Treatment Centers and Solariums

Hair Removal

Manicures/Pedicures

Make-up Artist

Massage Therapists

Dance & Fitness Studios

Yoga

Dry Cleaners

Mending & Alterations

Custom Tailor

Shoe & Leather Repairs

Trimmings (fabrics, lace, embroidery etc)

Key Cutters

Hairdressers (unisex)

Aldo Coppola **055 239 9402**
Via del Parione 65   Tues-Sat 10-6 (later by appointment)

Carlo Bay Hair Diffusion **055 681 1876**
Via Marsuppini 18 Tues-Sat 9-7

Gabrio Staff **055 214 668**
Via dei Tornabuoni 5 Tues-Sat 9-7

Gianni & Andrea **055 239 6525**
Via dei Pescioni 7 Tues-Sat 8:30-2, 3:30-7

I Parrucchieri di Firenze **055 216 007**
Borgo Santissimi Apostoli 50-52 Tues-Sat 9-7

Jean Louis David **055 216 760**
Lungarno Corsini 50 Tues-Sat 9-7

Mario **055 294 813**
Via della Vigna Nuova 22 Tues-Sat 9-6

Toni & Guy **055 264 5561**
Via Borgo Ognissanti 1? Tues-Sat 10-7

Barbers

Luigi **(no telephone)**
Via Calimaruzza 12 Tues-Sat 9-7:30

Pratesi **055 247 9814**
Borgo Pinti 47 Tues-Thurs 9-1, 3:30-7:30
Fri-Sat 9-7:30

Mario **055 294 813**
Via della Vigna Nuova 22 Tues-Sat 9-6

Beauty Treatment Centres and Solariums

Aldo Coppola **055 239 9402**
Via del Parione 65   Tues-Sat 10-6 (later by appointment)

Benessere **055 217 003**
Via Mondala 1 Mon 3:30-7:30, Tues-Fri 9-7:30, Sat 9-1

International Studio **055 281 838/293 393**
Via Porta Rossa 82 Tues-Sat 10-8

La Vanita **055 290 809**
Via Porta Rossa 55 Mon 3:30-7:30, Tues-Sat 9:30-7:30

La Vanita **055 217 536**
Via del Corso 15 Mon 3:30-7:30, Tues-Sat 9:30-7:30

Hair Removal

Benessere **055 217 003**
Via Mondala 1 Mon 3:30-7:30, Tues-Fri 9-7:30, Sat 9-1

Contrasto Hair **055 239 8553**
Via della Mosca 8-10 Tues-Sat 9-7

Giuliana Estetica **055 219 227**
Via de Benci 5 Tues-Sat 9-6

International Studio   **055 281 838/293 393**
Via Porta Rossa 82   Tues-Sat 10-8

Oasi   **055 234 6696**
Via degli Alfani 55   Mon-Sat 9:30-8:30

Manicures/Pedicures

Art Hair Studios   **055 238 1694**
Borgo Santissimi Apostoli 25   Tues-Wed 9-6, Thurs-Sat 9-7

Benessere   **055 217 003**
Via Mondala 1   Mon 3:30-7:30, Tues-Fri 9-7:30, Sat 9-1

Freni   **055 239 6647**
Via Calimala 1   Mon-Fri 9-6, Sat 9-12

Giuliana Estetica   **055 219 227**
Via de Benci 5   Tues-Sat 9-6

International Studio   **055 281 838/293 393**
Via Porta Rossa 82   Tues-Sat 10-8

La Vanita   **055 290 809**
Via Porta Rossa 55   Mon 3:30-7:30, Tues-Sat 9:30-7:30

Mario   **055 294 813**
Via della Vigna Nuova 22   Tues-Sat 9-6

Make-up Artist

Claudio Noto   **335 814 5973/338 151 5523**

Massage Therapists

Enrico Toccafondi at Blue Fitness   **055 238 2138**
Via il Prato 40   Mon-Fri 10-9

Hito Estetica   **055 284 424**
Via de' Ginori 21   Mon-Sat 9-7:30

International Studio   **055 281 838/293 393**
Via Porta Rossa 82   Tues-Sat 10-8

La Vanita   **055 290 809**
Via Porta Rossa 55   Mon 3:30-7:30, Tues-Sat 9:30-7:30

Tropos   **055 678 381**
Via Orcagnia 20a   Mon-Sat 9-9

Dance and Fitness Studios

Blue Fitness   **055 238 137**
Via il Prato 40   Mon-Sat 9-9

Centro Studi Danza   **055 351 530**
Via Monteverdi Claudio 3   Mon-Fri 9:30-9

Florence Dance Center   **055 289 276**
Borgo Stella 23   Mon-Fri 9:30-1, 3-10

Studio A   **055 292 887**
Via de' Ginori 19   Mon-Fri 10-10, Sat 10-1

Tropos   **055 678 381**
Via Orcagnia 20a   Mon-Sat 9-9

Yoga

Blue Fitness   **055 238 137**
Via il Prato 40   Mon-Sat 9-9

Studio A   **055 292 887**
Via de' Ginori 19   Mon-Fri 10-10, Sat 10-1

Yoga Centro   **055 234 2703**
Via de' Bardi 5   Mon-Sat (class times vary)

Dry Cleaners

Elensec   **055 483 415**
Via S. Gallo 50-52   Mon-Fri 8:30-1, 3:30-7:30
Sat 9-12:30

Elensec   **055 283 747**
Via dei Neri 46   Mon-Fri 8-1, 3-7:30

Lucy & Rita   **055 224 536**
Via dei Serragli 71   Mon-Fri 7-1, 2:30-7:30

Lucy & Rita   **055 224 536**
Via della Chiesa 19   (opening times as above)

O.M.   **055 248 0167**
Via Ghibellina 32   Mon-Fri 8:30-12:30, 3-7

Serena   **055 218 183**
Via della Scala 30 Mon-Sat 9-8
(general dry cleaning, also bridal, eveningwear and leather)

Zagros   **055 214 879**
Via delle Belle Donne 17   Mon-Fri 10-1, 3-8
Sat 10-1

Mending & Alterations

Arte del Rammendo   **055 238 2363**
Via Cavour Camillo Benso 32   Mon-Sat 9-1, 3:30-7:30
(invisible mending)

Punto Marina   **055 283 883**
Via dello Studio 7 Mon 3:30-7, Tues-Sat 8:30-12:30, 3:30-7

Custom Tailor

Milord   **055 280 739**
Piazza Strozzi 12-13   Mon-Sat 9:30-7:30

Shoe & Leather Repairs

Guido (shoes)   **(no telephone)**
Via Santa Monaca 9   Mon-Fri 7-1, 3-6

Il Ciabattino   **338 390 5792**
Via del Moro 88   Mon 2-7, Tues-Sat 8-1, 2-7

Il Veloce Ciabattino di Arezzo Vincenzo   **(no telephone)**
Via delle Terme 8   Mon-Fri 8:30-12:45, 3-7

Trimmings (fabrics, lace, embroidery etc)

Lisa Corti Home Textile Emporium　　　**055 264 5600**
Via de' Bardi 58　　　　　　　　　　　Mon 1:30-7:30
　　　　　　　　　　　Tues-Fri 10-1, 1:30-7:30

Lisa Corti Home Textile Emporium　　　**055 200 1200**
Via S. Niccolo 97　　　　　　　　　　Mon 3:30-7:30
　　　　　　　　　　　Tues-Sat 10-1, 3:30-7:30

Loretta Caponi　　　　　　　　　　**055 213 668**
Piazza Antinori 4　　　　　Mon-Fri 9-1, 3:30-7:30

Key Cutters

Masini　　　　　　　　　　　　　**055 212 560**
Via del Sole 19-21　　Mon-Fri 9-1, 3:30-7:30, Sat 9-1

Presto Service　　　　　　　　　**(no telephone)**
Via Faenza 77　　　　　　　　　　Mon 3:30-7:30
　　　　　　　　　　Tues-Sat 9-12:30, 3:30-7:30

Where to Wear Milan 2004

Best Picks

In-Store Restaurants

Restaurants

Milan Best Picks

10 Corso Como	Fiorucci Dept. Store
Antonia	Gio Moretti
Antonioli	Gucci
Armani Collezioni	La Vetrina di Beryl
Armani (Via Manzoni 31)	Paul Smith
Banner	Pineider
Biffi	Prada
Borsalino	Salvagente
Davide Cenci	Tim Camino
Diesel (Ticinese location)	Vergelio
Dolce & Gabbana (men)	Zap!
Du Pareil Au Même	Zara
Etro	

Milan In-Store Restaurants

10 Corso Como Caffè   02-2901 3581
Corso Como 10

Armani Caffè   02-7231 8680
Via Manzoni 31

Bistrot (in La Rinascente)   02-877 120
Via San Raffaele 2

Dolce & Gabbana Men's Bar   02-7601 1152
Corso Venezia 15

Globe Restaurant (in Coin)   02-5518 1969
Piazza 5 Giornate 1

Marino Alla Scala Ristorante (in Trussardi)   02-8068 8201
Piazza della Scala 5

Nobu (in Armani)   02-6231 2645
Via Pisoni 1

Milan Restaurants

BRERA / CORSO GARIBALDI / CORSO COMO

Al Garibaldi   02-659 8006
Viale Montegrappa 7
*wonderful rabbit on the menu, wonderful actresses
and producers on the chairs*

Beige   02-659 9487
Largo La Foppa 5
best little wine bar in town with focaccia to die for

Bushido   02-657 0565
Corso Como 6
sushi

Just Cavalli   **02-311 817**
Via Luigi Camoens at La Torre Branca
Cavalli's fashionable eatery in the middle of Parco Sempione

Le Langhe   **02-655 4279**
Corso Como 6
Piedmontese delicacies, and good for people-watching

La Torre di Pisa   **02-874 877**
Via Fiori Chiari 21
Tuscan

Pottery Caffè   **02-8901 3660**
Via Solferino 3
soups, sandwiches, desserts, herbal teas...and pottery!

Radetzky Caffè   **02-657 2645**
Corso Garibaldi 105
best for coffee and aperitivi

Santini   **02-655 5587**
Via San Marco 3
for a touch of Venice

Smeraldino   **02-659 5815**
Piazza XXV Aprile 1
pizzeria and restaurant

Topkapi   **02-8646 3708**
Via Ponte Vetero 21
pizzeria and restaurant

CORSO BUENOS AIRES

Asmara   **02-201 979**
Via Lazzaro Palazzi 5
Eritrean

Chandelier   **02-2024 0458**
Via Broggi 17
*Bohemian decor, comfort food, and everything is for sale
(including the chandeliers)*

Pizza OK   **02-2940 1272**
Via Lambro 15
as it says, pizzas only

Ristorante al Girarrosto   **02-7600 0481**
Corso Venezia 31
regional specialties, emphasis on meat dishes

CORSO DI PORTA TICINESE / CORSO GENOVA / NAVIGLI

360 degrees   **02-835 6706**
Via Tortona 12
creative buffet lunches in one of the city's hippest locales

Ape Piera   **02-8912 6060**
Via Lodovico il Moro 11
for haute Italian cuisine along the Naviglio

Gelateria Ecologica   (no telephone)
Corso di Porta Ticinese 40
hands down, the city's best and purest ice cream

Le Biciclette   02-5810 4325
Via Torti I
trendy cocktail bar/restaurant, known for Sunday brunch

Exploit   02-8940 8675
Via Pioppette 3
elegant restaurant with a popular happy hour

Osteria dell'Operetta   02-837 5120
Corso di Porta Ticinese 70
pasta galore—try the "tris", a dish of three kinds

Premiata Pizzeria   02-8940 6075
Via de Amicis 22
pizzeria and restaurant

Seven Steak and Wine   02-5810 1669
Corso Colombo 11
the name says it all

Sushi Koboo   02-5811 0956
Viale Col di Lana 1
the name says it all here too

MONTENAPOLEONE & SURROUNDINGS

Bagutta   02-7600 2767
Via Bagutta 14
Tuscan and international cuisine, with a literary tradition

Bice   02-7600 2572
Via Borgospesso 12
if you just want a salad for lunch, this is your place

Caffè Cova   02-7600 5599
Via Montenapoleone 8
charming turn-of-the-century tea room

Paper Moon   02-7602 2297
Via Bagutta 1
pizzeria and restaurant

Rêve Caffè   02-7600 1505
Via della Spiga 42
fusion frontrunners (big selection of teas)

Salumaio di Montenapoleone   02-784 650
Via Montenapoleone 12
for local specialties, e.g. risotto with saffron

CORSO VITTORIO EMANUELE / DUOMO (CENTER)

Da Giacomo   02-7602 3313
Via Sotto Corno 6
*serious specialists in fish, porcini, white truffles;
Madonna has been known to spoil herself here*

Luini   02-8646 1917
Via S.Radegonda 16
panzerotti, standing only

Pizzeria Ristorante Flash   02-5830 4489
Via Larga (corner of Via Bergamini)
pizzeria and restaurant

Sant' Ambroeus   02-7600 0540
Corso Matteotti 7
*exceptional espressos and pastries at one of
the city's oldest restaurants*

Santa Lucia   02-7602 3155
Via San Pietro all'Orto 3
*authentic Neapolitan pizzas, delicious pasta, and the company
of numerous stars whose photographs grace the walls*

Taverna Morigi   02-8645 0880
Via Morigi 8
wine, cheese and cold cuts in a lovely old Milanese tavern

Vecchia Latteria   02-874 401
Via dell'Unione 6
vegetarian

CORSO VERCELLI / MAGENTA

Bar Magenta   02-805 3808
Via Carducci 13
*another favorite turn-of-the-century place,
for sandwiches and aperitivi*

La Cantina di Manuela   02-439 83048
Via Raffaello Sanzio 16
great wines, cheeses and salads

Orti di Leonardo   02-498 3197
Corso Magenta 61
*a favorite with everyone from businessmen to footballers—
fried shrimp and zucchini flowers a specialty*

Milan Store Directory

Newcomers to Italy's proudest cities may be amazed to discover that many stores close during the lunch hour, and in
some cases the "hour" is in practice two or two and a half
hours. Don't despair, they will re-open! It's just that having
invented one of the world's greatest cuisines, they see no
reason why they shouldn't enjoy it. Our advice is to join
them, and for each of the cities in this book we have provided a select list of restaurants, sidewalk cafés, salad bars,
pizzerias etcetera, ideal for your shopping excursions.

We have also listed the opening hours for each store,
though these may vary considerably; to avoid frustration,
we recommend checking by telephone if in doubt. And
finally, while Italian fashion and Italian clothing stores are
among the most stylish in the world, you may be disappointed if you plan your shopping in August. The Italians
have a special relationship with August (which is often
fiendishly hot), and are happy to forsake retail in favor of
the beach. To the regular astonishment of workaholic
Protestant-ethic northern Europeans and Americans, many
Italian stores happily close for weeks—yes, weeks!—at a
time. It's a Mediterranean thing…

2Link

In this bare industrial setting dominated by glass and steel, minimalist fashion is the major statement. 2Link features modern-minded designers like Dries Van Noten and Driade. Beautiful Tibetan-style wraps and Asian-inspired homewares give the selection an earthy feel, but in general the offerings, such as deconstrucuted T-shirts, are consciously cool. The sleek assortment also includes the latest CDs and trendy style magazines like *Dazed and Confused* and *The Face*.   www.2link.it

Largo La Foppa 4   **02-6269 0325**
20121 Milan   Daily 10-8 (Sun-Mon 3-8)

2Link Black Label

There simply weren't enough racks at 2Link to divvy up all the Marras, Van Notens and Bikkembergs in demand, so the men get their own hall of style around the corner—a box-like space covered in wall to wall ebony. Just like the other store, this new men's arm attracts only those majoring in advanced dressing. That requires a full appreciation of Marras' asymmetrical cuts, the irregular stitching on a Dries Van Noten shirt, and of course the super crotch hike in a pair of J. Lindberg's slim trousers. It's serious business for serious fashion fans. A distinctive members-only vibe permeates the space, heightened by the staff of aloof cool magnets who aren't interested in holding hands with the uninitiated.

Via Solferino 46   **02-8907 6833**
20021 Milan   Sun-Mon 3-8, Tues-Sat 10:30-8

☆ 10 Corso Como

Carla Sozzani struck a chord when she opened this eclectic boutique-cum-bookstore-cum-art-gallery way back in 1991. Since then, fashionistas have maintained it as a favored destination for everything from candles and cookbooks to Prada and Gucci, and as of this year Y3 by Yohji Yamamoto. If you start to feel like you've tried on one label too many, take some respite with a cappuccino in the courtyard café. Or, if you're really in the mood to dig for treasures, head to the outlet store in Via Tazzoli, about five minutes away by foot, where you'll find discounted designer clothing and shoes.

Corso Como 10   **02-654 831**
20154 Milan   Mon 3:30-7:30, Tues
                              Fri-Sun 10:30-7:30, Wed-Thurs 10:30-9

Via Tazzoli 3   **02-2900 2674**
20154 Milan   Sat-Sun 11-7 (except in sales periods)

Acqua di Parma

No trip to Milan is complete without a visit to Acqua di Parma. First launched in the Thirties, Acqua di Parma's classic cologne for men and women remains a quintessential Italian luxury—and now there's a whole range of goodies to choose from. The shop on Via Gesu (just a short hop from the Four Seasons Hotel) is a calm oasis of soothing smells, with candles glowing and two floors of heavenly beauty products beckoning. From soaps and massage oils to shaving foam and talcum powder, everything exudes the subtle fresh scent that embodies this company's fame. If the stunning aromas of Sicilian citrus fruits, verbena, lavender and the rare Bulgarian rose don't seduce you, perhaps you'll be tempted by the cashmere dressing-gowns, gorgeous soft towels or caramel leather traveling bags. In typically Milanese style all purchases are exquisitely wrapped, with Parma's yellow paper and thick black ribbons bearing the crest of the Duke of Parma. Beauty doesn't get much smarter than this.

Via Gesu 3	**02-7602 3307**
20121 Milan	Mon 2:30-7, Tues-Sat 10-1:30, 2:30-7

Agnona

The word venerable could have been invented for this brand, which began 50 years ago as a world-class cashmere producer for the likes of Dior and Balenciaga. These days, the exquisite tradition founded by Francesco Ilorini Mo continues with a ready-to-wear collection crafted in superbly spun fabrics, including a very rare fleece taken from the tummies of Peruvian vicuñas. You'll find butter-soft blends and understated elegance in double-face cashmere coats, alpaca sweatshirts, superfine merino wool tops and camel hair pants. The look is tailored and luxurious, and is accompanied by every accessory needed—pashmina scarves, felt hats, shearling gloves—for a supremely refined weekend getaway.

Via della Spiga 3	**02-7631 6530**
20121 Milan	Mon 3-7, Tues-Sat 10-7

Alan Journo

Follow the stairs, with their rubberband-like banisters, down to the depths of this funky Spiga store. On your descent, you may pass handbags plastered with images of Marilyn Monroe, Philip Treacy's Andy Warhol hats, luggage swirling with planetary patterns, and other kitschy bits. On the fashion front, you'll find crisp black and white suits and skirts, bustiers and long flowing dresses with feathered stoles for the evening.

Via della Spiga 36	**02-7600 1309**
20121 Milan	Mon 3-7, Tues-Sat 10:30-2, 3-7

Alberta Ferretti

Growing up in her mother's dressmaking shop, Ferretti developed a passion for fashion. Every season reinvigorates her gift for girlish style in sweet pleated skirts and floaty chiffon dresses. Decorative details like ribbons and ruffles frequently appear. She also produces some decidedly more masculine options: tailored blazers, wide-leg trousers and practical pea coats, in shades of black, plum and government-issue green. Philosophy, the somewhat quirkier diffusion line, has loads of lovely bits.   www.albertaferretti.com
www.philosophy.it

Via Montenapoleone 19   **02-796 034**
20121 Milan   Mon 3-7, Tues-Sat 10-7

Via Montenapoleone 21   **02-7600 3095**
20121 Milan   Mon-Sat 10-7

Alberto Guardiani

Pointy mules striped with circus colors, basic leather lace-ups and trendy two-tone, sneaker-shoe hybrids are some of the styles you're liable to find from Alberto Guardiani. His disciples are young and style-savvy, particularly at the shop in Corso Ticinese, the stomping ground of Milan's hip teens, twenty- and thirtysomethings.

www.albertoguardiani.it

Via Montenapoleone 9   **02-7602 1697**
20121 Milan   Mon 3-7, Tues-Sat 10-1:30, 2:30-7

Corso di Porta Ticinese 67   **02-8324 1650**
20123 Milan   Mon 3-7:30, Tues-Sat 10:30-1, 3-7:30

Alexander McQueen

British "bad boy" Alexander McQueen is one of the hottest young designers around—an iconoclast who pummels the boundaries of creativity and style with his consistently cutting-edge, innovative clothing. Although McQueen's runway shows (dramatic affairs flaunting outrageously theatrical clothes) will have you thinking that he designs only for gothic princesses plowing through snow storms, one visit to his store will prove to you just how retail-savvy his backers, the Gucci group, have been. McQueen's over-the-top vision which explodes on one-of-a-kind cascading gowns and slashed formalwear translates remarkably well into a wearable collection of sharply tailored suits, hip trousers and sexy tops. It is still, of course, expensive, but that's a small price to pay for a brush with creative genius.

Via Verri 8   **02-7600 3374**
20121 Milan   Mon-Sat 10-7

Alviero Martini

Here is one Italian designer who takes the notion of going global to fashion extremes. Just about everything in his collection—suits, shoes, leather goods, even motorcycle helmets—is decorated with maps, from the antique geographical type to the brightly-colored modern classroom globe. If all this continent-spotting makes your head spin, there's plenty of plain-patterned ready-to-wear (from striped suits to spotted shift dresses to ruched and ruffled eveningwear) to bring you back down to earth.   www.alvieromartini.it.

Via Montenapoleone 26   **02-7600 8002**
20121 Milan   Mon-Sat 10-7

Andrea Pfister

His shoes have been the subject of exhibitions—"art for the feet"—which makes the starting price of $200 a pair seem relatively modest. Pfister is widely celebrated for his most concept-driven designs, from the Mondrian pump, decorated with the primary colors favored by the painter, to his Martini stiletto which features a heel shaped like the classic cocktail glass, complete with bulging lemon wedge. He has a gift for whimsy, but he does the decorative basics equally well, so flats with bright buttons look cool rather than cutesy while flower-patterned pumps are feminine but still refined. Matching bags are also available.

Via Montenapoleone 25   **02-7600 2036**
20121 Milan   Mon-Sat 10-1:30, 2:30-7

Anna Molinari Blumarine

The Anna Molinari and Blumarine labels hang side by side in this Spiga store. For the signature collection gender bending has been the theme of recent seasons, from satin lingerie-style sleeveless tops to pinstripe jackets with matching schoolboy shorts. Velvet, flapper-style minidresses come with skirts of feathers while creamy V-neck sweaters make a subtler style statement. In the more universally feminine Blumarine collection, bright colors and floaty romantic fabrics are the flavors of everydaywear.

Via della Spiga 42   **02-795 081**
20121 Milan   Mon 3-7, Tues-Sat 10-1:30, 2:30-7

Anteprima

It's an Italian brand but the designer, Izumi Ogino, is strictly Japanese. So it's no surprise that the store, as well as the clothes in it, is a study in quiet beauty best appreciated up close. Ogino keeps both her palette and cuts super-clean, using black, white and gray (sometimes a shot of rose) on her simply designed sheath dresses, shells and straight pants. Dresses and tops are fluid, never indecently tight. While the clothes may verge on the over-simplistic, Anteprima retains its cutting-edge status with its conceptual accessories which look like little pieces of artwork. Odd shapes, unique cut-outs and innovative construction are all wrought on flats, heels and handbags in a way that makes them a favorite of women looking to stand out, but quietly.

Corso Como 9   **02-655 2373**
20154 Milan   Mon-Sat 10-2, 3-7

☆ Antonia

Certified girl-about-town and junior princess of Italian multi-brand fashion, pint-size Antonia's got one little finger firmly clamped on the pulse of the global fashion scene. Her store, a mecca for Milan's most stylish, fashion-forward women, brings on board all the usual suspects—Dolce & Gabbana, Missoni, Valentino, Chloé, Ungaro—but whittles the selection down to a masterly and supremely original edit which will have you wondering why you don't own every piece on the shelves. Alongside Balenciaga trousers and Borbonese dresses, you'll come upon some new finds like the super-cool Haute label. Antonia Accessori next door (02-869 0216) supplies Milan with its only truly international offering of the season's best stilettos, hottest boots

Milan Directory

or this year's must-have bag by names like YSL, Marc Jacobs, Gucci and Rene Caovilla. Not one detail is over-looked, from the fantastic shopping bags with 3-D appliqués, to the window displays worthy of an art-gallery.

Via Ponte Vetero 1   **02-8699 8340**
20121 Milan   Mon 3-7, Tues-Sat 10-2, 3-7

☆ Antonioli

With its black rubber walls, cement skateboard ramp and Mohawked sales girls, this store is almost more fashionable than its roster of edgy designers. Its dark vibe epitomizes underground chic and so does its location—the store is nearly impossible to find along an odd street way off in Milan's canal district. But finders will be keepers at this treasure-chest packed full of original works by Alexander McQueen, London label Preen, Rick Owens, Ann Demeulemeester and Dries Van Noten. The only big brand name to make it past owner Claudio Antonioli's iron wall is a highly edited selection of Dolce & Gabbana. Accessories like J.A.S. handbags, Martin Margiela chains and even Japanese teddybear gadgets add a quirky twist to the oth-erwise somber mood.   www.antoniolishop.com

Via Pasquale Paoli 1   **02-3656 6494**
20143 Milan   Mon 3-8, Tues-Sat-11-8

Antonio Fusco

Women and men seeking Forbes 500 businesswear will find a tempting selection here, where luxurious fabrics and love-ly natural colors take classic Italian tailoring one better. Fusco's creations are conventional in essence but with the occasional flourish, which lends a sense of individuality to the collection. For after hours, there's a stylish selection of eveningwear.   www.antoniofusco.it

Via Sant' Andrea 11   **02-7600 2957**
20121 Milan   Mon-Sat 10-7

☆ Armani Collezioni

The godfather of sleek, Italian style has made a cozy home for his everydaywear collection smack in the middle of Milan's most exclusive shopping district. You'll find plenty of the leg-endary tailored jackets, lovely knits and soft, simple evening-wear in his favored neutral colors. Among the best, and most enduring, of Italian designers.   www.giorgioarmani.com

Via Montenapoleone 2   **02-7639 0068**
20121 Milan   Mon-Sat 10:30-7:30

Armani Jr

In a courtyard a step off the main thoroughfare, Armani grooms the next generation of fashion followers. Here you'll find his classic pared down style, well, pared down (fortunate-ly, the prices are a bit smaller, too). Mini leather jackets, pants and willowy knit skirts are just a bit more playful but no less chic than their adult counterparts.   www.giorgioarmani.com

Via Montenapoleone 10   **02-783 196**
20121 Milan   Mon 3-7, Tues-Sat 10-7

☆ Armani/Via Manzoni 31

Armani dubbed his modern megastore in Via Manzoni, opened in October 2000, an anniversary present to himself, celebrating his 25 years in fashion. Fans of Italy's most famous designer will find the men's and women's diffusion collections from Emporio Armani and Armani Jeans. There's also plenty to pick from the Armani Casa household collection, plus a florist, a bookstore, and the Armani Caffè. Budgeting diehards who can't bear to leave empty-handed could go for the Armani pralines or assorted Armani chocolates. On the way out, Nobu's sushi bar makes an inviting recuperation station. www.giorgioarmani.com

Via Manzoni 31	**02-7231 8600**
20121 Milano	Mon-Sat 10:30-7:30

Ars Rosa

This is one of those shops that seems almost too precious to be real, specializing in everything for the trousseau, known to Italians as the corredo. But you don't have to be a blushing bride to appreciate the luxurious custom-made lingerie and bathrobes, made in materials like silk and cashmere and embellished with touches of lace and embroidery. Christening gowns and other special occasion babywear can also be found here, plus beautiful household linen.

Via Montenapoleone 8	**02-7602 3822**
20121 Milan	Mon 2:30-7, Tues-Sat 9-12:30, 2:30-7

Atelier Aimée

Top-of-the-cake traditional gowns can be custom-made or bought ready-to-wear at this bridal boutique just off the Montenapoleone. Planning a winter wedding? Think ivory, off-the-shoulder, beaded bodice with three-quarter sleeves and layers of skirt that blossom gently like calla lilies. For summer, a ballerina gown with a petal-pink skirt and straps as thin as spaghettini comes with delicate jeweled sandals to match. Every year brings 300 new designs to choose from, so you won't have to worry about looking last-season, and wedding party attire is also available. www.aimee.it

Via Montenapoleone 27e	**02-799 300**
20121 Milan	Mon 3-7, Tues-Sat 10-1, 2-7

A.Testoni

Amedeo Testoni founded his Bologna-based shoemaking business nearly 75 years ago. Today, the third generation of the Testoni family is still turning out classic, handcrafted shoes in the finest Italian leather. The men's collection has acquired a world-class clientele, including such luminaries as Ronald Reagan, John McEnroe and Luciano Pavarotti. Business shoes as well as more leisurely but still luxurious styles are available, along with a women's collection and a range of leather bags, brief-cases and belts. www.testoniusa.com

Via Montenapoleone 19	**02-7600 3697**
20121 Milan	Mon 3-7, Tues-Sat 10-7

Avant

With its interior painted to resemble a cityscape—complete with building fronts, street signs and a twinkling night sky—Avant lures the gaggles of passers-by touring the Corso Buenos Aires, Milan's cheaper shopping alternative to Montenapoleone. Once inside, the nooks and crannies of this labyrinthine shop offer up-to-the-minute dresses, pants, shoes, lingerie and bikinis, as well as the occasional suit. Trendy looks and generally modest prices keep the crowds coming back for more.   www.avantinternational.it

Corso Buenos Aires 39   **02-2951 1115**
20124 Milan   Mon 2:30-7:30
           Tues-Sat 10:30-7:30

B-Fly

With jeans jackets carefully and sparingly displayed around the store, and an assortment of denim treated with the care afforded precious works of art, it's hardly surprising that the ambiance in B-Fly is more like a museum than a clothing shop. Around here it's known as the Levi's Kult store (we'd say Cult), with plenty of vintage and one-of-a-kind designs to choose from, so connoisseurs of the classic American label will do particularly well.

Corso di Porta Ticinese 46   **02-8942 3178**
20123 Milan   Mon 3-8, Tues-Sat 11-1, 3-8

Baldinini

From the heart of Italy's shoemaking district in San Mauro Pascoli come Baldinini's high-quality loafers, lace-ups, stilettos and boots. Most have a strong element of design and are accompanied by matching handbags, briefcases and other leather accessories.   www.baldinini.it.

Via Montenapoleone 15   **02-7602 2002**
20121 Milan   Mon 3-7, Tues-Sat 10-7

Bally

Swiss label Bally has found a firm footing in leather accessories, particularly in the matching shoes and bags. From classic flats to comfy bowling shoes to Roman sandals, simple styles and a neutral palette keep them from any faux pas. There are plenty of business basics as well, and they've recently launched a ready-to-wear collection. www.bally.com

Via Montenapoleone 8   **02-7600 8406**
20121 Milan   Mon-Sat 10-7

☆ Banner

Owned by the Biffi family (of Biffi boutique fame) and designed by renowned Italian architect Gae Aulenti, the Banner store is one of those must destinations for women on the hunt for sophisticated chic. Designer standbys like Ralph Lauren polos, Pucci capris and Burberry checks are intertwined with the latest being turned out by the cutting-edge designer crowd, like the beautiful suede jackets courtesy of Brazil's Patricia Viera. All with that same assurance of quality the Biffi name inspires around these parts.

Via Sant' Andrea 8a   **02-7600 4609**
20121 Milan   Mon 3-7:30, Tues-Sat 10-2, 3-7:30

Barbara Bui
Franco-Vietnamese designer Barbara Bui introduced her Milan boutique, and her sensibility for precisely tailored urban style, to the Via Manzoni back in 1999. It's still a good spot to find a beautiful pair of trousers or a close-cut leather blazer, with plenty of tailored shirts and simple knits to match. Colors stick to the basics—black, brown and beige—and there's an ample supply of pointy stilettos and leather sneaker-shoes to complete the sleek city look.   www.barbarabui.com

Via Manzoni 45   **02-2906 0216**
20121 Milan   Mon 3-7, Tues-Sat 10-1:30, 2:30-7

Benetton
This major Italian label is no minor presence in Milan, with shops spread all over the city. For the widest variety of men's, women's and childrenswear head to the Corso Vittorio Emanuele, Corso Buenos Aires or Corso Vercelli locations. You'll find all the bright knits, classic denim and colorful T-shirts that have made Benetton a consistently popular spot for European shoppers (though some might argue that the quality of the products has suffered a bit at the cost of chasing trends). Sheets, blankets and other items in the household collection are also available at Corso Vercelli.   www.benetton.com

Corso Vittorio Emanuele II 9   **02-771 2941**
20122 Milan   Daily 10-8

Corso Buenos Aires 19   **02-202 2911**
20124 Milan   Daily 10-8

Corso Vercelli 8   **02-4335 1121**
20145 Milan   Mon 3-7:30, Tues-Sat 10-7:30

☆ Biffi
Since the Sixties the Biffi boutique has been a consistent source for up-and-coming designers as well as those already arrived. Their mix of established labels ranges from classics like Fendi and Tod's to the more fashion-forward Helmut Lang, Hedi Slimane and Yohji Yamamoto. Women's and classic menswear are found in the main boutique, while men's sportswear is housed across the street at Corso Genova 5.   www.biffi.com

Corso Genova 6   **02-831 1601**
20123 Milan   Mon 3-7:30, Tues-Sat 9:30-1:30, 3-7:30

Bipa
The latest women's clothing and shoe collections are on display at this boutique. Anna Molinari, See by Chloé, Nokita and Les Tropeziennes are some of the names you

might find. We also spotted a few size 46s (American size 12), not a common sight in this part of the continent.

Via Ponte Vetero 10 **02-878 168**
20121 Milan Mon 3-7, Tues-Sat 10-7

Blunauta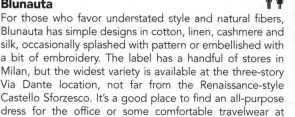

For those who favor understated style and natural fibers, Blunauta has simple designs in cotton, linen, cashmere and silk, occasionally splashed with pattern or embellished with a bit of embroidery. The label has a handful of stores in Milan, but the widest variety is available at the three-story Via Dante location, not far from the Renaissance-style Castello Sforzesco. It's a good place to find an all-purpose dress for the office or some comfortable travelwear at prices that won't break il banco. There is a small selection of informal jackets, pants, shirts and sweaters for men upstairs. www.blunauta.com

Via Dante 11 **02-8645 4266**
20123 Milan Mon-Sat 9:30-7:30

Boggi

Milan's local males, among the best turned-out men on the planet (though, naturally, the Romans won't agree, nor perhaps the signori in half a dozen other Italian cities), have long appreciated the good quality and fair prices at Boggi's boutiques. Tailored jackets and trousers and crisp cotton shirts get high marks, though those in the know say there are better sources for knitwear. Tiny concession stores dedicated to shirts and ties dot Milan's fashion center, while a few larger spaces offer the wider business selection in addition to sportswear. For women's clothing, visit the Via Durini location. www.boggi.it

Via Durini 28 **02-7600 5582**
20122 Milan Mon-Sat 10-7:30

Largo Augusto 3 **02-7600 1489**
20122 Milan (opening times as above)

Via Caretta, 1 **02-2952 6458**
20124 Milan Mon 3-7:30, Tues-Sat 10-7:30

Bonpoint

If you're feeling broody, beware. The precious smock dresses, itsy-bitsy overalls and sweet sweaters with Peter Pan collars from this premier French label could melt even the hardest heart. For girls, the collection goes up to age 16 while boyswear stops at 12, but the smallest-size selection is the best. If you bring the bambini with you, don't expect to leave without one of the tiny stuffed bears. www.bonpoint.com

Via Manzoni 15 **02-8901 0023**
20121 Milan Mon 3-7, Tues-Fri 10-7, Sat 10-2, 3-7

Borbonese

You may not have heard of this old-school Italian accessories brand but the Arpels family, who bought the company in 2000 and hired Alessandro Dell'Acqua to dream up a ready-to-wear line, has set out to change that. With Arpels signing the checks and Dell'Acqua sketching the sizzle, the rest of the world will soon join the Italians in coming to know and covet Borbonese's signature bird's-eye print. That unmistakable spotted suede fabric, made iconic in the Seventies, covers all the house's best accessories like the "sexy bag" (the mini version is an obligatory purchase), wallets, key chains, travel cases and even the linings of stiletto sandals. Dell'Acqua has ensured that the famous deconstructed bags get a make-over in the hottest colors, details and fabrics each season, and has whipped up a collection of sexy but very wearable clothing to cap the jet-set look. www.borbonese.it

Via Santo Spirito 26   **02-7601 7202**
20121 Milan   Mon 3-7, Tues-Sat 10-7

☆ Borsalino 👫

For nearly 150 years Borsalino has been the top name among fine Italian hatters. It was even honored by a classic Franco-Italian spoof-gangster film (*Borsalino*, in 1970) starring Alain Delon and Jean-Paul Belmondo—how many shops have had films named after them? So this is the place to come if you want panamas, cloche hats, berets, English caps, fedoras as worn by Humphrey Bogart and a zillion screen stars, goodies and baddies, or indeed that elegant wide-brimmed floppy Ingrid Bergman wore in *Casablanca*. Ladies are likely to find the perfect number for a summer wedding or a day at the Ascot races. www.borsalino.it

Galleria Vittorio Emanuele II 92   **02-8901 5436**
20121 Milan   Tues-Sat 10-2, 3-7

Via Verri 5   **02-7639 8539**
20121 Milan   Tues-Sat 10-2, 3-7

Boss Hugo Boss 👨

When they're not on the pitch, members of AC Milan football team get their kicks shopping at Hugo Boss, the official clothing supplier to the club. Boss's look, from suits to sportswear, is suave with a bit of structure and very euro-male. Outerwear, underwear and watches are also available. www.hugoboss.com

Corso Matteotti 11   **02-7639 4667**
20121 Milan   Mon 3-7, Tues-Sat 10-7

Bottega Veneta

Under the guidance of creative director Tomas Maier this Venetian shoe and accessories label, known for its woven intrecciato handbags, has found its way right back onto the fashion map and straight into the best shopping district in town. And it's no wonder. Those ultra-luxe handbags, which plague top editors' hit lists every season, are the result of Maier's extremely precise and innovative eye. It's not just the bags, shoes and luggage that come dripping in gorgeous rare skins, though. The store itself, swathed in dark woods, lush carpets and animal-skin furniture, puts a Schrager hotel to shame and provides the perfect setting for the highly original and top-grade product.

Via Montenapoleone 5   **02-7602 4495**
20121 Milan   Mon-Sat 10-7

Braccialini

Bright colors and bohemian handiwork make Braccialini's selection stand out in the sea of sleek Italian leather goods. Embroidery, patchwork and floral appliqués are some of the techniques long favored by company founder Carla Braccialini who has been designing since 1954. Today, she and her son Massimo maintain their signature collection, in addition to creating accessories for British fashion icons Vivienne Westwood and Patrick Cox.   www.braccialini.it

Via Montenapoleone 19   **02-7601 8162**
20121 Milan   Mon 3-7, Tues-Sat 10-1:30, 2:30-7

Brloni

Many a high-rolling man (James Bond included) has slid into a Brioni made-to-order suit, only to start a lifetime love affair with this venerable Italian label. What makes these custom get-ups so special? For starters, the impeccable tailoring, super-luxe fabrics and tireless attention to detail, which have put them on the backs of film stars and society bigwigs since 1945. Women were finally inducted into the club in 2001, with luxurious suits and separates powerful enough for a CEO but posh enough for cocktails. The men's and women's stores in Milan—both of which also offer sportswear, accessories and small leather goods—sit opposite one another in Via Gesu, allowing for simultaneous his-and-hers power-suiting.

Via Gesu 4 (women)   **02-7639 4019**
20121 Milan   Mon-Sat 10-7

Via Gesu 3 (men)   **02-7639 0086**
20121 Milan   (opening times as above)

Bruno Magli

The firm founded by three brothers in a Bologna basement in 1936 has a lot to show for its 68 years. Today, in addition to their men's lace-ups and loafers, the label boasts an extensive women's collection of clothing, handbags and other leather accessories. There's also an assortment of sneakers and casual suede and leather shoes available from Magli Sport. The store on Via Manzoni is new this year and beautifully designed in Magli's rich orange and brown signature colors.   www.brunomagli.it

Via San Paolo 1   **02-865 695**
20122 Milan   Mon-Sat 10-7:30
Via Manzoni 14   **02-7631 7478**
20121 Milan   Mon-Sat 10-7

Burberry

All the frumpiness of this classic London label got swept right out the door when Saks exec Rose Marie Bravo took charge, wisely hiring former Gucci designer Christopher Bailey to shoot up the top Prorsum line with authentic London street edge. Luckily, the 150-year-old baby didn't get thrown out with the bathwater. On the contrary, founder Thomas Burberry's most famous outerwear recipes are still going strong, like the world-renowned trenchcoat which is now available in custom-made formats for Burberry's more discerning clientele. Bailey has proved to be more than competent at drawing from Burberry's rich sportswear heritage while designing the kinds of frocks and jumpers that London's coolest club kids want to wear on their nights off. And for the traditionalists, there is the more conservative and affordable Burberry London line packed with bright and sporty pants and jackets. As we went to press the first Milan store was preparing to open.   www.burberry.com

Via Bigli 2   **n/a at press time**
Milan 20121

Cacharel

This French label, which made a big splash back in the Sixties with its colorful Liberty-print dresses, fell into a deep fashion sleep throughout the Eighties and Nineties. But the brand is now alive again and kicking up its hip heels, thanks to the design ingenuity of husband and wife team Suzanne Clements & Ignacio Ribeiro who were tapped by founder Jean Bousquet in 2000. With its girly eccentricity, suddenly the brand is a haven for trendy types who snap up the feminine dresses and tops which have a mild spike of London edge. Bold color combinations and wacky op-art prints abound on the cute sweaters and floaty blouses, but more serious toned-down fare can be found on straightforward suits and trenches. Cacharel's knack for the sweetly stylish also plays out in a perfectly charming line of children's clothing which will have you buying everything in sets of two.

Via San Paolo 1   **02-8901 1429**
20121 Milan   Mon 3:30-7:30, Tues-Sat 10-7:30

Camper

They've been selling Spaniards comfortable footwear for 125 years but Camper's arrival in Milan dates back just a few years. The label best known for bubble-soled bowling shoes also offers a selection of men's and women's loafers, clogs, sneakers and sandals. But back to those bowling shoes: they come in a range of trendy two-tones and are the perfect shoe for touring a chic city like Milan—dressier than sneakers but comfortable enough to walk for hours in.   www.camper.com

Via Montenapoleone 6   **02-799 015**
20121 Milan   Mon-Sat 10-7:30

Via Torino 15   **02-805 7185**
20123 Milan   Mon 3-7:30, Tues-Sat 10-7:30

Canali   👤

When Giovanni and Giacomo Canali started this family tai-loring business back in the 1930s, the two brothers could-n't have imagined stitching 1,400 suits a day, but that impressive volume is now standard fare. Canali's look always has been and always will be rooted deeply in classic formal suiting. For die-hard traditionalists, there are rows and rows of beautifully finished, impeccable suits all boast-ing A-grade natural fabrics. Casual sportswear also makes it into the mix, but for Canali's core customer—the gentleman who turns his nose up at the concept of dress-down Friday—the sporty pieces are hardly what we'd call relaxed.

Via Verri 1   **02-7639 0365**
20121 Milan   Mon-Sat 10-7

Canziani   👤

Classic men, or at least those who want to dress in a classic style, can find both ready-to-wear and made-to-measure shirts here, along with ties to match. They can also find underclothes (but no suits to cover them up) and tradition-al pajamas, too.

Via Montenapoleone 26   **02-7602 2076**
20121 Milan   Mon 3-7, Tues-Sat 9:30-1, 2:30-7

Casadei   👤👩

Founded in the Fifties by Quinto Casadei, this renowned footwear label has managed to remain independent. Not for lack of suitors, though. Prada chief executive Patrizio Bertelli is said to have tried to get his foot in the door, and no wonder. Casadei's slim-heeled boots, slides and sling-backs score high marks with fashion followers and rank up there with Sergio Rossi for sex appeal. There is a small men's collection.

Via Sant' Andrea 17   **02-7631 8293**
20121 Milan   Mon 3-7, Tues-Sat 10-7

Cavalli e Nastri   👤

If you've got a passion for fashion's past, head to this shop in the artsy Brera district for authentic vintage dating from the turn of the century through to the 1970s. From Pucci to Gucci, there are plenty of designer names, some reason-ably priced, some not. If you prefer just to dip your toes in, you'll also find a wide variety of shoes, handbags and other accessories. And if you have a stack of vintage stuff surplus to requirements at home, they are in the market to buy.

Via Brera 2   **02-7200 0449**
20121 Milan   Mon 3:30-7:30, Tues-Sat 11-7

Via de Amicis 9   **02-8940 9452**
20123 Milan   (opening times as above)

Celine

American Michael Kors has reinvigorated this once-tired French fashion house, transforming it into a symbol of expensive "modern classic" style. Current pièces de résistance include inverted pleated trousers, gold-accented exotic tops, low-slung cropped boleros and, of course, those famous Boogie bags. For fall, expect more of their sophisticated sportswear and the Cruise line. There are also plenty of accessories, as well as a home collection.   www.celine.com

| **Via Montenapoleone 25** | **02-7601 5579** |
| 20121 Milan | Mon-Sat 9:30-7:30 |

Cerruti

Ever since the abrupt exit of legendary designer Nino Cerruti from the house that bears his name, this brand has flipped designers faster than a flapjack chef. But somehow the classic aura remains, and a flow of hunky Hollywood A-listers continues to walk down the red carpet in the house's perfectly cut tuxedos, if not gowns. Whoever happens to be at the design helm—last we checked it was Hollywood designer David Cardona—the task is to re-interpret Nino's sophisticated, classic looks and pull them together for a sophisticated wardrobe for the 21st century. Signature Cerruti territory—tuxedo detailing for women, sharply cut suits, luxurious fabrics—are almost always on display, but sprinklings of edgier, younger looks balance the mood.

| **Via della Spiga 20** | **02-7600 9777** |
| 20121 Milan | Mon-Sat 10-7 |

Cesare Gatti

This textiles shop spins its goods with mom-and-pop appeal. Every product—sweater, scarf, coat, cape or blanket—comes straight from the factory in Biella. This should add up to savings for the customer, so if you're in the market for authentic Italian cashmere and silk, take a look.

| **Via Montenapoleone 19** | **02-796 860** |
| 20121 Milan | Mon 3-7, Tues-Sat 10-1:30, 2:30-7 |

Cesare Paciotti

The silver dagger logo should serve as a warning: tread carefully, these heels can be lethal, particularly the signature knee-high stiletto boots which come laced with tassels in S&M-style slashed black leather or simple solid suede. For those who prefer to stay on safer ground, there are flat shoes and bohemian suede buckled boots. Men can choose from wingtips and brogues to snakeskin shoes and combat boots, while the kids can enjoy his brightly colored sneaker line. Paciotti is a distinct style.   www.cesare-paciotti.com

| **Via Sant' Andrea 8 (women)** | **02-7600 1338** |
| 20121 Milan | Mon 3-7, Tues-Sat 10-7 |

| **Via Sant' Andrea 8a (men)** | **02-7600 1164** |
| 20121 Milan | (opening times as above) |

Chanel

Designer Karl Lagerfield has given the most venerable of French fashion houses a modern makeover. While maintaining many of Coco's original concepts, like the wool suits and quilted bags, Lagerfield has injected a bit of whimsy: today, the suits come in brightly-colored tweeds, the bags in orange or turquoise terrycloth with white plastic chains. If this all sounds a bit too frivolous, not to worry. There's still plenty of earnestly elegant fashion to be had here.

Via Sant' Andrea 10a   **02-782 514**
20121 Milan   Mon-Sat 10-7

Chic Simple

From the store layout to the merchandise, the name about sums it up. If you need a break from the rampant streetwear style of Ticinese, stop in here for more understated fare from Helmut Lang, Plein Sud, Fendi Jeans, Philosophy by Alberta Ferretti, Laltramoda and other designers.

Corso di Porta Ticinese 48   **02-5810 0146**
20123 Milan   Mon 3:30-8, Tues-Sat 10-1, 3-8 (Thurs 8:30)

Chicco

Children's chain Chicco (pronounced Keeko) is an institution among new (and expecting) Italian parents, providing every basic bit for babies, from bibs to bottles to bath tubs. For older children, there's an extensive range of toys and clothing up to age 8. The store is immense, with a Chiccolandia playland in the basement for kids, a great distraction device while you get on with your shopping. Maternitywear and accessories are also available.   www.chicco.com

Piazza Diaz 2   **02-8699 8597**
20123 Milan   Mon 2-7:30, Tues-Fri 10-7:30

Christian Dior

John Galliano's flair for the dramatic has brought a modern, playful spirit to the famous house of Dior. Styles for fall are distinctly gothic hardcore, with zipped leather pants and vicious ruby red stilettos leading the pack. His ubiquitous saddle bags also feature heavily, done up this season in black patent leather, nutty-brown calfskin and deep blue nylon. As always, bold and adventurous tailoring abounds. Next door, however, in the modern, steel-enforced surroundings of No 14, the tone is a little more subdued. Here you'll find the cool, clean lines of Dior Homme, the menswear collection designed by Hedi Slimane. www.dior.com

Via Montenapoleone 12   **02-7631 7801**
20121 Milan   Mon-Sat 10-7

Via Montenapoleone 14   **02-7639 8530**
20121 Milan   Mon-Sat 10-7

Christies

A good place to find an intimate gift for yourself or your Valentine. This Italian lingerie label offers a range of bras

and panties, from the politely practical to the flagrantly frivolous. There's also swimwear and a small collection of
eveningwear. The Tatto line of underwear has no stitching
for a super-smooth silhouette. www.christieslingerie.it

Corso Vercelli 51　　　　　　　**02-4802 2152**
20144 Milan　　　　　　Mon 3-7, Tues-Sat 10-2, 3-7

Church's

This venerable British shoemaker has found a happy home-
away-from-home in Milan, under the watchful eye of its parent company, Prada. The owners may be Italian, but Church's
style remains resolutely English, featuring classic wingtips,
oxfords, lace-ups, loafers and brogues of the highest quality.
The only detectable difference is that the Milanese shop
assistants are dressed in Prada rather than the traditional tailored suits of Jermyn Street. www.churchshoes.com

Via Sant' Andrea 11　　　　　　**02-7631 8794**
20121 Milan　　　　　　　　Mon-Sat 10-7:30

Galleria Vittorio Emanuele II 84　　**02-7209 4454**
20121 Milan　　　　　　(opening times as above)

Cisalfa

A leader in Italian sports apparel and equipment, Cisalfa
has everything for weekend athletes and those who are
more fanatically fit. Italian labels like Fila can be found
among numerous popular imports, including Puma,
Adidas, Reebok and Nike. If you're more of a sideline sup-
porter and you've embraced the national passion for football (soccer, to Americans), you'll also find the jerseys for all
the Italian teams. www.cisalfasport.it

Corso Vittorio Emanuele II 1　　**02-8691 5319**
20122 Milan　　　　Mon 1-7:30, Tues-Sat 10-7:30

Clan

Clean, sleek walls and a fashionable staff serve as a cool
backdrop for this multi-brand outpost. The brands, almost
all homegrown, are on the small side, with a strong push
towards fashionable urban wear. It's sporty, it's cool and it
attracts a youthful, fashionable crowd that keeps the air
fresh. Guys will find sleek Daniele Alessandrini jackets to
pair with hip Frankie Morello pants. Hip young ladies venture toward shrunken John Richmond leather jackets, Jean
Paul Gaultier jeans and sexy tops and dresses by
Philosophy or Kristina T. The offering is mixed, the pieces
are often original and the prices never reach levels of
absurdity. www.clan-pontaccio.com

Via Pontaccio 15　　　　　　　**02-875 759**
20121 Milan　　　Mon-Fri 10-1, 2:30-7:30, Sat 10-7:30

Coccinelle

Got a handbag fetish? Then put this store on your short list
and get ready to stock up. Here handbags come simple,
stylish and, above all, safe—as in, a bank robbery is not

Milan Directory

required to exit with something special. Better still, Coccinelle has cornered the market in functionality, ensuring that these user-friendly bags perform for the woman who carries her life, not just her lipstick, inside her cherry-red carry-all. The vibe is cheerful and accessible, just like the product which comes in bright colors in addition to more sober classics. Each season you'll notice updates in small details, like beading or delicate embellishment, but the formula for this tried and true Italian brand stays firmly put—it's all about getting a good handbag without a major hassle.

Via Manzoni at Via Bigli   02-7602 8161
20121 Milan   Mon 3-7, Tues-Sat 10-7

Corso Buenos Aires 16   02-2040 4755
20124 Milan   Mon 3-7:30, Tues-Sat 10-7:30

Corso Genova   02-8942 1347
20123 Milan   Mon 3:30-7:30
      Tues-Sat 10:30-2:30, 3:30-7:30

Via Statuto 11   02-655 2851
20121 Milan   (opening times as above)

Co-Co

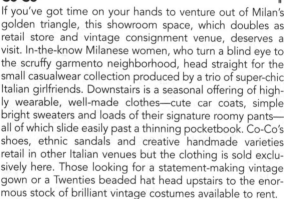

If you've got time on your hands to venture out of Milan's golden triangle, this showroom space, which doubles as retail store and vintage consignment venue, deserves a visit. In-the-know Milanese women, who turn a blind eye to the scruffy garmento neighborhood, head straight for the small casualwear collection produced by a trio of super-chic Italian girlfriends. Downstairs is a seasonal offering of highly wearable, well-made clothes—cute car coats, simple bright sweaters and loads of their signature roomy pants—all of which slide easily past a thinning pocketbook. Co-Co's shoes, ethnic sandals and creative handmade varieties retail in other Italian venues but the clothing is sold exclusively here. Those looking for a statement-making vintage gown or a Twenties beaded hat head upstairs to the enormous stock of brilliant vintage costumes available to rent.

Via Giannone 4   02-3360 6356
20154 Milan   Mon-Fri 10-7 (closed in August)

Coin

Coin's massive main store in Piazza 5 Giornate hosts a good mix of trendy and classic labels, such as Guess?, Diesel, Docker's, Fred Perry and Corneliani. But as you would expect of a department store, there is much diversity. On the ground floor you will find a wide selection of accessories, perfumes and cosmetics, and the Globe restaurant—there are two other cafés, including the macrobiotic New Age Caffè. And if you need a trim, there's an Aldo Coppola hair salon on the seventh floor. Selection at the Oviesse store doesn't look like much, but the stock is a lot less expensive and this is a good place to buy children's basics.   www.coin.it

Piazza 5 Giornate 1a   02-5519 2083
20129 Milan   Mon-Sat 9:30-8:30

Corso Buenos Aires 39 (Oviesse) 02-2040 4801
20124 Milan Daily 9-8

Corneliani

The Corneliani brothers founded this high-quality menswear label in Mantua in the Thirties and the company continues to turn out classic suits, shirts and ties. If you want made-to-measure, the materials are in the back and delivery time is three weeks. Customers more attentive to the whims of fashion go for the more casual clothes (such as leather jackets) from the Trend Corneliani line. www.corneliani.com

Via Montenapoleone 12 02-777 361
20121 Milan Mon-Sat 10-7

Costume National

Designer Ennio Capasa is a master of urban style, offering wearable fashion in high-tech fabrics and a basic color palette dominated by black, white and brown. Beautiful coats and finely cut leather figure prominently in a strong individualized collection that includes velvet smoking jackets with matching pants, belted micromini dresses, skinny tailored trousers and drapey blouses that soften the silhouette. Capasa's clientele are as individual as his pieces, ranging from hip fashion followers coveting the cool cuts to chic older women looking for clothing with character. www.costumenational.com

Via Sant' Andrea 12 02-7601 8356
20121 Milan Mon 3-7:30, Tues-Fri 10-2, 3-7, Sat 10-7

C.P. Company and Stone Island

It may be Italian-owned, but this men's sportswear label's head and heart are stuck smack dab in the Australian outback. The sporty, highly utilitarian clothing is perfect for a swift dismount from a mud-splattered 4X4, but the exceptional fabrications, the result of astute research by its Italian factories, will have you looking just as good strutting the streets of the concrete jungle. Joining the rugged linen shirts and washed cotton trousers is dressier fare from CP Company. Soft button-down sweaters and crews are a bonus, but the tour de force is the impressive selection of high-tech outerwear, expertly constructed and covered with stylish accoutrements.

Corso Venezia 12 02-7600 1409
20121 Milan Mon 3-7, Tues-Sat 10-7

DAAD Dantone

You'll be surpised to find one of Milan's most directional stores tucked rather sadly into a tourist-laden Galleria, but take one step into DAAD and all misgivings about the uncool entrance will disappear. Where else in Milan will you find deconstructed intellectual rags by Antonio Marras thrown together with Dsquared's sex-bomb sportswear? Trust us, you won't any place else. Here, underexposed and overpriced niche brands like Andrew McKenzie, John

Milan Directory

Richmond and Anne Demeulemeester get their well-deserved moment in the spotlight. It's a real melting-pot inside—cool T-shirts, sexy evening dresses, goth jewelry and funky shoes all collide—but there are unique finds to be had at every glance for hip guys and girls on the scout for something new.

Corso Matteotti 20   **02-7600 2120**
20121 Milan   Mon 3-7:30, Tues-Sat 10-7:30

D&G

The Corso Venezia home of Dolce & Gabbana's diffusion line is often packed to the door jambs. Among the racks and between the gilded columns you'll find fall's crisp shirts with just that touch of adventure, giant Alpine sweaters, wool vests and low-slung cargo pants. As always, these two know how to have fun with their fashion and still make it sexy. In the back is the cute D&G Jr line with its brightly-colored playful pieces.   www.dolcegabbana.it

Corso Venezia 7   **02-7600 4091**
20121 Milan   Mon-Sat 10-7

David Mayer

If you're looking for euro-style menswear with a Seventies flair, Rome-based designer David Mayer may have just the thing in one of his two Milan shops. Fitted sweaters with bold graphic patterns, white shirts with black embroidery, tight-fitting trousers and faded jeans with front patch pockets…it all may bring flashbacks of Eric Estrada going off-duty on ChiP's. If this sounds like your scene, you're in some suave company—football star Francesco Totti and actor Leonardo Di Caprio are among Mayer's fans. Other DM merchandise such as shirts, lotions and deodorants are also available.   www.davidmayer.com

Corso Buenos Aires 66   **02-2952 0134**
20124 Milan   Mon 3-7:30, Tues-Sat 10-7:30

Via Meravigli 16   **02-8698 4075**
20123 Milan   Mon 3:30-7:30, Tues-Sat 10:30-2, 3-7:30

☆ Davide Cenci

Attentive service is the big selling-point at this multi-brand men's and women's store in the burgeoning fashion district of Via Manzoni. Whether you're shopping for business or play, the brands on hand tend towards the classic so you'll never be taken for a trend-chaser. Polo shirts, long-pleated skirts, tailored jackets, Malo knitwear and Burberry's classic trench coats are complimented by footwear from Hogan and Tod's. The selection is slightly more male-oriented, particularly the beautiful suits.   www.davidecenci.com

Via Manzoni 7   **02-8646 5132**
20146 Milan   Mon 3:30-7:30, Tues-Sat 10-7:30

DEV

It's a shrine to Diego Della Valle's empire, a store which brings all the jewels of the Tod's group—Tod's, Hogan, and

Fay—into one neatly wrapped box. This store is quickly becoming one-stop shopping for Milano bene, the city's bourgeois elite, who pour in to snap up the newest pebble-soled Tod's loafer and Hogan handbag, then a quilted Fay jacket and sporty pair of trousers while they're at it. Sideline projects for Della Valle, like the irresistible Acqua di Parma fragrances and shirts and suiting by Brooks Brothers, also make it into the sophisticated but classic mix. Stay all day in this calm luxurious place and you won't see a single tourist enter the shop. Its location, outside the bounds of the city's traditional shopping center, and its refined concept, are both pure Milanese.

Corso Vercelli 8　　　　　　　　　**02-4802 8848**
20145 Milan　　　Mon 3-7:30, Tues-Sat 10-1, 3:30-7:30

☆ Diesel

This consistently successful Italian street brand has opened its house to the young and hip Ticinese crowd. Diesel's new domesticated concept store features cozy lounge areas with throw rugs, a chill-out patio and a friendly, laid-back staff to make customers feel right at home. For those who like to lead the fashion pack, here at Corso Porta Ticinese Diesel features prototype versions of its innovative jeans so you can pick your favorite styles and have them custom-made. Diesel guarantees that many of its products are on sale here before they reach other locations. The 55DSL line is found in Porta Ticinese 75, and the Diesel Style Lab collection is set to open in the same block. Diesel continues to do business outside the Ticinese area, of course, at its original Milan store in Galleria Passarella near Corso Vittorio Emanuele, and has also introduced its super-hip duds to the under 12 crowd with a new kids' store.　　www.diesel.com

Corso Porta Ticinese 44　　　　　　**02-8942 0916**
20123 Milan　Mon 3:30-7:30, Tues-Fri 11-1:30, 3:30-7:30
　　　　　　　　　　　　　　　　　　　Sat 11-7:30

Galleria Passarella 2　　　　　　　**02-7639 0583**
20122 Milan　　Sun-Mon 3:30-7:30, Tues-Sat 10:30-7:30

Corso Porta Ticinese 75　　　　　　**02-8324 1649**
20123 Milan　　　　　　　　　　　　Mon 2:30-7:30
　Tues-Fri 10:30-1:30, 3:30-7:30, Sat 10:30-1:30, 2:30-7:30

Corso Venezia 11 (kids)　　　　　　**02-7601 1701**
20121 Milan　　　　　　　　　Mon-Sat 10:30-7:30

Diffusione Tessile

Just a hop, skip and a jump off the Corso Vittorio Emanuele, Diffusione Tessile sells last season's collection from MaxMara at a discount. You'll also find the numerous other labels controlled by the MaxMara group, including Max & Co, Sportmax, Marella, Penny Black and Marina Rinaldi, the group's label for plus-size women. Since the store spans so many brands the range is enormous, from cozy knits to silky skirts to business basics to eveningwear. There are also plenty of lovely classic coats as well as a few shoes, bags and other accessories.

Galleria San Carlo 6   **02-7600 0829**
20122 Milan   Mon 3:30-7:30, Tues-Sat 10-7:30

DMagazine Outlet

A bargain-hunter's dream in the exclusive area of Montenapo, the tightly packed DMagazine offers past collections at a discount: Prada, Miu Miu, Romeo Gigli, Dsquared, Plein Sud, Costume National, Gucci, Cavalli, Armani, Jil Sander and many more. By all means go, but keep your expectations in check because a look through some of the stock might make it instantly apparent why it hasn't sold. And keep in mind that clothes that were extremely expensive to begin with, though reduced will not necessarily come cheap. But if you're in the mood to do some digging, there may be treasures to be found.

Via Montenapoleone 26   **02-7600 6027**
20121 Milan   Daily 9:45-7:45

Docks Dora

You'll find a seamless blend of new and secondhand clothing, much of it with a Seventies flair, at Docks Dora. There are loads of jeans, Seven and G-Star among the most prevalent, as well as flouncy Betsey Johnson dresses, vintage Burberry trenches and a selection of lingerie. You're slightly off the main fashion drag here but the store is hopping nonetheless. The psychedelic changing-room curtains are similar to those on sale in the shop.

Viale Crespi 7   **02-2900 6950**
20121 Milan   Mon 3-8, Tues-Sat 11-8, Sun 3-7:30

☆ Dolce & Gabbana

Since the late Eighties Dolce & Gabbana have layered lavish avant-gardism with their hot-blooded Sicilian fire to create some of the industry's steamiest concoctions. The brand has been a fashion phenomenon, exploding into the upper stratospheres of cool. Although they have the trademark to bombshell dressing, the duo's true genius lies in their ability to pour the hippest of street fashion into sophisticated get-ups, sending women home with all the ingredients for a modern lifestyle: a perfectly tailored cocktail suit, a va-va-vroom lace-up corset dress, and a hip-hop parka for beating the streets. Statement-making gowns splash on many a red carpet, but there's also plenty of fabulous camis, cargoes and trousers for your average cash-loaded young thing.

Via della Spiga 2   **02-7600 1155**
20121 Milan   Mon-Sat 10-7

Dolce & Gabbana (men's)

Now that the duo have become the kings of Italy's next fashion generation, they are taking Milan's shopping system by storm. In addition to the original women's store in Via della Spiga and the new accessories and vintage stores, Dolce & Gabbana have recently inaugurated this historic

palazzo as stage set for their sizzling menswear. With its
Sicilian barber shop, full-service spa and super-hip bar, this
landmark 18th-century building is a gentlemen's club as
well as a men's store. Yes, there are three beautifully
appointed floors dedicated to the best of Dolce's
menswear—the sleek trousers, the gangster-worthy suits,
the hip-hop-influenced streetwear—but the real joy is
being able to relax with a hot-towel shave or a glass of nero
d'Avola in the private courtyard to stave off a wave of shopping fatigue.

Corso Venezia 15   **02-7602 8485**
20121 Milan   (opening times as above)

Dolce & Gabbana (vintage)

They've only just celebrated their 18th birthday, but now
they have their very own vintage store. Filled with re-makes
of their most beloved signature looks, this tiny store is a
shrine to the Sicilian pair's biggest moments in the late
Eighties and early Nineties when Linda and Cindy ruled the
runways in show-stopping corset dresses, rhinestone-stud-
ded bustiers and mannish suits. Most of the merchandise
has been updated to fit a more modern silhouette, but the
basics—crisp white shirts, those bum-hugging pencil skirts
and loads of animal prints—are all on track for a second
round in the spotlight. If a blast from the past won't get
your heart racing, then dip into the adjoining accessories
store filled top to bottom with the newest eyewear, handbags and, yes, plenty of those wardrobe staple pointed
slingbacks with leopardskin lining.

Via della Spiga 26a/b   **02-799 950**
20121 Milan   (opening times as above)
(vintage & women's accessories)

Domo Adami

The lovely and unusual wedding dresses designed by
Mauro Adami could set you back anywhere from $2,000 to
$10,000—not bad if you're only going to do it once.
Located in a charming pebbled courtyard off Via Manzoni,
the Domo Adami studio can also offer a hand with accessories, make-up, hair and a wedding album. There are plenty of traditional gowns available, but for the less conventional bride Adami likes to experiment with pale colors and
fitted, rather than poofy, cuts. For the bride who can't bear
not to make a statement, there's a gown that's been splat-
ter painted, Jackson Pollock-style, with bright shades of
green and blue.   www.domoadami.com

Via Manzoni 23   **02-805 7207**
20121 Milan   Tues-Sat 10-6

☆ Du Pareil Au Même

Visiting mamans and a fair share of local mamme swear by
this French childrenswear label for cute, well-priced clothing from newborn to age 14. Like many other Milan stores
selling baby bits, Du Pareil Au Même offers a shower reg-

istry service for mothers-to-be. The Buenos Aires store is the larger of the two and has much key equipment like strollers, high chairs and stuffed toys.   www.dpam.com

Corso Buenos Aires 49   **02-2941 1607**
20124 Milan   Mon 12-7:30, Tues-Sat 10-7:30 (Friday 10-6)

Via Dante 5   **02-7209 4971**
20123 Milan   Mon-Sat 10-7:30

E-Play
Original, ironic and eye-catching designs dominate this spanking new urbanwear shop. Clothes hounds with an eye for unusual design details will find plenty of button-down shirts in crumpled fabric or featuring asymmetric collars, ruffled blouses with hems that look as if they've been burnt and jeans splashed with artistic decoration.   www.e-play.it

Corso Venezia 5   **02-7640 7198**
20121 Milan   Mon 3-7:30, Tues-Sat 10-7:30

Emanuel Ungaro
Ungaro himself continues to design his famed haute couture collection, but the ready-to-wear line is now under the direction of Giambattista Valli who is trying to build a bridge to a younger flock of fashion followers. For fall, there are ruffled floral dresses in lovely light chiffon, shearling coats, embroidered suede skirts and plenty of accessories, from leather mules to tasseled bags in tan-colored suede. The more traditional eveningwear and tailored suits are also always available, of course.

Via Montenapoleone 27   **02-7602 3997**
20121 Milan   Mon 3-7, Tues-Sat 10-7

Emilio Pucci
Unless you've been in a deep snooze for several seasons, you know that this legendary Sixties designer has made a comeback. Here you'll find the bright swirling signature prints on dresses, tops, trousers and scarves. The collection, now overseen by French designer Christian Lacroix, is part of the LVMH stable of luxury goods companies.
                                        www.emiliopucci.com

Via Montenapoleone 14   **02-7631 8356**
20121 Milan   Mon 3-7, Tues-Sat 10-7

Energie
It may not look like much from the outside, but all five floors of Energie are packed with the latest in Italian streetwear, from tiny T-shirts to long, low-waisted flared jeans to platform shoes. It's a great source for girly brands like Killah Babe and Miss Sixty, while guys go for the Energie and Sixty Pro-Tec labels. There's a lot here to sift through, but when your own energie starts to flag, the thumping background music might get it going again.   www.energie.it.

Via Torino 19   **02-7202 0077**
20123 Milan   Mon-Fri 10-7:30, Sat 9:30-8
                                    Sun 10:30-1:30, 2:30-7:30

Eral 55

Ever wondered how Milanese men manage to whip up that rumpled chic look—totally undone but somehow flawlessly chic—for every low-key public appearance? This store, a granddaddy of polished sportswear for the last 25 years, must have something to do with it. Here, casualwear has nothing to do with droopy sweats or rumpled T-shirts, but is instead a carefully crafted mix of high-end, low-end and vintage styles expertly edited for your benefit. Exceptionally tailored Italian shirts and colorful ties are played off against urban essentials like cargo pants and vintage inspired leather jackets. Bright trainers tone down washed twill blazers or Baracuda Blue jackets from London. The staff have an annoyingly low tolerance for out-of-towners, but if you act as smooth as the shots of Steve McQueen and Frank Sinatra which line the walls you can finesse your way into a pair of Eral's wild two-tone cowboy boots, modeled after the Texan "Grey Jones" but handmade in Italy.

Piazza XXV Aprile 14   **02-659 8829**
20124 Milan   Mon 3:30-7:30, Tues-Sat 10:30-7:30

Ermenegildo Zegna

One of the most famous names in Italian menswear, Zegna offers lovely tailored suits in the finest fabrics. When Giorgio Armani first produced his menswear collection for Armani Collezioni, he turned to Zegna for advice. Mere mortals can get some expert guidance of their own while selecting the best fit in a made-to-measure suit or the most flattering button-downs from a refreshing range of colors. For smaller wallets, Zegna offers sportswear, ties and other accessories.   www.zegna.com

Via Verri 3   **02-7600 6437**
20121 Milan   Mon-Sat 9:30-7

☆ Etro

Fashionistas fanatical about wearing only black might change their minds after visiting this men's and womenswear boutique. Beautifully made suits, shirts, scarves and accessories in a rainbow of colors and patterns leap off every rack. The brilliant palette has also spilled over onto chairs, sofas, candles and vases in Etro's home furnishing store next door.   www.etro.it.

Via Montenapoleone 5   **02-7600 5049**
20121 Milan   Mon-Sat 10-7

Extè

In the short eight years of its existence Italian brand Extè has picked up and dropped designers as fast as a fashion editor dismisses last season's accessories. But throughout the varied twists and turns of its fashion concept, one element is assured: if you don't have a set of legs that come up to your armpits, you might be hard pressed to find anything suitable in this store. The skirt hems are itty-bitty, tops come cropped

Milan Directory

and slashed up, and pulling on a pair of skin-tight pants is often a two-person undertaking. If a sexed-up, sometimes trashy, look is your ticket to happiness, look no further. Better yet, the prices, a bit lower than most designers, will leave plenty of cash left over for a set of killer stilettos to complete your vixen look. www.exte.it

Via della Spiga 6 **02-783 050**
20121 Milan Mon 3-7, Tues-Sat 10-7

Fatto a Mano

On the Corso Porta there's a strong Asian influence taking hold. Fatto a Mano helped launch this trend, beckoning to countries like China and Thailand for their comfortable range of drawstring trousers, button-down shirts and summer dresses. They also have loads of colorful scarves, silk slippers, beaded purses and belts.

Corso di Porta Ticinese 76 **02-8940 1958**
20123 Milan Mon 3-7:30, Tues-Sat 9:30-7:30

Fausto Santini

Fausto Santini's fans are glad that this former lawyer has forsaken the pursuit of justice for the art of shoe design. Women seeking comfort and style in equal measure will find some beautiful ballerina shoes, flats and boots, many with lovely little embellishments like fur trim. Drawstring leather bags and other accessories are also available, in addition to an appealing men's selection, and prices are relatively reasonable given the quality and the neighborhood. www.faustosantini.it

Via Montenapoleone 1 **02-7600 1958**
20121 Milan Mon 3:30-7:30, Tues-Sat 10-7:30

Fay

These are the clothes that keep half of Italy's population—the impeccably dressed half—looking photo-grade for all their luxury leisure time. The story of the brand's unexpected boom started with Tod's group CEO, Diego Della Valle, who went pazzo for a fireman's-style jacket which he saw in America in the late Eighties—so much so, that he brought the coat back home, gave it an Italian makeover and created an entire brand around the sporty chic look. Now the company offers a whole line of sporty jackets, all featuring exquisite detailing, plus scores of impossibly refined casualwear. Italy's elite can't get enough of it. For a polished look perfect for jaunts to Portofino or St. Moritz, you'll find quilted jackets, tailored cotton pants, preppy sweaters, plus an assortment of handbags pristine enough to make papa Diego proud.

Via della Spiga 15 **02-7601 7597**
20121 Milan Mon-Sat 10-7

Fedeli Red and Blue

Choose from a wide range of fabrics for made-to-measure shirts, sweaters and pullovers or select from the ready-to-wear. Cotton is the watchword in spring and summer, while cashmere and knits come in when the sun gets low. Ties and other accessories are also available.

Via Montenapoleone 8　　　　　　　　　**02-7602 3392**
20121 Milan　　　　Mon-Fri 10-1:30, 2:30-7, Sat 10-1, 2:30-7

Fendi

From the Baguette to the Ostrik, Fendi always have a waiting list as long as the King James Bible for their latest handbag designs. Revered primarily for their accessories, this prestigious label has plenty more to offer. Make the pilgrimage to Via Sant' Andrea for their famous furs, luggage and luxurious ready-to-wear.　　　　　　www.fendi.it

Via Sant' Andrea 16　　　　　　　　　**02-7602 1617**
20121 Milan　　　　　　　　　　　　　Mon-Sat 10-7

Fila

Fila remains a good source for sportswear. Its five floors are filled with shorts, sweats, swimsuits, T-shirts, running shoes and other athletic gear, plus watches, duffle bags and sunglasses. Fila has collaborated with Ferrari on a line of mod sportwear, including red patent-leather shoes, polo shirts and other items embellished with the galloping horse.　　　　　　　　　www.fila.com

Piazza Liberty 8　　　　　　　　　　**02-7601 1293**
20121 Milan　　　　　　　　　　　　　Mon-Sat 10-8

☆ Fiorucci Dept. Store

More kitsch that your average department store, Fiorucci offers a selection of clothing that ranges from cute to classic, mingled among pink plastic flamingos, Japanese cookbooks and the soaps, candles and other homey treats that make Fiorucci a great spot for gift shopping. Organized like a bazaar, the store houses the Fiorucci collections, including Safety Jeans and Target for Fiorucci, as well as labels like Le Petit Prince, Pinko, Kent, Killah Babe and Simonetta. The baby clothes are particularly cute, if a bit overpriced. Relocating at press time.　　www.fiorucci.it

Corso Europa　　**(no further details available at press time)**

Fogal

This Swiss hosiery label has hit its stride with a selection of reliable luxury stockings. In more than 80 colors, plain and patterned, Fogal features fabrics from soft silk and cashmere to the hard-working Lycra. A small selection of classic cotton, wool and cashmere men's socks is available along with body suits and bustiers and sticky-soled Froggies socks for kids.　　　　　　　　　www.fogal.com

Via Montenapoleone 1　　　　　　　　**02-7602 1795**
20121 Milan　　　　　　Mon 1-7:30, Tues-Sat 10-7:30

Fornarina

Anyone with a weakness for the Eighties revival will find plenty to please from this sexy, youth-infused Italian label.

Milan Directory

The look for fall includes flared denims, low-slung tapered ankle pants, pleated skirts in cotton and stripy longsleeved tees. It's one part pretty little girl, one part hard-partying punk, with plenty of trimmings—jewelry, sunglasses and hair accessories—to complete the look.   www.fornarina.com

Corso di Porta Ticinese 78   **02-8320 0759**
20123 Milan   Mon 3:30-7:30, Tues-Fri 10-1, 3:30-7:30
                                            Sat 10-1, 3-8

Fratelli Rossetti

Fratelli Rossetti broke fashionable footwear ground in the Fifties when they introduced their brown moccasin in an era that revered basic black. Today the collection is classic with some trendy twists. Men will find styles ranging from traditional oxfords to buckled leather loafers with a long tapered toe. Women will find slingbacks with straps that snake around the ankle, woven leather slides and two-tone oxfords in bright color combinations. Leather and suede jackets, handbags and belts are also available.   www.rossetti.it

Via Montenapoleone 1   **02-7602 1650**
20121 Milan   Mon-Sat 10-7:30, Sun 10-1, 2:30-7

Corso Magenta 17   **02-8645 4284**
20123 Milan   Mon 3-7:30, Tues-Fri 10-2, 3:30-7:30
                                            Sat 10-7:30

Frette

These are the famed bed linens on which the world's richest and most decadent have demanded to lay their heads for well over a century. The supreme quality and extravagant luxury of the brand first wooed the Italian royal household in 1881, and later the Vatican, but today Frette's linens and homewear are requisite for anyone with impeccable taste. Now, next to sheets with stratospheric thread-counts and silk duvets, you'll find a full line of homewear that will make you want to stay locked behind closed doors for the next century. Retreat to bliss in cashmere or velvet robes lined in heavy satin, warm up in a fur-trimmed wrap sweater, or trollop around your boudoir in a pair of mink-lined crocodile mules. The spectacle doesn't come cheap, but if Frette is good enough for the Pope, you better believe it's worth the tag.

Via Montenapoleone 21   **02-783 950**
20121 Milan   Mon 3-7, Tues-Sat 10-7

Via Manzoni 11   **02-864 433**
20121 Milan   Mon 3-7, Tues-Sat 10-1:30, 3-7

Corso Buenos Aires 82   **02-2940 1072**
20124 Milan   (opening times as above)

Corso Vercelli 23/25   **02-498 9756**
20145 Milan   (opening times as above)

Furla

Furla has done for handbags what Heinz did to ketchup: they've taken a simple, good-looking and tasty product and brought it to the masses at shockingly decent prices. Like most established Italian brands, the Bologna-based company has kept things in the family since its foundation back in 1927. Today Giovanna Furlanetto, surrounded by a brood of children and extended family, spins out boatloads of calfskin or glossed leather bags which skew high on function and medium on fast fashion. The same no-nonsense approach goes into the brand's line of accessories which includes jewelry, watches, small leather goods and scarves. Also new for the label is a burgeoning shoe line.

Corso Vittorio Emanuele II 2   **02-796 943**
20122 Milan   Mon-Sat 10-7:30

Corso Vercelli 11   **02-4801 4189**
20145 Milan   Mon 3-7:30, Tues-Sat 10-7:30

Corso Buenos Aires 18   **02-204 3319**
20124 Milan   Mon 2:30-7:30, Tues-Sat 10-7:30

Geox

They call them the shoes that breathe. Geox has a patented sole which, they claim, releases moisture without letting moisture seep in. Heels for the office, summer flats, classic loafers to kick around on the weekend...you name it, it's here. But while some Geox wearers attest to their comfort, they also admit that these shoes are not built to last a lifetime. Look out for their new store in Galleria Vittorio Emanuele II due to open later this year.   www.geox.com

Via Montenapoleone 26   **02-7600 9372**
20121 Milan   Mon 3-7:30, Tues-Sat 10-7:30

Corso Buenos Aires 2   **02-2953 1626**
20124 Milan   (opening times as above)

Via Speronari 8   **02-8699 5608**
20123 Milan   Mon 11-7:30, Tues-Sat 10-7:30

Giacomelli Sport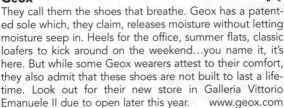

The giant action photo of Paolo Maldini, Milan's striking football star, is reason enough to visit this sportswear shop. Other sporting greats, like Boris Becker and Michael Jordan, get face time too. Among the brands on sale, you'll find the latest models from Nike, Adidas and Asics. Beware of visiting during the sales when the competition is fierce.   www.giacomellisport.com

Piazza Argentina 4   **02-2940 9806**
20124 Milan   Mon 2:30-8, Tues-Sat 9:30-8

Gianfranco Ferré

As if being a first-rate couturier and top of the line ready-to-wear designer weren't enough, maestro Gianfranco Ferré also has an architectural degree which he put to work in his brand-new store and adjoining day spa. Waxed stucco walls and a glass mosaic floor house both super-luxe men's and women's collections. Although Ferré's outrageously priced clothes appeal greatly to the heavily-jeweled ladies-who-do-nothing-but-lunch set, the designer has taken a stab at wooing a younger crowd. So, locked in between the structured shoulders and heavy lapels, you'll find some mighty fine leather pieces and dramatic evening looks. Classic customers and sweet young things alike will find consolation in a post-shopping hot-stone facial or detoxification wrap at the in-store spa—an immediate antidote to post-spending woes.   www.gianfrancoferre.com

Via Sant' Andrea 15   **02-794 864**
20121 Milan   Mon 3-7, Tues-Sat 10-7

Gianni Campagna

In a majestic 19th-century building near Milan's public gardens, Gianni Campagna offers personalized precision tailoring in the finest fabrics. Sharon Stone, Pierce Brosnan and Jack Nicholson are among the fans of his famous suits. A financially friendlier ready-to-wear collection is also available, and the womenswear is produced under the Baratta label.   www.sartoriacampagna.it

Via Palestro 24   **02-778 811**
20100 Milan   Mon-Sat 9:30-7

Gianni Versace

Avid Versace fans will be delighted that the fashion house famed for its pursuit of excess has all but abandoned its brief foray into the slightly more subdued world. Shocking colour and vibrant patterns are back with a vengeance in this season's selection of sheer knit tops, boldly striped dresses, embroidered blouses and tailored pants. But you can still find simple black and white trousers and turtlenecks in the mix, along with just a touch of gothic for women and a fusion of Cuban style and heavy metal for the men. The perennial supply of sexy slit-to-the-nethers evening dresses plus skincare products and accessories also feature heavily. Head to nearby Via San Pietro all'Orto for the younger and more affordable Versus label and the home collection. www.versace.com

Via Montenapoleone 11   **02-7600 8528**
20121 Milan   Mon-Sat 10-7

Via San Pietro all'Orto 10   **02-7601 4722**
20121 Milan   Mon-Sat 10-7

Gibo by Julie Verhoeven

She's been a fashion illustrator, set designer, stylist and art teacher, but now the wildly creative hands of London-based Julie Verhoeven are busy whipping up collections for Italian manufacturer Gibo. Gibo, a veteran of Italian moda who produces for such wanted labels as Paul Smith, Hussein Chalayan, Viktor & Rolf, Marc Jacobs, Michael Kors and Antonio Berardi, is a proponent of young, edgy designers and its own newly released collection is no exception. Expect the same kind of remixes—like jersey dresses paired with Eighties sportswear pieces—that you'd find in the hippest of London street fashions. There will also be plenty of bright color and the same kind of kinky sensuality that infuses Verhoeven's own psychedelic illustrations.

Via Sant' Andrea 10a   **n/a at press time**
20121 Milan

☆ Gio Moretti

If you're tired of traipsing up and down the golden streets of la moda Milanese from one fashion house to the next, head to Gio Moretti and find all the la-la-luxe labels under one convenient roof. Strategically located in Via della Spiga, Moretti has already done all that time-consuming editing for you, bringing the best of Jean Paul Gaultier, Roberto Cavalli, Ralph Lauren, Jil Sander, Chloé, DKNY, Rene Caovilla or whatever strikes her fancy for the season. Downstairs, a sporty yet chic collection of menswear is enlivened with funky home objects, art books and obscure CDs. To cap off an envy-evoking family portrait, head just a few doors down the street and scoop up some of the most irresistible—and pricey—baby clothing Milan has to offer.

Via della Spiga 4   **02-7600 3186 (women)**
                                          02-7600 2172 (men)
20121 Milan   Mon 3-7, Tues-Sat 10-7
Via della Spiga 9 (Gio Moretti Baby)   **02-780 089**
20121 Milan   (opening times as above)

Giorgio Armani

With gentle tailoring and a subtle color palette, Giorgio Armani continues to churn out classic, comfortable clothing in the finest fabrics. In this (understated, of course) sand-colored boutique, you'll find lovely, simple day and eveningwear for women on the ground floor, with the menswear downstairs. Around the corner on Villa della Spiga sits a second store, entirely devoted to Armani leather goods, eyewear and other accessories.

                                          www.giorgioarmani.com

Via Sant' Andrea 9   **02-7600 3234**
20121 Milan   Mon-Sat 10:30-7
Via della Spiga 19   **02-783 511**
20121 Milan   Mon-Sat 10:30-7

☆ Gucci

Gucci fans rejoice! Your sadistic fashion dream of being crushed to near-death by piles of Tom Ford's brilliant hand-iwork can now come true. This brand-new behemoth store, Gucci's largest in the world, is an endless labyrinth featuring more product than any Gucci addict could possibly hope for. Rows and rows of Gucci's hard-core, sexed-up ready-to-wear, the same pieces which regularly throw fashion editors and celebrities into seasonal seizures, grace the entire basement level. The ground floor is jam-packed with every coveted bag on the planet. If you're feeling snooty about seeing your same croc clutch in the hands of your best friend, do what any proper slave to statement would do and snag a limited-edition piece or whip up your own personalized delight from Gucci's made-to-order collection. Be sure to bring your man along for the eye-popping ride, either to test out the Gucci saddle or to relish in the made-to-measure men's shoes which will have him looking like a slick Forties gangster in no time.   www.gucci.com

Via Montenapoleone 5-7   **02-771 271**
20121 Milan   Mon-Sat 10-7

Guess?

It's hard to miss this store, prominently located in San Babila. Naturally, there's an ample supply of denim, as well as T-shirts, sweatpants, jackets and a range of accessories from the Eighties jeans label that is still simmering if not quite sizzling hot.   www.guess.com

Piazza San Babila 4b   **02-7639 2070**
20122 Milan   Mon-Sat 10-7:30

H&M

As we went to press plans were well advanced for this giant Swedish retailer, the champion of fast fashion at inconceivably low prices, to swoop into town. Their new location—the landmark Fiorucci store in San Babila—has a few Italians bent out of shape, as the historic Italian brand has been forced to move. All three floors of the enormous outpost will be transformed into a showcase for H&M's usual fare: instant trends, catwalk copies, and prices good enough to eat. But there's never a free lunch. The chain is notorious for its merchandise mayhem, uncontrollable crowds and mile-long lines for dressing-rooms and check-out.

Galleria Passerella 2   **n/a at press time**
20122 Milan

Helmut Lang

For a designer as universally acclaimed as Helmut Lang, it's always been a mystery that he has been conspicuously off fashion's retail radar. Luckily, die-hard fans of the reclusive designer's cult classics have a new outpost where they can scoop up his famed stove-pipe trousers and other deconstructed minimalist goodies. The Milan boutique, an urban oasis graced by simple architecture and a light exhibit which runs down an awesome stairwell, was conceived by Lang himself. The severely modern style is an ode to his hardcore fashion offering—the kind of stuff that's great for edgy girls looking to stand out, but quietly. Two floors house both the men's and women's artfully constructed ready-to-wear as well as a small offering of Lang's quirky shoes and accessories.   www.helmutlang.com

Via della Spiga 11   **02-7639 0255**
20121 Milan   Mon-Sat 10-7

Hermès

Amid prints of bucolic hunting scenes and leather saddles tacked to the wall, this lofty French house delivers all the luxe you can lap up. Luggage, wallets, belts, handbags, scarves, ties, watches, perfume, socks and even towels are carefully displayed alongside a small clothing collection. The style statement has not always been totally au courant, but now that they have access to Jean Paul Gaultier's creative ideas this may change. Always a lovely place to splurge on a lasting gift.   www.hermes.com

Via Sant' Andrea 21   **02-7600 3495**
20121 Milan   Mon 3-7, Tues-Sat 10-7

Hogan

Part of the Diego Della Valle empire, Hogan's shoes are characterized by the same high quality that has given big brother label Tod's such solid standing over the years. The styles are generally casual and comfy, from bowling shoes to loafers, though there are a few high heels. The handbags have also touched a recent peak in popularity, and there are some shoes for children.

Via Montenapoleone 23   **02-7601 1174**
20121 Milan   Mon-Sat 10-7

Iceberg

This Italian brand, designed by Paolo Gerani, has earned a following for its brightly-colored knitwear. The store attracts a largely thirtysomething crowd that has grown weary of basic black and white and comes for a bold dose of style from the brand that is not afraid to play with pattern.   www.iceberg.com

Via Montenapoleone 10   **02-782 385**
20121 Milan   Mon-Sat 10-7, Sun 10-1, 2-7

I Pinco Pallino

The windows of this children's shop never cease to halt the otherwise concentrated shoppers endlessly parading up and down tony Via della Spiga. The trendy creations are wildly extravagant—often outlandish—but Italian mamas with a lot of cash revel in spoiling their bambini in up-to-the-minute style. It's all highly original. Skirts and dresses are intricately constructed and detailed, while suits and jackets in fine fabrics have a men's-like tailoring. If you're trying to run as far away from Gap Kids as possible, a stop-off here will make you a very happy mama indeed.   www.pincopallino.it

Via della Spiga 42   **02-781 931**
20121 Milan   Mon 3:30-7, Tues-Sat 10-7

Jeanseria del Corso

Known simply as JDC, this den of denim attracts a generally young and trendy crowd. You'll find JDC's own collection, along with labels like Guru (known for its bright floral designs), Levi's, Lonsdale and Diesel, plus the bags from sportswear companies that have been sweeping streetwear for a year or two.

Piazza Duomo 31   **02-8646 1737**
20122 Milan   Daily 10-7:30 (Mon 12-7:30)

Corso Buenos Aires (corner of Pergolesi) 1   **02-2940 6990**
20124 Milan   Mon 3-7:30, Tues-Fri 10-1:30, 3-7:30
     Sat 10-7:30

Jil Sander

As we went to press, Jil Sander fans were rejoicing worldwide and emptying their closets top to bottom. Why? To make room for the unmatched designs of the minimalist German designer who had just announced the return to her company. After a three-year hiatus Jil is back in the saddle, promising to deliver the same exquisitely crafted, simple designs that made Sander-slaves out of millions of women throughout the Nineties. Other designers can only aspire to the purity which Sander effortlessly achieves on her flawless suits and easy daywear, as well as on chic accessories and shoes. But simplicity certainly doesn't imply a wallflower existence for its wearers. Put on anything from Jil Sander—including the planned new line of eveningwear—and you will instantly feel the sensuality, the glamour and, above all, the price tag of these exceptional clothes.

Via Verri 6	**02-777 2991**
20121 Milan	Mon-Sat 10-7

Jimmy Choo

Nothing arouses unadulterated passion more consistently than a set of Jimmy Choo's stiletto heels. This cult-like British label, founded out of a couture shoe business by former British *Vogue* accessories editor Tamara Mellon, is now required foot candy for uptown ladies and red carpet divas alike. Designer Sandra Choi consistently whips up colorful strappy sandals, elegant pumps and sexy slingbacks that elongate the leg like no other. These towering pieces of foot-art don't come cheap, but the surge of instant glamour is worth every last penny. The Milan shop—due to open in early 2004—will also feature the new line of leather handbags, ladylike but very modern bags to complete your well-heeled look.

Via San Pietro all'Orto 17	**n/a at press time**
20121 Milan	

John Richmond

Rock 'n' roll rebels can hone their style at British designer John Richmond's Via Verri shop. Greatest hits include studded denim dresses for female groupies and jeans and tees for the guys. The staff resemble bouncers at a concert, all in T-shirts emblazoned with the John Richmond logo, but they're far friendlier. A selection of CDs and magazines adds to the vibe.

Via Verri (corner of Via Bigli)	**02-7602 8173**
20121 Milan	Mon 3-7:45, Tues-Sun 10-7:45

Joost

We love this small stylish men's store, located just down from Via Torino. And what's not to love? All the labels, including the striking proprietary brand Joost, have a chic individual quality to them which signals a modern but not overly made-up man. A highly personalized mix can be had from the G-star denim or twill trousers, Pringle sweaters, rumpled button-downs and Spanish-style shoes. There's a revolving door of small trendy labels, but consistency is found in the strong innovative knitwear, led by the quirky Joost brand itself.

Via Cesare Correnti 12　　　**02-7201 4537**
20123 Milan　　　　　Mon 3-7, Tues-Sat 10-2, 3-7

Julien

Newly-opened Julien has everything most Milan stores don't: well-edited vintage clothing, hard to find niche sportswear labels, home-made items and a hip vibe. There's Sixties-style knitwear, wacky shoes you never thought you'd need (but do), creative tanks and tees by Mail project, Mambo, Puma, lots of denim and even a vintage camera collection. The band of friends who opened the store, three underground guys and one with-it girl, also sew original handbags or T-shirts and can whip up anything to your specification. This cool-kid gang also had the brains to open up a chic bar across the street from the store where you'll want to stop for a panino or aperitivo. By a stroke of genius, and convenience, both venues are open until midnight.

Via C.M.Maggi 3　　　　**02-349 1392**
20100 Milan　　　　　　Mon-Sat 12-12

Kallisté - Un Dimanche à Venise

Italian shoemaker Kallisté has its portfolio pockets full of brands, but its French moniker "Un Dimanche" happens to be the most upscale and interesting. At first glance the shoes in this small shop all look a bit crooked, as if they've been washed or warped, but when you wear them those quirks add to a charming and unique look. Prices stay relatively reasonable, even for the intricate shelled lace-up sandals in summer or a pair of fierce metallic boots come fall.

Corso Matteotti 22　　　　**02-7631 7447**
20121 Milan　　　　Mon 3-7:30, Tues-Sat 10-7:30

Kenzo

A subtle Asian influence reverberates from the collections of Gilles Rosier (womenswear) and Roy Kejberg (men's). Unfinished borders are a key feature of this fall's trousers, coats and shirts, and knits are chunky and cuddly in cashmere. Along with the ready-to-wear collections, Kenzo's Milan boutique offers perfumes and accessories like the brilliantly colored scarves that are synonymous with Kenzo himself, who stepped down in 1999.

Via Sant' Andrea 11　　　　**02-7602 0929**
20121 Milan　　Mon 3-7:30, Tues-Sat 10-2, 3-7:30

Kristina Ti

Turin-based designer Cristina Tardito's soft approach to lingerie design has helped her earn the nickname "designer of the invisible". Invisible because her handiwork is usually hidden under layers of clothing, and because of the careful attention she pays to even the smallest details. The Kristina Ti boutique offers her beautiful unfussy lingerie and swimwear, along with a small but growing and very feminine ready-to-wear collection.　　www.kristinati.it

Via Solferino 18　　　　**02-653 379**
20121 Milan　　　　Mon 3-7, Tues-Sat 10-7

Krizia

Mariuccia Mandelli's fashion formula hasn't changed much since she founded her company nearly 50 years ago. The same soft, deconstructed clothes for which she became famous in the Sixties still grace the walls of Krizia's recently refurbished Milan outpost. On any given outing to Krizia, in any given era, you are guaranteed face-to-face shopping time with a wide-leg palazzo pant, a hip-length knit sweater and a jungle's worth of tiger or leopard motifs. Today's models have, of course, been given the requisite trend update but the collection does sway slightly senior. The women's collection, which includes everything from beaded evening dresses to swimwear, is accompanied by a smaller collection for men which includes innovative knitwear and colorful shirts and ties.

Via della Spiga 23	**02-7600 8429**
20121 Milan	Mon 3-7, Tues-Sat 10-7

La Boule de Neige

Fashion globetrotters, after an afternoon of style binging at 10 Corso Como, undoubtedly make a beeline for this boutique situated across the street to see what's new from a handful of American and Italian designers. The sweet as pie white walls, which feature doodles or cartoons of seasonally-rotating artists, are a perfect backdrop for the prim-chic clothing which hangs neatly on floating racks. Crisp suits by Michael Kors, silky slip dresses by Calvin Klein and plenty of cashmere by Malo and Gentry Portofino almost always make it into the mix. Things get spiced up with colorful flats and ladylike heels by Sigerson Morrison, Christian Louboutin and Jimmy Choo, plus hand-painted bags by Anya Hindmarch.

Corso Como 3	**02-6291 0777**
20154 Milan	Mon 2:30-7:30, Tues-Sat 10-7:30

L'Armadio di Laura

Laura has been in the vintage business longer than most of us have been alive. She was the first signora to set up a secondhand shop in Milan, much to the horror of the by-the-book fashionistas at the time. Since then attitudes concerned "used" clothing have relaxed and Milan does have its vintage community, in which Laura and her courtyard boutique flourish. Her take on the vintage phenomenon, however, is extremely broad and encompasses the big business of recent designer goods at heavy discounts. With last season's Prada and Dolce at 50% off, Laura's closet is like one big outlet store. But you'll also find thrift variety (soccer shirts and beat-up cords) as well as more classic vintage items like beaded dresses from the Forties.

Via Voghera 25	**02-836 0606**
20125 Milan	June 15-Sept 15: Mon-Fri 10-6
	Sept 15-June 15: Tues-Sat 10-6

La Perla

The pearl of fine Italian lingerie, this luxury label offers every style from sensibly seamless to sex-kitten. Bras and panties, lacy bustiers, sheer body suits, swimsuits and a selection of ready-to-wear are all available. The addition of a coat collection means they've got you fully covered, bottom layer to top. www.laperla.com

Via Montenapoleone 1   **02-7600 0460**
20121 Milan   Mon 3-7, Tues-Sat 10-7

Corso Vercelli 35   **02-498 7770**
20144 Milan   Mon 3:30-7:30, Tues-Sat 10-7:30

La Rinascente

This massive department store traces its history in Milan's Via Radegonda back to 1865, a few years before Italy even became a republic. A major fashion destination ever since, La Rinascente is full of mid and upper-range brands for adults and children, from Nike and Adidas to Dockers and Diesel to Missoni and Moschino. The lingerie selection on the mezzanine floor is extensive, with homegrown labels La Perla and D&G alongside the imports. Near the top level, you'll find an Estée Lauder Spa and a café with a view of the Duomo's spikes and gargoyles. For those travelling by car, there is ample parking in the store's garage. www.rinascente.it

Via Radegonda 3   **02-88521**
20121 Milan   Mon-Sat 9-10, Sun 10-8

Larusmiani

Fabric manufacturers for their own label, Larusmiani maintains tight quality control over the cotton, linen and wool used to create their menswear collections. This Gucci neighbor is a good source for sportswear and casualwear, with a varied color scheme and all the accessories a guy could need. www.larusmiani.it

Via Verri 10   **02-7600 6957**
20121 Milan   Mon-Sat 10-7:30, Sun 10:30-1:45, 2:45-7

☆ La Vetrina di Beryl

For nearly 20 years, Barbara di Beryl and her brother Norman have presided as the reigning couple of the hottest shoe kingdom in Milan. Di Beryl, herself an accomplished shoe designer, is known to make special requests and even design changes before buying from the world's most exclusive cobblers. The result is a window filled with only the best, most creative foot candy from Alain Tondowski, Pierre Hardy, Costume National, Michel Perry, Marni, Marc Jacobs, Miu Miu and Prada. In the back room there's a mixed bag of one-off vintage pieces, unique—and wildly costly—handmade shoes by Paul Harnden, as well as a strong showing of ethnic clothing and accessories from Indonesia and Afghanistan.

Via Statuto 4   **02-654 278**
20121 Milan   Mon 3-7:30, Tues-Sat 10:30-7:30

Les Copains

For sexy knitwear with seasonal twists, look no further than Italian label Les Copains. Both lines, the classic Les Copains and the more fashion-forward Trend Les Copains, are spun from beautiful wools, cashmeres and silk blends, creating sweater looks in nearly every incarnation. The mix is always eccentric in this brightly lit store, providing vampy evening options next to non-statement tailored sportswear. Undoubtedly, you'll walk away with a great V-neck something. For guys, the offering is less fashion-oriented, but a crisp polo or a wool sweater can't be beat. There is a slight lack of coherency, but the very fair prices make small sins forgivable.

Via Manzoni 21   **02-7208 0092**
20121 Milan   Mon 3-7 Tues Sat 10-7

Le Solferine

If Milan's main streets are known for one thing, it's the staggering number of women's shoe stores. Add this one to the list. Towering stilettos, simple slingbacks, funky sandals and cool boots abound from such names as Jimmy Choo, Emilio Pucci and Rene Caovilla. The stock is predominantly for women though you may spot the occasional men's shoe and there are a few leather clothes.   www.lesolferine.com

Via Solferino 2   **02-655 5352**
20121 Milan   Mon 3:30-7:30, Tues-Sat 10-7:30

Via Meravigli 16   **02-7200 4433**
20123 Milan   Mon 3-7:30, Tues-Sat 10:30-2, 3-7:30

Levi's

It's the classic American denim label that never seems to go entirely out of style. Maybe it's because they're always the first to revolutionize a new method of fading, a new place for a pocket or a cool new way to taper a leg. From 501s to Twisted you'll find all variety of jeans here, as well as skirts, jackets and sporty tees.   www.levi.com

Via Silvio Pellico 6   **02-8646 4609**
20121 Milan   Mon 3:30-7:30, Tues-Sat 10-7:30

Lorella Braglia

Soft, subtle touches and the occasional departure from standard tailoring make this womenswear collection very feminine and very chic. A pleat in a jacket, a tuck in a skirt...odd, unexpected details convey a sense of originality. Braglia's clothing is manufactured by Dielle, a knitwear company she founded in the mid-Eighties before starting to design her own ready-to-wear.   www.lorellabraglia.com

Via Solferino (corner of Via Ancona)   **02-2901 4514**
20121 Milan   Mon 3:30-7:30, Tues-Thurs 10-2, 3:30-7:30
                                                Fri-Sat 10-7:30

Lorenzo Banfi

Sylvester Stallone, Harrison Ford, Eddie Murphy, Tom Cruise...some of Hollywood's most lusted-after have slipped into a pair of Lorenzo Banfi's handmade loafers, lace-ups or ankle boots. You'll find plenty of head shots downstairs in the Via Spiga store, along with the shoes, briefcases and a small selection of knitwear. Banfi also has a few loafers for women.   www.lorenzobanfi.it

Via della Spiga 42   **02-7601 4011**
20121 Milan   Mon 3-7, Tues-Sat 10-1, 2-7

Via Montenapoleone 10   **02-7601 3710**
20121 Milan   (opening times as above)

Loro Piana

For generations the Loro Piana family has been producing fine men's suits, beautiful blankets and the softest sweaters and scarves. The name is known for their lovely raw materials—from cashmere to vicuña wool—and highly skilled handiwork. Their made-to-measure suits are top-notch, and come with prices to match.

Via Montenapoleone 27   **02-777 2901**
20121 Milan   Mon-Sat 10-7

Louis Vuitton

No matter the city, no matter the day, there never ceases to be a label-hungry crowd lingering at Louis Vuitton. The classic luggage, wallets and handbags are the biggest draw, but much has been made in recent seasons of Marc Jacobs' ready-to-wear. Fall brings another round of sophisticated ladylike luxurywear—silk camisoles and embellished, beaded dresses, eveningwear trimmed in sequins and fur, and square-toed shoes with cylindrical attachments. Even if you can't afford to buy, it's lovely to look at.   www.vuitton.com

Via Montenapoleone 2   **02-777 1711**
20121 Milan   Daily 9:30-7:30 (Sun 11-7:30)

Luisa Beccaria

Designer Luisa Beccaria would seem to lead a very charmed life indeed, retreating when she pleases from the hustle and bustle of Milan to her family's Sicilian estate. No wonder her clothing reverberates with romanticism, from exquisite tailleurs to flowing dresses to a selection of bridal gowns. There is also an adorable selection for children.

Via Formentini 1   **02-8646 0018**
20121 Milan   Mon 3-7, Tues-Sat 10-7

Luisa Spagnoli

Here's a name to remember if you struggle to find fashionable clothing to fit the fuller figure. Sizes here begin at an Italian size 42 (American size 8) and go up to about 52. Spagnoli has revamped its look recently and has a bit more attitude. You'll see some very sexy pieces in the shop windows, along with slightly ethnic get-ups.

Corso Vittorio Emanuele II   **02-795 064**
(corner of Galleria San Carlo)   Mon 3-7:30
20122 Milan   Tues-Sat 10-7:30

Milan Directory

Corso Buenos Aires 39 **02-2953 7033**
20124 Milan (opening times as above)

Malo

Malo's bright and cheery store is a key destination for luxurious cashmere sweaters so soft you'll want to sleep in them. Lovely accessories like scarves and gloves are also available in a rainbow of colors, along with an expanding ready-to-wear collection.

Via della Spiga 7 **02-7601 6109**
20121 Milan Mon-Sat 10-7

Mancadori

Mancadori's philosophy is simple: use natural fibers to maximum effect. This means cotton and viscose in summer and wool and cashmere in winter for their appealing collection of sweaters, tops and twinsets. Look for cashmere gloves as the days grow shorter.

Via Montenapoleone 1 **02-7600 0031**
20121 Milan Mon 3-7, Tues-Sat 10-7

Mandarina Duck

Durable high-tech fabrics provide the raw material for Mandarina Duck's modern selection of luggage, rucksacks, briefcases, messenger bags and wallets. They're also the foundation for the men's and women's sportswear; watches and other assorted accessories are also on hand. www.mandarinaduck.com

Galleria San Carlo (Corso Europa) **02-782 210**
20122 Milan Mon 3-7:30, Tues-Sat 10-7:30

Mariella Burani

Women who covet the seductive glamour of historic Hollywood—think Rita Hayworth and Marilyn Monroe—will find plenty of romantic dresses, lovely skirts and smart tailored jackets, all designed by Mariella herself. Some of the selection is sheer and lacy, cut short or with strategically placed slits which reveal perhaps a bit more flesh than might have been prudent in the past. For more classic tastes, Burani also knows how to leave a little more to the imagination. www.mariellaburani.it

Via Montenapoleone 3 **02-7600 3382**
20121 Milan Mon 3-7, Tues-Sat 10-7

Marilene

When you're sick and tired of dropping boatloads of dough at Prada and Gucci for a flavor-of-the-minute shoe, make a beeline for this multi-brand footwear store where rapid-fire trends explode and prices barely make a peep. The window boasts a wide selection of seasonal pumps and sandals, but head downstairs in the Vittorio Emanuele flagship for a full oasis offering. Somehow this store manages to cater to women of all ages and styles, drawing them in with high-quality, up-to-the-minute looks that have enough of their own personality not to be labeled dreaded knock-offs.

Corso Vittorio Emanuele II 15	**02-7600 0665**
20122 Milan	Mon 3:30-7:30, Tues-Sat 10-7:30
Via Torino 13	**02- 8646 0732**
20123 Milan	Mon 3-7:30, Tues-Sat 10-7:30
Corso Buenos Aires 25	**02-201 251**
20124 Milan	(opening times as above)

Marina Rinaldi

For those who need more breathing room than most Italian fashion affords, the Marina Rinaldi collection starts at an American size 12. Part of the MaxMara empire, the Rinaldi aesthetic is similarly classic: suits, knits, and tailored basics for day with some bolder bits for the evening and a sporty selection of casualwear—appealing to a demographic that is typically thirty plus. Pretty shoes and handbags are also available. (The Galleria Passarella address is actually on the main Corso Vittorio Emanuele.)

Galleria Passarella 2	**02-782 065**
20122 Milan	Mon 2-7:30, Tues-Sat 10-7:30
Corso Buenos Aires 77	**02-669 2691**
20124 Milan	Mon 3:30-7:30, Tues-Sat 10-1, 3:30-7:30

Marisa

Marisa Lombardi is one of the few long-reigning dames of Milanese retail. Although she's no longer a spring chicken at the crest of the fashion food chain, her multi-brand stores continue to churn out cutting-edge fashion for mature chic ladies. After decades in the business Marisa still maintains a healthy roster of top international designers, but she's edited out all the absurd skirt lengths and skin-tight ensembles that are best left to young things. Sant' Andrea houses the most edgy and experimental brands like Issey Miyake, Commes des Garçons and Balenciaga. The boutique in Via della Spiga, on the other hand, takes a trip down country roads offering earthy and more casual fare by several smaller designers.

Via Sant' Andrea 10a	**02-7600 0905**
20121 Milan	Mon 2:30-7, Tues-Sat 10-1:30, 3-7
Via Sant' Andrea 1	**02-7600 1416**
20121 Milan	(opening times as above)
Via Della Spiga 52	**02-7600 2082**
20121 Milan	(opening times as above)

Marni

Designer Consuelo Castiglioni was doing vintage-inspired looks and bohemian romance before it was chic again. Every fashion house has toyed with the gypsy theme, but at Marni it's the thread for every season. Breezy peasant blouses, chiffon scarves, floral dresses and patchwork coats capture an old-fashioned flavor. Accessories like Forties-style pumps, knit hats and bohemian handbags are also available.

Via Sant' Andrea 14	**02-7631 7327**
20121 Milan	Mon-Sat 10-7

Martin Luciano

Feeling a hard-core military moment coming on? Or maybe you just forgot to pack your cargo pants for an afternoon stroll along the navigli. Whatever the trigger for your camo-craving, this warehouse filled with vintage duds from the authentic reserves of Italian, American and German armed forces is sure to provide the fix. Located along one of Milan's canals, the giant space offers wall-to-wall stalls of flight suits, bomber jackets, trench-style coats, padded sweaters—some battered and abused, others hauled out of storage in spanking new condition. Best is the large variety of great-fitting fatigues and cargoes. There's enough product here to put an entire brigade back in the trenches—or send a fashion-hungry pack off in ruggedly authentic style. For tried and true classics, the front room also offers a decent selection of used and new jeans by Levi's and Wrangler.

Alazaia Naviglio Grande 58　　　　　　**02-5810 1173**
20143 Milan　　　　　　　　Tues-Sat 9-12:30, 3:30-7:30

Martino Midali

Richly textured knitwear and comfortable clothing are featured in Martino Midali's boutiques. The Milanese designer offers tailored and more casual clothing under the Midali Toujours label and although the roomier styles are not meant to be maternitywear per se, women who are expecting might find a few pieces to keep them comfortably in fashion.

Corso di Porta Ticinese 60　　　　　　**02-8940 6830**
20123 Milan　　　　　　Mon 3:30-7:30, Tues-Sat 10-7:30

Ponte Vetero 9　　　　　　　　　　**02-8646 2707**
20121 Milan　　　　　　Mon 3-7:30, Tues-Sat 10-2, 3-7:30

MaxMara

This Italian group has cornered the market in wearable designer clothing at a notch below designer prices. They are a good source for classic jackets, pants, skirts and knits, and also cover the field from casualwear to elegant evening clothes. Right next to the main store, a younger, trendier crowd heads for a second outlet and the Max & Co line.

Piazza del Liberty 4　　　　　　　　**02-7600 8849**
20121 Milan　　　　　　　　　　　Mon-Sat 10-7:30

Piazza del Liberty 4 (Max & Co)　　　　**02-780 433**
20121 Milan　　　　　　　　(opening times as above)

Missoni

The Missonis, first Ottavio and Rosita and now their daughter Angela, have gained fame for creating unique, boldly-colored, zig-zag knits. Here you'll find plenty of the geometric patterns vibrating off sweaters, skirts, dresses and bikinis and housewares like platters, blankets and pillows.　　　　　　　　　　www.missoni.it

Via Sant' Andrea 2　　　　　　　　**02-7600 3555**
20121 Milan　　　　　　　　Mon 3-7, Tues-Sat 10-7

Miu Miu

More whimsical than big sister Prada, Miuccia's Miu Miu collection has a sense of play expressed in cuts to suit the best body types and in a bevy of bright colors. Despite a selection of childish styles—khaki culottes with purple patch pockets, corduroy coats, halter romper-suits and bright yellow boots—the clothing looks sleek rather than silly, though much depends on the wearer. Men should head to the back of the store for mod minimalist suits and black ankle boots. www.miumiu.it

Corso Venezia 3   **02-7600 1799**
20121 Milan   Mon-Sat 10-7:30

Mortarotti

From the outside, it looks like a quaint townhouse, but inside you'll find one of the few Montenapoleone multi-brand stores, with clothing, shoes and accessories from such labels as Gérard Darel, Hugo Boss, Gianfranco Ferré and Cavalli. The names may be high-designer but the selection is pleasantly subdued, with a style sensibility that's just this side of conservative. You're liable to find some lovely options for everyday and special occasions.

Via Montenapoleone 24   **02-7600 3839**
20121 Milan   Mon 3-7:30, Tues-Sat 10-7:30

Corso Magenta 29   **02-8645 2253**
20123 Milan   Mon 3:15-7, Tues-Sat 10-7

Moschino

This playful Italian label likes to deliver sexy womenswear with a wink. Fall's coquettish selection includes short tailored jackets, wool pants, knit tops, flippy skirts and Thirties-style satin evening dresses. The Via Spiga location also carries the Moschino Cheap & Chic collection, featuring cute baby-doll dresses and pretty overcoats. Follow the red carpet downstairs to find Moschino jeans, menswear, childrenswear and lingerie. Via Sant' Andrea has only the women's signature collection. www.moschino.it

Via della Spiga 30   **02-7600 4320**
20121 Milan   Mon-Sat 10-7

Via Sant' Andrea 12   **02-7600 0832**
20121 Milan   (opening times as above)

Nadine

Style-savvy thirtysomethings come to Nadine for fashionable wardrobe staples, from the indispensable pair of black pants to that tailored jacket you'll wear every week, with a few sexy extras like form-fitting stretch pullover tops thrown in. Prices are mid-range.

Corso Vittorio Emanuele II 34   **02-7600 9028**
20122 Milan   Daily 9:30-8

Corso Buenos Aires 38   **02-2024 1642**
20124 Milan   Mon-Sat 9:30-7:30, Sun 1-7:30

Naj-Oleari

Way back when, Naj-Oleari was a top brand name with its own stores dedicated to its earthy, feminine wares. We're not exactly sure what caused its fall from the fashion radar, but this store in Via Brera has been transformed to sell a hodge-podge of clothing, accessories and novelty items, all in the brand's original bohemian spirit. It's now almost entirely dedicated to the French bohemian line Antik Batique and is one of the few places in town to carry that flirty label. They've got colorful, ethnic-looking jackets, billowing blouses, piles of Japanese stationery, the complete assortment of Moleskine notebooks and a children's clothing section—almost all French labels—that is cute as pie.   www.najoleari.com

Via Brera 8   **02-805 6790**
20121 Milan   Mon 3-8, Tues-Sat 10-8

Napapijri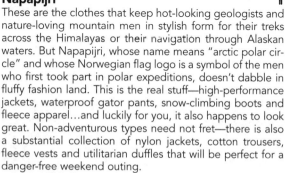

These are the clothes that keep hot-looking geologists and nature-loving mountain men in stylish form for their treks across the Himalayas or their navigation through Alaskan waters. But Napapijri, whose name means "arctic polar circle" and whose Norwegian flag logo is a symbol of the men who first took part in polar expeditions, doesn't dabble in fluffy fashion land. This is the real stuff—high-performance jackets, waterproof gator pants, snow-climbing boots and fleece apparel…and luckily for you, it also happens to look great. Non-adventurous types need not fret—there is also a substantial collection of nylon jackets, cotton trousers, fleece vests and utilitarian duffles that will be perfect for a danger-free weekend outing.

Via Manzoni 46   **02-782 413**
Milan 20121   Mon-Sat 10-7

Narciso Rodriguez

He's been on the fashion radar for some time but is best known for designing the late Carolyn Bessette's wedding dress. With a design education that includes stints at Calvin Klein, Cerruti and Loewe, Rodriguez has cultivated a collection that tends towards chic minimalism. You're likely to find tailored trousers, silky blouses, pencil skirts and lightly embellished satin dresses for evening. Colors are generally neutral and styles fashionably restrained.   www.narcisorodriguez.com

Via Montenapoleone 21   **02-7631 7072**
20121 Milan   Mon 3-7, Tues-Sat 10-7

No Season

This lifestyle emporium for modern urbanites has a selection of music (lounge, house and garage), books (fashion, design and photography), as well as plenty of clothes, shoes and accessories. Fashion comes courtesy of high designers like Jean Paul Gaultier, Antonio Berardi, Vivienne Westwood and Helmut Lang, plus plenty of sporty brands like Adidas, Nike and Puma that never seem to go out of style.   www.noseason.com

Corso di Porta Ticinese 77   **02-8942 3332**
20123 Milan   Mon 3-8, Tues-Sat 10:30-1, 3-8

Onyx Fashion Store

One of Milan's hot spots for trendy teenage girls, Onyx features jeans, sweats, skirts and tube tops for fashionistas-in-training and tomboys alike. The latest style in backpacks, thongs, handbags and loads of other accessories that any 15-year-old would flip for are also on hand. There is also a younger section for the 5-11 set.

Corso Vittorio Emanuele II 24   **02-7601 6083**
20122 Milan   Mon-Thurs 10:30-7:30, Fri-Sat 10:30-8
Sun 12-8

Via Torino 2   **02-8909 5140**
20123 Milan   Mon 3-7:30, Tues-Sat 10:30-7:30
Sun 3-7:30

Patrizia Pepe

The up-to-the-minute styles at this Florentine company strike nearly every hit seen on ready-to-wear runways plus some new ones you never thought possible. Whatever is hot for the season—a feminine dress, a sharp trouser, the perfect belt, a slouchy sweater—you can count on finding a morphed version of it here, but at a price which is head and shoulders below designer level. This may be knock-off territory, but you'll find none of the usual mass-market mayhem. The vibe is distinctively cool and the spacious store staffed by a friendly bunch ready to whip you into this season's trends.

Via Manzoni 38   **02-7601 4477**
20121 Milan   Mon-Sat 10-7:30

Paul & Shark

This Italian label specializes in hi-tech sailing clothes, using its own sailing team to test the designs for seaworthiness under the harshest conditions. But landlovers will also find plenty to please, including pullovers, windbreakers, jackets, turtlenecks and corduroy pants.   www.paulshark.it

Via Montenapoleone 15   **02-7600 8565**
20121 Milan   Mon 3-7, Tues-Sat 10-7

☆ Paul Smith

Irreverent British designer Sir Paul Smith has enlivened Via Manzoni with his retro-spirited boutique designed by Sophie Hicks. Every collection is a cocktail of colorful kitsch and classic English tailoring, with plenty of playful patterns served straight up. In addition to men's and women's ready-to-wear, you'll find shoes, underwear, swimwear, cufflinks and ties, plus a small section for children.   www.paulsmith.co.uk

Via Manzoni 30   **02-7631 9181**
20121 Milan   Mon-Sat 10-7

P-Box

Visions of a high-class stroll in perfectly dainty heels will dance in your head after an obligatory visit to this store created by Italian clothing manufacturer Aeffe. It's one big hot box for Aeffe labels' shoes and bags, all produced by legendary leather goods maker, Pollini. Besides the impeccably crafted, classic Pollini pumps, you'll get a flirty dose of Alberta Ferretti and Philosophy's strappy sandals, an irreverent kick from Moschino's creative designs and plenty of sexy, mile-high slingbacks by Narciso Rodriguez, the new poster boy of minimalism. High-end product placed sparsely around the dark room creates a moody, artistic ambiance which makes dropping piles of cash a calming, almost zen-like experience.

Via Manzoni 13   **02-8901 3000**
20121 Milan   Mon 3:30-7:30, Tues-Sat 10-7:30

Via Pontaccio 19   **02-8646 4991**
20121 Milan   (opening times as above)

☆ Pineider

Walking into the Pineider store is like taking a trip to your rich auntie's cozy château in the countryside—pure bliss. Designer Rebecca Moses has waved her magic creative wand and cast a fabulous spell over this historic Italian stationery company which dates from the 18th century. The precious papers, hallmarks of the brand, still line the walls in their pristine glory, but Moses has added a complete lifestyle collection, including leather goods and homeware, which is irresistibly charming and chic. An afternoon winding through the charming nooks and crannies of the three-story building, Pineider's very first refreshed concept store, is an exercise in pure delight.

Via Manzoni 20   **02-7639 4680**
20121 Milan   Mon 3:30-7:30, Tues-Sat 10-7:30

Piombo

If you didn't know any better, you would walk right past this gem of a store tucked down an inconspicuous alley off of Via della Spiga, but take our advice and drag your boyfriend here immediately. What lies behind the somewhat perplexing entrance is an explosion of color, pattern and creativity, a testament to Massimo Piombo's flamboyant flair and his friendship with fellow fashion colorist Sir Paul Smith. A full wardrobe for a fashionable guy's busy calendar—chic wool suits, hip cotton printed shirts, faded cotton jackets and pants—is on display throughout the maze of yellow-carpeted art deco rooms. The workmanship is evident on every piece and, best of all, most garments are made from fabrics whose wild originality can't be beat. Piombo cuts his striped suits and patterned sweaters slim and sleek, so linebackers and muscle buffs will have to settle for originality with one of the zany retro-inspired ties.

Via della Spiga 34   **02-7631 8902**
20121 Milan   Mon-Sat 10-1, 2-7

Plus

Just a step from the Piazza Duomo, women will find a very wearable medley of up-to-date (but not imminently outdated) tailleurs, separates and knits. The idea is to be both in style and at ease. Philosophy by Alberta Ferretti and Strenesse are among the labels you may expect to find.

Piazza Missori 2   **02-8646 1820**
20121 Milan   Mon 3-7, Tues-Sat 10-7

Pollini

With over 100 years of cobbling practice, the Pollini family knows a thing or two about stitching a well-crafted shoe. The highly polished footwear and leather goods are churned out after a painstaking process of modeling, cutting, stitching and hand-finishing high-grade leather hides in the Pollini factories in the Emilia Romagna region. The result is top quality and the prices tend to swing right along. Some of the styles tiptoe towards fashion-forward, but the majority are in the safe zone which helps Italy's well-heeled, conservative set—men and women—maintain their style status quo.

Piazza Duomo 31   **02-875 187**
20121 Milan   Mon 2:30-7:30, Tues-Sat 10-7:30

Corso Vittorio Emanuele II 30   **02-794 912**
20122 Milan   (opening times as above)

☆ Prada

The fashion editors' anointed one for more than a decade, it's no wonder Prada is a prominent presence in Milan's fashion triangle. From the black nylon bags that swept the style pages of the early Nineties to today's satin lingerie-inspired eveningwear, Miuccia Prada never seems to stop setting trends. Along with men's and women's ready-to-wear, you'll find plenty of the coveted shoes, handbags and wallets as well as the skincare collection. Prada sportswear is available at the Sant' Andrea location. www.prada.com

Via Montenapoleone 8 (women)   **02-777 1771**
20121 Milan   Mon-Sat 10-7:30

Via Montenapoleone 6 (men)   **02-7602 0273**
20121 Milan   (opening times as above)

Via della Spiga 1 (accessories)   **02-7600 2019**
20121 Milan   (opening times as above)

Via della Spiga 5 (lingerie)   **02-7601 4448**
20121 Milan   (opening times as above)

Via Sant' Andrea 21 (sportswear)   **02-7600 1426**
20121 Milan   (opening times as above)

Galleria Vittorio Emanuele II 63-65   **02-876 979**
20121 Milan   (opening times as above)

ProMod

It's been described as a supermarket of fashion, but the store also stands out for the relative durability of its designs. The two Milan locations of this French chain are good sources for clothing that will last longer than a single season, from suits and dresses to more casual everydaywear. www.promod.com

Milan Directory

Via Mazzini 2   **02-8901 4745**
20123 Milan   Daily 10-8 (Sun 3-8)

Corso Buenos Aires 41   **02-2952 0575**
20124 Milan   Daily 9:30-8 (Sun 10-8)

Purple

It may sit opposite the columns of San Lorenzo, Milan's anointed gathering place for scruffy teen drop-outs, but only the most stylish of the nose and lip-pierced crowd venture into this store. Here, they stock up on Fake London shirts and jackets, studded belts, limited-edition Adidas accessories and hard core D&G pieces. It's one of the city's few spots that offer a healthy mix of underground, smaller design labels, which is refreshing. The staff come rigged with spiked hair and combat boots, but you'll find none of the pomp or attitude that is obligatory in the boutiques which line the luxury thoroughfares.

Corso di Porta Ticinese 22   **02-8942 4476**
20122 Milan   Mon 3:30-7:30
                              Tues-Sat 10:30-1:30, 3:30-7:30

Ralph Lauren

Across the Atlantic he may have to share the limelight with the likes of Calvin and Donna, but here in Italy Ralph's reign as the king of American casualwear goes undisputed. The Milanese are so gaga, they nearly genuflect before the logo'd merchandise that epitomizes preppy chic laced with old-world aristocracy. This store, due to open late this year, will be Lauren's first freestanding venture in Italy. The locals were drooling for months in anticipation of the four floors filled with sporty prepster classics ablaze with American flags and polo shirt tailoring. With the complete offering of Ralph's luxury apparel and accessories, including all the top labels and the coveted home line, no one will be going back to the casa empty-handed.   www.polo.com

Via Montenapoleone 4   **n/a at press time**
20121 Milan

Replay

Replay is considered one of the leaders in Italian street style. The store's layout is innovative, with wide punctured-metal stairs and a pebble-covered floor. The collection features Italian denim in a variety of sizes, shapes and styles, with tanks, sweatshirts and other casual tops to match. You'll also find skirts, minis, jean jackets and more, but prices are a bit high for streetwear.   www.replay.it

Largo Corsia dei Servi 11   **02-7631 0196**
20122 Milan   Mon 3-7:30, Tues-Sat 10-7:30

Roberto Cavalli

Who wants to marry a millionaire? The same lady who covets Cavalli's snakeskin pants, white to-the-floor fur coats, and sexy evening dresses splashed with his animal prints. Never one for understated style, Cavalli extends his reputation for excess to a rich range of shoes and accessories and a home collection.   www.robertocavalli.net

Via della Spiga 42   **02-7602 0900**
20121 Milan   Mon 3-7, Tues-Sat 10-7

Romeo Gigli
Unbuttoned types will find alternatives to basic business
attire at Romeo Gigli, where splashes of color and imagina-
tive patterns abound. Among the selection are bright
patchwork and pinstripe suits, Thirties-style bias-cut dresses and velvety green coats.   www.romeogigli.it

Via della Spiga 30   **02-7601 1983**
20121 Milan   Mon-Sat 10-2, 3-7

Ruffo
When the world's top fashion houses demand your leather
hides for their exclusive product, you know you're the
industry's gold standard. But Ruffo, who counts Prada and
Dolce & Gabbana among clients, also has its own clothing
label to boast its high-quality hides. The brand's mastery of
highly innovative leather techniques—they pleat it, burn it,
wash it, smash it and transform it into inconceivable
states—used to be on display with the niche Ruffo Research
line. Now that that line has been suspended, the company
is bringing all its out-of-the-box leather brainpower to the
main Ruffo line which offers a wide variety of sporty clothing and accessories. A funky edge is given to the women's
line with suede sweatsuits, metallic motorcycle jackets and
reversible leather shirts, while the men's line veers towards
classic territory. Sprinkled throughout both mixes are non-
leather pieces like cotton shirts and knit sweaters.

Via della Spiga 48   **02-7601 5523**
20121 Milan   Mon 3-7, Tues-Sat 10-7

☆ Salvagente/Salvagente Bimbo
Inconspicuously located in a residential block off the main
fashion track, Salvagente is perhaps Milan's most famous
designer discount store. It might take some rummaging
through the racks of suits, dresses, sweaters, pants and
skirts, but most people find something to take home. At
Salvagente Bimbo about ten blocks away the same concept
is applied to babies' and kids' clothes.

Salvagente   **02-7611 0328**
Via Fratelli Bronzetti 16   Mon 3-7
20129 Milan   Tues, Thurs-Fri 10-12:30, 3-7, Wed, Sat 10-7

Salvagente Bimbo   **02-2668 0764**
Via Balzaretti 28   Mon 3-7, Tues, Thurs-Sat 10-1, 3-7
20133 Milan   Wed 10-7

Salvatore Ferragamo
Long a symbol of the very highest style in leather goods
and accessories, the venerable fashion house is now
expanding its ready-to-wear. The women's location also
has ties and a few gift items for men, so you might save
yourself a trip to the men's shop at the other end of
Montenapo.   www.ferragamo.com

Via Montenapoleone 3 (women)   **02-7600 0054**
20121 Milan   Mon 3-7, Tues-Sat 10-7

Via Montenapoleone 20 (men)   **02-7600 6660**
20121 Milan   (opening times as above)

Samsonite

This sleepy American luggage company made an impressive cool-factor recovery in 2000 when it re-launched the brand and annihilated its boring-as-beige image. With a super-sleek line of accessories and travel-inspired clothing, Samsonite made Sixties "flight attendant chic" something to talk about. Although some of the initial buzz has died down, there are still plenty of high-quality creative finds for a globetrotting fashion nomad in this store. In addition to the tried and true luggage—including the indispensable stainless steel trolley—there are streamlined sporty clothes for guys and girls on the run.

Corso Matteotti 12   **02-7602 0264**
20121 Milan   Mon 3-7:30, Tues-Sat 10-7:30

Sergio Rossi

Women with a soft spot for sexy stilettos have been known to lose all control at Sergio Rossi. Gucci creative director Tom Ford and chief executive Domenico De Sole were themselves seduced back in 1999 when they added this Italian footwear label to the group's stable. Now it's not just required shopping for female foot aficionados. Rossi has just opened its first men's store a few doors down from the Via della Spiga location, where the slip-ons are butter-soft, the lace-ups panther-sleek and the designs couldn't be cooler.   www.sergiorossi.com

Via della Spiga 15   **02-7600 2663**
20121 Milan   Mon 3-7, Tues-Sat 10-7

Via Montenapoleone 6a   **02-7600 6140**
20121 Milan   (opening times as above)

Via della Spiga 5 (men)   **02-7639 0927**
20121 Milan   (opening times as above)

Sermoneta Gloves

A good source of leather gloves (and other accessories), whether you want the classic driving type or cozy lined styles for winter. One of the most affordable stores on the fashion triangle.

Via della Spiga 46   **02-7631 8303**
20121 Milan   Mon-Sat 10-7

Shabby Chic

It's neither super-shabby nor super-chic, but this vintage store is worth a trip just for its terrific selection of Burberry trenches and cashmere sweaters. The brightly lit, well kept nook is another plus, although you won't find any high-end designer hits in the neat piles of pastel Lacoste or along the racks of Fifties-style floral skirts. It's simple and cute, and it's right next to one of the best fish restaurants in the city, Da Giacamo. So you can shop cheaply and spend the money right before taking in a salt-crusted branzino. www.shabby.it

Via B. Cellini 21   **02-7601 8149**
20129 Milan   Mon 3-7:30, Tues-Sat 10:30-7:30

Simonetta Ravizza   ♀

If you make it to the top of the beautiful white staircase you'll be rewarded with Simonetta Ravizza's designer furs. Mink, sable and chinchilla come in small doses on jacket trim or full-strength in long, luxurious coats. www.annabella.it/simonetta

Via Montenapoleone 1   **02-7601 2921**
20121 Milan   Mon 3-7, Tues-Sat 10-1:30, 2:30-7

Sisley   ♂♀

Sisley began back in 1968 as a Parisian denim manufacturer before being acquired by Benetton in 1974. Known in particular for their knitwear, they are also a source of classic casual and sportswear for the young of both sexes, and the selection occasionally spills over into business basics and the odd bit of eveningwear. The Dogana location is their latest outlet, a megastore by the Piazza Duomo.   www.sisley.com

Galleria Passarella 1   **02-763 881**
20122 Milan   Daily 10-8

Corso Buenos Aires 3   **02-204 6446**
20124 Milan   Mon 12-8, Tues-Sat 10-8

Via Dogana 4   **02-763 881**
20123 Milan   Daily 10-8

Sportmax   ♀

Each and every season Sportmax takes its trend-savvy customer on a rocking road trip through fashion's best fantasyland and yet still manages to pull together a collection of highly wearable clothing. The label, if you haven't made the connection, is the swinging little sister brand to the older and more uptight MaxMara. It's fun, it's light, and it's affordable. The young ladies who flock to this store all relish the denim line, the funky shoes and accessories and the sexy evening pieces. And, lucky for you, Milan is the only city in the world with a freestanding store fully dedicated to the fashion frenzy.

Via della Spiga 30   **02-7601 1944**
20121 Milan   Mon-Sat 10-7:30

Stefanel   ♂♀

Once a small knitwear company, Stefanel has matured into a major force in Italy's mid-range casualwear market. Knitwear remains the core business but you'll also find denim jeans and leather coats. The look is generally young, with a nod to the latest trends, but styles tend not to stray too far from the classics.   www.stefanel.it

Corso Vittorio Emanuele II 28   **02-7631 8722**
20122 Milan   Mon-Sat 10-8, Sun 10-2, 3-8

Via Spadari 1   **02-809 279**
20123 Milan   Mon 1:30-8, Tues-Sat 10-8, Sun 3-7

Strenesse

German designer Gabrielle Strehle is as rigorous with her pared-down designs as she is with the bare bones architecture of this Milan store. Raw wood and cement give the space an industrial feel, playing off the absolute simplicity of the clothes. Strehle's a purist by heart and an intellectual by head. One look at the clean lines on men's and women's suits, the relaxed cut of the pants and the simplicity of flowing dresses and you'll see that selling sex is not on her agenda. There are good finds, but summertime shoppers beware—the walls of this deconstructed store generate more heat than a greenhouse, creating a steamy oven in summer months.

Via Manzoni 37   **02-657 2401**
20121 Milan   Mon-Fri 10-2, 3-7, Sat 10-7

Taboo

Somehow this shop manages to convey a feeling of faraway lands, though the designers on display are 100% homegrown. Quirky new collections from Kristina Ti can be found here, along with raku ceramics, candles and a selection of jewelry. Fun fashion and a little bit more.

Piazza Generale Cantore 3   **02-837 3814**
20123 Milan   Mon 3-7:30, Tues-Sat 10-1, 3-7:30

Tanino Crisci

This family-owned firm has its roots in riding boots, as the mounted-horse logo might suggest, but there are also plenty of shoes to choose from including wingtip pumps and classic loafers. And you'll find a full range of accessories—scarves, ties, belts, bags and briefcases.   www.taninocrisci.com

Via Montenapoleone 3   **02-7602 1264**
20121 Milan   Mon 3-7, Tues-Sat 10-2, 3-7

☆ Tim Camino

With its downtown cool, vintage vibe and mix-matched philosophy, Tim Camino's shop would fit in much better in Nolita than in Milan but the misplaced geography is helping many a local girl with her hard to find hip-fix. Cropped pants, shredded or patchwork skirts and oversized velvet driver hats are constant fixtures. The staff look permanently dazed but don't take their slackish attitude for lack of interest. They're just mellow and will be more than pleased to help you dig for your size in Camino's cult-style jeans, a patchwork skirt, or the perfect shade of their retro washed-twill jackets.

Via de Amicis 3   **02-836 0124**
20123 Milan   Mon 3:30-7:30, Tues-Sat 10-7:30

Tod's

Their handstitched leather moccasins are a stylish staple for any shoe closet. Ferrari fans can also go for the red Ferrari driving shoes with Tod's trademark pebbled soles. A few high heels are also available, as well as a Junior Tod's collection for kids. Beautiful leather bags are another draw. www.tods.com

| **Via della Spiga 22** | **02-7600 2423** |
| 20121 Milan | Mon-Sat 10-7 |

Trussardi

Now at the helm of her family's leather-based fashion company, Beatrice Trussardi is blossoming creatively and zooming ahead with her own feminine style. For women, that means loads of color on the girly, playful clothes and plenty of trinkets on the top-notch leather accessories. Men will find a modern take on the natty dresser in pin-striped trousers, smoking jackets and tailored waistcoats. The boutique next to La Scala is a Trussardi lifestyle store: there's the ready-to-wear, a large cache of accessories on the ground floor and a restaurant and café upstairs. The more casual Trussardi Jeans and Sportswear collections are at the Galleria Strasburgo store on the corner of Via Durini.   www.trussardi.it

| **Piazza della Scala 5** | **02-8068 8242** |
| 20121 Milan | Mon-Sat 10-7 |

| **Via Sant' Andrea 3 (women)** | **02-7602 0380** |
| 20121 Milan | Mon-Sat 10-7 |

| **Via Sant' Andrea 5 (men)** | **02-7602 0380** |
| 20121 Milan | Mon-Sat 10-7 |

| **Galleria Strasburgo 3** | **02-7601 1313** |
| 20121 Milan | Mon 3-7, Tues-Sat 10-2, 3-7 |

Valentino

The name is synonymous with timeless luxury…tweed and camel suits, delicate silk blouses, gold sequined evening gowns and coats trimmed in fur. There are also plenty of gilded bits here, from boots to belts and bags, and the finest examples of the designer's haute couture actually hang in glass cases. Men will find classic suits and their own selection of accessories.   www.valentino.it

| **Via Montenapoleone 20** | **02-7600 6182** |
| 20121 Milan | Mon-Sat 10-7 |

Valextra

Just utter the word "Valextra" and Italians pause in com-munal tribute, just long enough to give this A-list Milanese brand its rightful respects. A collective breakout of oohs and aahs then follows over the incomparable quality and style of these top-notch leather goods which have been accessorizing Europe's elite since 1937. It's not just the rig-orously clean lines on briefcases, suitcases and overnight bags which make a first-class ticket absolutely obligatory. Valextra's signature cross-hatched leathers, which come in apple red and logan green in addition to more traditional blacks and mahoganies, are so smooth, so delightful, that you'll be petting your purse or wallet more often than your

Milan Directory

mate. Handstitching featuring impeccable seams and Sherlock Holmes-style locks are an added bonus, as well as the made-to-measure service offered at the Via Cerva location. www.valextra.it

Piazza San Babila 1   **02-7600 5024**
20122 Milan   Mon 3-7, Tues-Sat 10-7

Via Cerva 11   **02-760 0103**
21021 Milan   Mon 3-7, Tues-Sat 10-1:30, 2:30-7

☆ Vergelio

This luxury shoe seller offers a wide choice of designer brands—from Tod's to Marc Jacobs to Roberto Cavalli—at its handful of locations in Milan. While brands do overlap between stores, the chicest (and most expensive) selection is found in Vittorio Emanuele, but we'd suggest you head towards Buenos Aires if your aim is to find reasonably priced top-quality shoes. The Buenos Aires store also shares space with Timberland—walk in one side, it's Vergelio; walk through to the other, it's Timberland—so you can also find those walking shoes for trekking round the sights.

Corso Vittorio Emanuele II 10   **02-7600 3087**
20122 Milan   Mon 3-7:30, Tues-Sat 10-7:30

Corso Buenos Aires 9   **02-2940 6272**
20124 Milan   Mon 3-7:30, Tues-Sat 9:30-7:30

Vicini

Giuseppe Zanotti's sequined mules, jeweled evening shoes and satiny stilettos with butterfly appliqués have found a firm footing on the fashion scene. His latest collection is verging on the sadomasochistic with heavily buckled leather straps riding up the leg. There's also a selection of eyewear, bags and belts. Britney's a devotee. www.vicinishoes.com

Via della Spiga 1   **02-7600 2828**
20121 Milan   Mon-Sat 10-7

Vierre

Men and women on the hunt for designer shoes will find a dense population in this pretty Montenapo store: Alain Tondowski, Michel Perry, Roberto Cavalli, Gianni Barbate, Antonio Berardi, Miu Miu, Rene Caovilla, Jil Sander, Giorgio Armani, Costume National and D-Squared are just some examples. Styles range from impossibly high heels to comfortable walking shoes.

Via Montenapoleone 29   **02-7600 1731**
20121 Milan   Mon 3:30-7, Tues-Sat 10-7

Vito Nacci

In a beautiful art deco building just off Piazza San Babila, you'll find this source of stylish fur. The selection includes ready-to-wear and haute couture coats and jackets, along with such accessories as stoles and fur-trimmed winter scarves, gloves and hats. www.vitonacci.it

Via Durini 11   **02-7600 4001**
20122 Milan   Mon 3-7, Tues-Sat 9-1, 3-7

Yves Saint Laurent

The French may have turned up their noses at Tom Ford when he arrived on the scene, but they can't deny the magical effect the American designer has had on their homeland's most classic brand. Since being bought by the Gucci group in 1999, YSL has been transformed from a stylish grandma boutique into a supernova of supreme style. The utterly sophisticated designs are coveted by the chicest of Hollywood icons like Nicole Kidman who regularly wears drop-dead gorgeous YSL gowns for her paparazzi appearances. For the rest of us Ford continues to whip up irresistible suits, great coats and killer heels, all oozing with a deep, dark glamour that is oh-so-French. The entire YSL collection, featuring men's and women's ready-to-wear, watches, eyeglasses, jewelry and shoes, in addition to an enormous selection of hit-list handbags, fills all 850 square metres of this newly renovated store, Europe's largest YSL outpost.

Via Montenapoleone 27   **02-7600 0573**
Milan 20121   Mon-Sat 10-7

☆ Zap!

Beneath giant chandeliers in a funky bazaar-like setting, this multi-brand store offers Anna Sui, Santa Croce, Gaetano Navarro, Holly, Kookaï and many more. There are books, gadgets and even collectors' Barbie dolls. Upstairs you'll find vintage clothing, even including a few very expensive Pucci shirts. There are some children's clothes and an Aldo Coppola hair salon.

Galleria Passarella 2   **02-7606 7501**
20122 Milan Mon 1-7:30, Tues-Sat 10-7:30

☆ Zara

This Spanish chain only landed in Milan two years ago, but judging by the interminable wait for dressing-rooms it has been eagerly received. Always inspired by the latest trends, Zara offers a huge variety of up-to-the-minute shirts, pants, dresses, suits, coats and accessories at knock-off prices. Perfect for capturing a look from the catwalk.   www.zara.com

Corso Vittorio Emanuele II 11   **02-7639 8177**
20122 Milan   Daily 10-8

Zeus

Blumarine, Blugirl, Just Cavalli, Plein Sud and Paola Frani are some of the brands you might find at this trendy boutique, alongside lesser-knowns like local label LCY. Swimwear and lingerie are also available, and styles tend towards the feminine and romantic.

Corso Genova 24   **02-8940 8267**
20123 Milan   Mon 3:30-7:30
   Tues-Sat 9:30-1, 3:30-7:30

Milan Stores by District

Brera / Corso Garibaldi / Corso Como

Corso Buenos Aires

Corso di Porta Ticinese / Corso Genova

Via Montenapoleone & neighborhood

Corso Vittorio Emanuele / Duomo / Via Torino

Corso Vercelli / Magenta

Piazza 5 Giornate and outwards

Milan—City Center

Milan—City Center

ORTO BOTANICO

V. Borgonuovo

V. F.lli Gabba

Monte di Pieta

V. A. Manzoni

Central Station

GIARDINI PUBLICI

V. del Becchio Politecnico

V. Borgospesso

V. S. Spirito

V. della Spiga

V. Gesu

V. Monte Napoleone

Four Seasons

V. Sant'Andrea

Palazzo di Senato

Corso Buenos Aires

V. Bigli

V. P. Verri

V.G.Morone

V. Bagutta

Corso Venezia

Teatro Alla Scala

Corso G. Matteotti

Piazza della Scala

V. Agnello

V. S. Paolo

V. S. Pietro all'Orto

Piazza San Babila

V.Radegonda

Piazza del Liberty

Corso Vittorio Emanuele II

V. Silvio Pellico

Corso Europa

V. Durini

Piazza del Duomo

Duomo

Palazzo del Capitano di Giustizia

Lgo. Augusto

Piazza dei Bersaglieri

Piazza Diaz

V.Paolo da Cannobio

Piazza S. Stefano

V. Larga

V. Francesco Sforza

V. Andreani

Piazza Velasca

Universita

V. S. Barnaba

V. della Commenda

Corso Porta di Romana

Hospital

SCALE in metres

0   100   200   300

Milan Districts

233

Milan—Largo La Foppa

Milan—Corso Buenos Aires

Brera / Corso Garibaldi / Corso Como
See map page 232

2Link	Largo La Foppa 4
2Link Black Label	Via Solferino 46
10 Corso Como	Corso Como 10
Anteprima	Corso Como 9
Antonia & Antonia Accessori	Via Ponte Vetero 1
Bipa	Via Ponte Vetero 10
Cavalli e Nastri	Via Brera 2
Coccinelle	Via Statuto 11
Co-Co	Via Giannone 4
Clan	Via Pontaccio 15
Docks Dora	Viale Crespi 7
Eral 55	Piazza XXV Aprile 14
Julien	Via C.M.Maggi 3
Kristina Ti	Via Solferino 18
La Boule de Neige	Corso Como 3
La Vetrina di Beryl	Via Statuto 4
Le Solferine	Via Solferino 2
Lorella Braglia	Via Solferino (corner of Via Ancona)
Luisa Beccaria	Via Formentini 1
Martino Midali	Via Ponte Vetero 9
Naj-Oleari	Via Brera 8

Corso Buenos Aires *See map page 234*

Avant	Corso Buenos Aires 39
Benetton	Corso Buenos Aires 19
Boggi	Via Caretta 1
Coccinelle	Corso Buenos Aires 16
David Mayer	Corso Buenos Aires 66
Du Pareil Au Même	Corso Buenos Aires 49
Frette	Corso Buenos Aires 82
Furla	Corso Buenos Aires 18
Geox	Corso Buenos Aires 2
Giacomelli Sport	Piazza Argentina 4
Jeanseria del Corso	Corso Buenos Aires (at Pergolesi)
Marilene	Corso Buenos Aires 25
Marina Rinaldi	Corso Buenos Aires 77
Nadine	Corso Buenos Aires 38
Oviesse	Corso Buenos Aires 35
ProMod	Corso Buenos Aires 41
Salvagente Bimbo	Via Balzaretti 28
Sisley	Corso Buenos Aires 3
Vergelio	Corso Buenos Aires 9

Corso di Porta Ticinese / Corso Genova
See map page 232

55DSL (Diesel)	Corso di Porta Ticinese 75
Alberto Guardiani	Corso di Porta Ticinese 67
Antonioli	Via Pasquale Paoli 1

Milan Districts

B-Fly	Corso di Porta Ticinese 46
Biffi	Corso Genova 6
Cavalli e Nastri	Via de Amicis 9
Chic Simple	Corso di Porta Ticinese 48
Coccinelle	Corso Genova 6
Diesel	Corso di Porta Ticinese 44
Fatto a Mano	Corso di Porta Ticinese 76
Fornarina	Corso di Porta Ticinese 78
Joost	Via Cesare Correnti 12
L'Armadio di Laura	Via Voghera 25
Martin Luciano	Alazaia Naviglio Grande 58
Martino Midali	Corso di Porta Ticinese 60
No Season	Corso di Porta Ticinese 77
Purple	Corso di Porta Ticinese 22
Taboo	Piazza Generale Cantore 3
Tim Camino	Via de Amicis 3
Zeus	Corso Genova 24

Via Montenapoleone & neighborhood
See map page 233

Agnona	Via della Spiga 3
Alberta Ferretti	Via Montenapoleone 21a
Alberto Guardiani	Via Montenapoleone 9
Alexander McQueen	Via Verri 8
Alviero Martini	Via Montenapoleone 26
Andrea Pfister	Via Montenapoleone 25
Anna Molinari Blumarine	Via della Spiga 42
Antonio Fusco	Via Sant' Andrea 11
Armani Collezioni	Via Montenapoleone 2
Armani Jr	Via Montenapoleone 10
Armani/Via Manzoni 31	Via Manzoni 31
Ars Rosa	Via Montenapoleone 8
Atelier Aimée	Via Montenapoleone 27e
A.Testoni	Via Montenapoleone 19
Baldinini	Via Montenapoleone 15
Bally	Via Montenapoleone 8
Banner	Via Sant' Andrea 8
Barbara Bui	Via Manzoni 45
Bonpoint	Via Manzoni 15
Borbonese	Via Santo Spirito 26
Borsalino	Via Verri (corner of Via Bigli)
Boss Hugo Boss	Via Matteotti 11
Bottega Veneta	Via Montenapoleone 5
Braccialini	Via Montenapoleone 19
Brioni	Via Gesu 3 & 4
Bruno Magli	Via Manzoni 14
Burberry	Via Bigli 2
Camper	Via Montenapoleone 6
Canali	Via Verri 1
Canziani	Via Montenapoleone 26

Casadei	Via Sant' Andrea 17
Celine	Via Montenapoleone 25
Cerruti	Via della Spiga 20
Cesare Gatti	Via Montenapoleone 19
Cesare Paciotti	Via Sant' Andrea 8
Chanel	Via Sant' Andrea 10a
Christian Dior	Via Montenapoleone 12 & 14
Church's	Via Sant' Andrea 11
Coccinelle	Via Manzoni at Via Bigli
Corneliani	Via Montenapoleone 12
Costume National	Via Sant' Andrea 12
C.P. Company and Stone Island	Corso Venezia 12
Davide Cenci	Via Manzoni 7
DMagazine Outlet	Via Montenapoleone 26
Dolce & Gabbana	Via della Spiga 2 & 26a-b
Dolce & Gabbana	Corso Venezia 15
Domo Adami	Via Manzoni 23
Emanuel Ungaro	Via Montenapoleone 27
Ermenegildo Zegna	Via Verri 3
Etro	Via Montenapoleone 5
Extè	Via della Spiga 6
Fausto Santini	Via Montenapoleone 1
Fay	Via della Spiga 15
Fedeli Red and Blue	Via Montenapoleone 8
Fendi	Via Sant' Andrea 16
Fogal	Via Montenapoleone 1
Fratelli Rossetti	Via Montenapoleone 1
Frette	Via Montenapoleone 21
Frette	Via Manzoni 11
Geox	Via Montenapoleone 26
Gianfranco Ferré	Via Sant' Andrea 15
Gianni Versace	Via Montenapoleone 11
Gibo by Julie Verhoeven	Via Sant' Andrea 10a
Gio Moretti	Via della Spiga 4
Gio Moretti Baby	Via della Spiga 9
Giorgio Armani	Via della Spiga 19
Giorgio Armani	Via Sant' Andrea 9
Gucci	Via Montenapoleone 5-7
Helmut Lang	Via della Spiga 11
Hermès	Via Sant' Andrea 21
Hogan	Via Montenapoleone 23
Iceberg	Via Montenapoleone 10
I Pinco Pallino	Via della Spiga 42
Jil Sander	Via Verri 6
Jimmy Choo	n/a at press time
John Richmond	Via Verri (corner of Via Bigli)
Kenzo	Via Sant' Andrea 11
Krizia	Via della Spiga 23
La Perla	Via Montenapoleone 1
Larusmiani	Via Verri 10

Milan Districts

Les Copains	Via Manzoni 21
Lorenzo Banfi	Via Montenapoleone 10
Lorenzo Banfi	Via della Spiga 42
Loro Piana	Via Montenapoleone 27c
Louis Vuitton	Via Montenapoleone 2
Malo	Via della Spiga 7
Mancadori	Via Montenapoleone 1
Mariella Burani	Via Montenapoleone 3
Marisa	Via Sant' Andrea 1 & 10a
Marisa	Via Della Spiga 52
Marni	Via Sant' Andrea 14
Missoni	Via Sant' Andrea 2
Mortarotti	Via Montenapoleone 24
Moschino	Via della Spiga 30
Moschino	Via Sant' Andrea 12
Napapijri	Via Manzoni 46
Narciso Rodriguez	Via Montenapoleone 21
Patrizia Pepe	Via Manzoni 38
Paul & Shark	Via Montenapoleone 15
Paul Smith	Via Manzoni 30
P-Box	Via Manzoni 13
Pineider	Via Manzoni 20
Piombo	Via della Spiga 34
Prada	Via della Spiga 1 & 5
Prada	Via Montenapoleone 6 & 8
Prada	Via Sant' Andrea 21
Ralph Lauren	Via Montenapoleone 4
Roberto Cavalli	Via della Spiga 42
Romeo Gigli	Via della Spiga 30
Ruffo	Via della Spiga 48
Salvatore Ferragamo	Via Montenapoleone 3 & 20
Sergio Rossi	Via della Spiga 5 & 15
Sergio Rossi	Via Montenapoleone 6a
Sermoneta Gloves	Via della Spiga 46
Simonetta Ravizza	Via Montenapoleone 1
Sportmax	Via della Spiga 30
Strenesse	Via Manzoni 37
Tanino Crisci	Via Montenapoleone 3
Tod's	Via della Spiga 22
Trussardi	Piazza della Scala 5
Trussardi	Via Sant' Andrea 3 & 5
Valentino	Via Montenapoleone 20
Versus (Gianni Versace)	Via San Pietro all'Orto 10
Vicini	Via della Spiga 1
Vierre	Via Montenapoleone 29
Yves Saint Laurent	Via Montenapoleone 27

Corso Vittorio Emanuele II /Duomo / Via Torino
See map page 233

Benetton	Corso Vittorio Emanuele II 9
Blunauta	Via Dante 11
Boggi	Via Durini 28
Boggi	Largo Augusto 3
Borsalino	Galleria Vittorio Emanuele II 92
Bruno Magli	Via San Paolo 1
Cacharel	Via San Paolo 1
Camper	Via Torino 15
Chicco	Piazza Diaz 2
Church's	Galleria Vittorio Emanuele II 84
Cisalfa	Corso Vittorio Emanuele II 1
DAAD Dantone	Corso Matteotti 20
D&G	Corso Venezia 7
David Mayer	Via Meravigli 16
Diesel	Galleria Passarella 2
Diffusione Tessile	Galleria San Carlo 6
Du Pareil Au Même	Via Dante (corner of Via Cairoli)
Energie	Via Torino 19
E-Play	Corso Venezia 5
Fila	Piazza Liberty 8
Fiorucci Dept. Store	Corso Europa
Furla	Corso Vittorio Emanuele II 2
Geox	Via Speronari 8
Geox	Galleria Vittorio Emanuele II
Gianni Campagna	Corso Venezia 53a
Guess?	Piazza San Babila 4b
H&M	Galleria Passerella 2
Jeanseria del Corso	Piazza Duomo 31
Kallisté—Un Dimanche à Venise	Corso Matteotti 22
La Rinascente	Via Radegonda 3
Le Solferine	Via Meravigli 16
Levi's	Via Silvio Pellico 6
Luisa Spagnoli	Corso Vittorio Emanuele II *(corner of Galleria San Carlo)*
Mandarina Duck	Galleria San Carlo *(corner of Corso Europa)*
Marina Rinaldi	Galleria Passarella 2
Marilene	Corso Vittorio Emanuele II 15
Marilene	Via Torino 13
Max & Co	Piazza Liberty 4
MaxMara	Piazza Liberty 4
Miu Miu	Corso Venezia 3
Nadine	Corso Vittorio Emanuele II 34
Onyx Fashion Store	Corso Vittorio Emanuele II 24
Onyx Fashion Store	Via Torino 2
Plus	Piazza Missori 2
Pollini	Piazza Duomo 31
Prada	Galleria Vittorio Emanuele II 63

Milan Districts

ProMod	Via Mazzini 2
Replay	Largo Corsia dei Servi 11
Samsonite	Corso Matteotti 12
Sisley	Via Dogana 4
Sisley	Galleria Passarella 1
Stefanel	Corso Vittorio Emanuele II 28
Stefanel	Via Spadari 1
T'store (Trussardi)	Galleria Strasburgo
	(corner of Via Durini)
Valextra	Piazza San Babila 1
Vergelio	Corso Vittorio Emanuele II 10
Vito Nacci	Via Durini 11
Zap!	Galleria Passarella 2
Zara	Galleria Vittorio Emanuele II 11

Corso Vercelli / Magenta

Benetton	Corso Vercelli 8
Christies	Corso Vercelli 51
DEV	Corso Vercelli 8
Fratelli Rossetti	Corso Magenta 17
Frette	Corso Vercelli 23-25
Furla	Corso Vercelli 11
La Perla	Corso Vercelli 35

Piazza 5 Giornate and outwards

Coin	Piazza 5 Giornate 1a
Salvagente	Via Fratelli Bronzetti 16
Shabby Chic	Via B. Cellini 21

Milan Stores by Category

Women's

Men's

Unisex

Children's

Women's Accessories

10 Corso Como
Antonia Accessori
Armani/Via Manzoni 31
Bottega Veneta

Coccinelle
Coin
Dolce & Gabbana

Fiorucci Dept. Store
Giorgio Armani
Gucci
La Rinascente

Prada
Sermoneta Gloves
Valextra

Women's Bridal

Atelier Aimée
Domo Adami

Luisa Beccaria

Women's Career

Antonio Fusco
Brioni
Coin
Davide Cenci

Emporio Armani
Giorgio Armani
La Rinascente
MaxMara

Women's Cashmere/Knitwear

Agnona
Blunauta
Cesare Gatti
Fedeli Red and Blue
Krizia

Les Copains
Loro Piana
Malo
Mancadori Missoni

Women's Casual

Armani/Via Manzoni 31
Benetton
Co-Co
Coin

Diesel
Emporio Armani
Energie
E-Play

Fay
Fiorucci Dept. Store
Fornarina
Guess?

Jeanseria del Corso
La Rinascente
Levi's
Max & Co

Nadine
Onyx Fashion Store
Paul & Shark
Prada

ProMod
Replay
Sisley
Stefanel

Women's Classic

Brioni
Coin
Davide Cenci
Fay

Gianni Campagna
La Rinascente
Loro Piana
Piombo

Women's Contemporary

2Link
10 Corso Como
Antonia
Antonioli

Avant
Biffi
Bipa
Chic Simple

Clan
Coin
DAAD Dantone
Fiorucci Dept. Store

Gio Moretti
Julien
La Boule de Neige
La Rinascente

Lorella Braglia
Marisa
MaxMara
Mortarotti

Nadine
Naj-Oleari
Patrizia Pepe
Plus

Purple
Samsonite
Sportmax
Taboo

Tim Camino
Zap!
Zara
Zeus

Women's Designer

Alan Journo
Alexander McQueen
Anna Molinari Blumarine
Anteprima

Armani Collezioni
Armani/Via Manzoni 31
Banner
Barbara Bui

Borbonese
Burberry
Celine
Cerruti

Chanel
Christian Dior
Costume National
D&G

Dolce & Gabbana
Emanuel Ungaro
Emilio Pucci
Etro

Extè
Fendi
Gianfranco Ferré
Gianni Campagna

Gianni Versace
Gibo
Giorgio Armani

Gucci
Helmut Lang
Hermès
Iceberg

Jil Sander
John Richmond
Kenzo
Krizia

Les Copains
Louis Vuitton
Marni
MaxMara

Missoni
Miu Miu
Moschino
Narciso Rodriguez

Paul Smith
Prada
Ralph Lauren
Roberto Cavalli

Ruffo
Salvatore Ferragamo
Strenesse
Trussardi

Valentino
Yves Saint Laurent

Milan Categories

Women's Discount

Avant
Diffusione Tessile

DMagazine Outlet
Salvagente

Women's Ethnic

Fatto a Mano

Women's Eveningwear & Special Occasions

Alexander McQueen
Christian Dior
Coin
Emanuel Ungaro
Giorgio Armani

La Rinascente
Salvagente
Valentino
Versace

Women's Furs

Fendi
Simonetta Ravizza

Vito Nacci

Women's Handbags

Alviero Martini
A.Testoni
Baldinini
Bally

Fausto Santini
Fendi
Furla
Gucci

Borbonese
Bottega Veneta
Braccialini
Bruno Magli

Hermès
Hogan
La Rinascente
Louis Vuitton

Chanel
Christian Dior
Coccinelle

Mandarina Duck
Prada
Tod's

Coin
DEV
Etro

Trussardi
Valentino

Women's Hats

Borsalino
La Rinascente

Women's Hosiery

Coin
Fogal

La Rinascente

Women's Leather

Fendi
Ruffo

Trussardi

Women's Lingerie

Christies
Coin
Frette
Kristina Ti

La Perla
La Rinascente
Pineider
Prada

Maternity

Chicco
Martino Midali

Women's Plus Sizes

Luisa Spagnoli
Marina Rinaldi

Women's Shirts

Coin
Fedeli Red and Blue

La Rinascente
Mancadora

Women's Shoes

Alberto Guardiani
Andrea Pfister
A.Testoni
Baldinini

Jimmy Choo
Kallisté—Un Dimanche
  à Venise
La Rinascente

Bally
Barbara Bui
Bottega Veneta
Bruno Magli

La Vetrina di Beryl
Le Solferine
Marilene
Miu Miu

Camper
Casadei
Cesare Paciotti
Coin

P-Box
Pollini
Prada
Salvatore Ferragamo

Davide Cenci
DEV
Fausto Santini
Fratelli Rossetti

Sergio Rossi
Tanino Crisci
Tod's
Vergelio

Geox
Gucci
Hogan

Vicini
Vierre

Women's Swimwear

Cisalfa
Christies
Coin

Fila
Giacomelli Sport
La Rinascente

Milan Categories

Women's Vintage & Retro

B-Fly
Cavalli e Nastri
Co-Co

Docks Dora
Dolce & Gabbana Vintage

Julien
L'Armadio di Laura
La Vetrina di Beryl

Shabby Chic
Zap!

Women's Young & Trendy

Diesel
Energie
Fornarina
H&M

Jeanseria del Corso
Onyx Fashion Store
ProMod
Zara

Men's Business Apparel

Biffi
Boggi
Brioni

Canali
Coin
Corneliani

Davide Cenci
Ermenegildo Zegna
Gianni Campagna

La Rinascente
Loro Piana

Men's Cashmere/Knitwear

Cesare Gatti
Fedeli Red and Blue
Loro Piana

Malo
Missoni

Men's Casual

Armani/Via Manzoni 31
Benetton
Biffi
Coin

C.P. Company &
  Stone Island
Diesel
Energie

E-Play
Ermenegildo Zegna
Fay
Guess?

H&M
Jeanseria del Corso
La Rinascente
Larusmiani

Levi's
Napapijri
Paul & Shark
Prada

Replay
Sisley
Stefanel

Men's Contemporary

2Link
2Link Black Label
10 Corso Como
Antonioli

Biffi
Boss Hugo Boss
Clan

Coin
DAAD Dantone
David Mayer

Eral 55
Gio Moretti
Joost
Julien

La Rinascente
No Season
Piombo

Purple
Samsonite

Men's Designer

Alviero Martini
Antonio Fusco
Armani Collezioni
Burberry

Cerruti
Christian Dior
Costume National
D&G

Dolce & Gabbana
Extè
Gianfranco Ferré/GFF
  Gianfranco Ferré

Gianni Versace
Giorgio Armani
Gucci
Helmut Lang

Hermès
Iceberg
Jil Sander

John Richmond
Kenzo
Krizia
Les Copains

Louis Vuitton
Missoni
Miu Miu
Paul Smith

Prada
Ralph Lauren
Romeo Gigli
Ruffo

Salvatore Ferragamo
Strenesse
Trussardi
Valentino

Yves Saint Laurent Rive
  Gauche

Men's Discount

DMagazine Outlet
Salvagente

Men's Hats

Borsalino
La Rinascente

Milan Categories

Men's Leather & Leather Goods

A.Testoni
Baldinini
Bally
Bottega Veneta

Coin
Gucci
Hermès

La Rinascente
Prada
Ruffo
Salvatore Ferragamo

Trussardi
Valextra

Men's Shirts

Boggi
Brioni
Canziani

Coin
Corneliani

DEV
Fedeli Red and Blue
La Rinascente

Paul Smith
Piombo

Men's Shoes

Alberto Guardiani
A.Testoni
Baldinini
Bally

Bottega Veneta
Bruno Magli
Camper
Casadei

Cesare Paciotti
Church's
Davide Cenci

DEV
Fausto Santini
Fratelli Rossetti
Hogan

Lorenzo Banfi
Pollini
Sergio Rossi
Tanino Crisci

Tod's
Vergelio
Vierre

Men's Swimwear

Cisalfa
Coin
Fila

Giacomelli Sport
La Rinascente

Men's Undergarments

Coin
D&G

La Rinascente

Men's Vintage & Retro

B-Fly
Docks Dora
Julien

Martin Luciano
Zap!

Men's Young & Trendy

DAAD Dantone
Diesel
Energie

H&M
Jeanseria del Corso
Zara

Unisex Athletic

Cisalfa
Fila

Giacomelli Sport
La Rinascente

Unisex Athletic Accessories

Cisalfa
Fila

Giacomelli Sport

Unisex Outdoor Sports Apparel

Paul & Shark

Children's Clothing

Armani Jr
Ars Rosa
Benetton
Bonpoint

Du Pareil Au Même
Fiorucci Dept. Store
Gio Moretti
La Rinascente

Cacharel
Coin
D&G
Diesel

Moschino
Naj-Oleari
Replay

Children's Shoes

Hogan
Tod's

Milan Services

Beauty Salons

Hairdressers

Make-up Artists

Skin Treatments

Manicures

Day Spas

Fitness Studios

Dry Cleaners

Mending & Alterations

Shoe & Leather Repairs

Trimmings (fabric, ribbons, buttons etc)

Personal Shopper

Italian Fashion Website

Beauty Salons

Aldo Coppola
Corso Garibaldi 110

02-655 2144
Tues-Sat 9-6

Aldo Coppola
Via Manzoni 25

02-8646 2163
Tues-Sat 9-5:30

Aldo Coppola
Piazza San Babila 1

02-7600 7299
Tues-Sat 9-5:30

Aldo Coppola
in Coin, Piazza 5 Giornate 1a

02-5411 6026
Mon 1-8:30
Tues-Sat 9:30-8:30

Aldo Coppola
in Zap!, Galleria Passarella 2

02-798 464
Mon 3-7:30, Tues-Fri 10-7

Downtown
Piazza Cavour 2

02-7601 1485
Mon-Fri 7-midnight, Sat-Sun 10-9

Intrecci
Via Larga 2

02-7202 2316
Mon 11-8, Tues-Fri 10-11, Sat 10-9

Orea Maglia
Via Marghera 18

02-469 4976
Tues-Wed, Fri 9:30-7:30
Thurs 11-10, Sat 9-7

Orea Maglia
Via Castaldi 42

02-204 6584
Tues-Sat 9:30-7

Tony & Guy
Via Vincenzo Monti 27

02-4802 7137
Mon 9:30-3:30, Tues-Sat 9:30-7:30

Tony & Guy
Galleria Passarella 1

02-7601 8360
Tues-Sat 10-7:30 (Thurs 10-8:30)

Hairdressers

Aldo Coppola
Corso Garibaldi 110

02-655 2144
Tues-Sat 9-6

Aldo Coppola
Via Manzoni 25

02-8646 2163
Tues-Sat 9-5:30

Aldo Coppola
Piazza San Babila 1

02-7600 7299
Tues-Sat 9-5:30

Aldo Coppola
in Coin, Piazza 5 Giornate 1a

02-5411 6026
Mon 1-8:30
Tues-Sat 9:30-8:30

Aldo Coppola
in Zap!, Galleria Passarella 2

02-798 464
Mon 3-7:30, Tues-Fri 10-7

Antica Barbiera Colla
Via Gerolamo Morone 3

02-874 312
Tues-Sat 8:30-12:30, 2:30-7

Intrecci
Via Larga 2

02-7202 2316
Mon 11-8, Tues-Fri 10-11, Sat 10-9

Jean Louis David
Via Plinio 5

02-2024 1065
Tues-Sat 9:30-7

Jean Louis David
Via Moscova 29

02-659 9993
Tues-Sat 9-6:30

Jean Louis David **02-7200 2912**
Passaggio Duomo 2 Tues-Sat 9-7

Orea Maglia **02-469 4976**
Via Marghera 18 Tues-Wed, Fri 9:30-7:30
Thurs 11-10, Sat 9-7

Orea Maglia **02-204 6584**
Via Castaldi 42 Tues-Sat 9:30-7

Rolando **02-655 1527**
Via Manzoni 31 Tues-Sat 9-6:30

Piergiuseppe Moroni **02-7602 1631**
Via S.Pietro all'Orto 26 Tues-Sat 9:30-7

Tony & Guy **02-4802 7137**
Via Vincenzo Monti 27 Mon 9:30-3:30, Tues-Sat 9:30-7:30

Tony & Guy **02-7601 8360**
Galleria Passarella 1 Tues-Sat 10-7:30 (Thurs 10-8:30)

Make-up Artists

Diego Dalla Palma **02-876 818**
Via Madonnina 13-15 Mon 1:30-5:30
Tues-Fri 10-11, 12:30-5:30

MAC **02-8699 5506**
Via Fiori Chiari 12 Mon-Sat 10-8

Madina **02-7601 1692**
Corso Venezia 23 Mon 3-7:30, Tues-Sat 10-7:30

Madina **02-860 746**
Via Tivoli 8 (opening times as above)

Shu Uemura **02-875 371**
Via Brera 2 Mon-Fri 10:30-7

Skin Treatments

Estée Lauder Skincare Center **02-801 480**
in La Rinascente (7th floor) Mon-Sat 9:30-10
Piazza del Duomo

Manicures

Enhancements **02-6269 4537**
Via Solferino 46 Mon-Sat 10-8

Just Nails **02-4634 98**
Via G. Washington 76 Tues-Sat 9-7

Day Spas
(all provide massages, facials and other treatments)

Arte del Benessere **02-2906 2000**
Via Moscova 24 Mon-Fri 10-8, Sat 9-3:30
(ayurvedic treatments)

Blissful Club **02-8901 2820**
Via Unione 1 Mon-Sat 11-8

Milan Services

Centro Benessere (in Jean Louis David)   **02-659 9993**
Via Moscova 29   Tues-Sat 9-6:30

Centro di Estetica   **02-2953 1173**
Corso Buenos Aires 36   Mon 3:30-7:30
Tues-Fri 9:30-7, Sat 9:30-7:30

Club 10   **02-62301**
Hotel Principe di Savoia   Mon-Fri 7-10
Piazza della Repubblica 17   Sat-Sun 9-8
(*a huge range of beauty treatments*)

Dolce & Gabbana Grooming   **02-7640 8888**
Corso Venezia 15   Mon-Sat 10-7

E'Spa @ Gianfranco Ferré   **02-7601 7526**
Via Sant' Andrea 15   Mon-Fri 10-10, Sat 10-9, Sun 11-6

Navigli Beauty Center   **02-835 6601**
Via Mortara 5   Mon-Sat 10-8

Fitness Studios

Cairoli Health Club   **02-7602 8517**
Via Senato 11   Mon-Fri 7-11, Sat 9-9, Sun 10-9

Downtown   **02-7601 1485**
Piazza Cavour 2   Mon-Sat 7-midnight, Sun 6-9

Dry Cleaners

Campista Antonina   **02-655 2201**
Via Moscova 15   Tues-Fri 8-12:30, 2-7:30, Sat 8-12

De Leo Carmine   **02-8646 1931**
Via Rovello 8   Mon-Fri 9-7

Lavaderia Automatica Carillon   **02-5519 2315**
Corso di Porto Vittoria 51   Mon-Fri 8-12:30, 3-7, Sat 8-12:30

Lavarapido o.k.   **02-653 421**
Viale Crispi Francesco 5a   Mon-Fri 8:30-6:30

Lavasecco Fontana   **02-545 7934**
Via Fontana 5   Mon-Fri 8-12:30, 3-7:30, Sat 8-12:30

Lavasecco S.Croce di Altavilla Francesca   **02-832 2471**
Via Santa Croce 1   Mon-Fri 8-12:30, 2:30-7, Sat 8-12:30

Lavasecco Tintoria   **02-5831 5898**
Via dei Pellegrini 6   Mon-Fri 8:30-1, 2:30-7, Sat 9-12:30

Rinnovapel   **02-506 5321**
Via degli Umiliati 7   Mon-Fri 9-6
(*cleaning and repair of leather clothing*)

Tintoria D'Elite   **02-782 333**
Viale Piave 12   Mon-Fri 8:30-6:30, Sat 9-12:30
(*general dry cleaning, also bridal, eveningwear and leather*)

Mending & Alterations

Bottega Artiginale di Rimedi e Stile 02-4801 2026
Via Ruggiero Settimo 4 Mon-Fri 3:30-7
(specialist in vintage and bridal) Sat by appointment

Carabella Ceccato Anna Maria 02-659 2790
Corso Baribaldi Giuseppe 93 Mon-Fri 8-12:30, 3-7

Colella Nicoletta 02-2951 4699
Viale Regina Giovanna 28 Mon 2-6, Tues-Fri 9-1, 2-6
Sat 9-1

Scarpa Maria 02-331 3028
Via Sarpi Paolo 50 Mon-Fri 9:30-12, 3:30-6:30
Sat 9:30-12, 3:30-5

Te lo 6 Rotto 02-545 8089
Via della Commenda 28 Mon 3:30-7
Tues-Sat 9:30-12:30, 3:30-7

Shoe & Leather Repairs

Alvisi Milano 02-740 413
Via Mameli 24 Mon 3-7:30, Tues-Sat 8:30-12:30, 3-7:30

Artigianoteca 02-5519 2855
Viale Premuda 1 Mon-Fri 8-7, Sat 8-12

Di Litta Francesco 02-5519 2221
Corso di Porto Vittoria 49 Mon-Fri 8:30-12:50, 2:30-6:50

Margarita Vincenzo 02-5831 0161
Corso Italia 46 Mon-Fri 8-1, 2:30-7:30

Milito Giuseppe 02-836 1149
Piazzale Cantore Antonio 5 Mon-Fri 8:30-12:30, 3-6
Sat 8:30-12:30

Ruffa Pasquale 02-8645 3020
Via Meravigli 18 Mon-Fri 9-1, 3-7, Sat 9-1

Valentini 02-8645 2589
Corso Italia 14 Mon-Fri 10-2:30, 3:30-7
Sat 10-12:30, 3:30-7

Trimmings
(fabrics, buttons, ribbons, cross stitch and embroidery kits, etc)

Binacchi Angelo 02-5519 4556
Via della Commenda 25 Mon-Fri 8-1, 3-6:30, Sat 8-1

Bonetti Domenica Miriam 02-864 376
Via Arco 1 Mon 3-7, Tues-Sat 10-2, 3-7

Gandini Tessutti Alta Moda 02-7600 8641
Via Gesu 21 Mon, Fri 9-1, 2-5
Tues-Thurs 9-1, 2-6

Ida del Castillo Tessutti 02-5811 2137
Corso di Porta Ticinese 105 Mon 3:30-7:30
Tues-Fri 10:35-1, 3:30-7:30

Il Mondo di Alice	**02-5405 0066**
Via Orti 4	Mon 3-7:30, Tues-Sat 10-7:30
Isabella Ottolenghi	**02-7600 1622**
Piazza San Babila 3	Mon 2-7, Tues-Sat 10-1, 2-7
Le Mercerie	**02-8645 4338**
Via San Vittore 2	Mon 3-7, Tues-Sat 9:30-1:30, 3-7
Mimma Gini Tessutti	**02-8940 0722**
Via Croce 21	Mon 3-7, Tues-Sat 10-7
Tuttomodo	**02-2900 3718**
Via Statuto 18	Mon 2-7, Tues-Fri 9-1:30, 2-7

Personal Shopper

Barbara Lessona   **www.personalshoppersinitaly.com**
348 450 3655 / 06-855 1630 / 06-4423 7225

Italian Fashion Website

Logan Bentley   **www.made-in-italy.com**

Fashion Speak

Avant-garde: forward-thinking or advanced. When referring to art or costume, sometimes implies erotic or startling. Derived from the French for "advance guard".

Bridge collection: a collection that is priced between designer and mass market.

Couture: French word used throughout fashion industry to describe the original styles, the ultimate in fine sewing and tailoring, made of expensive fabrics, by designers. The designs are shown in collections twice a year—spring/summer and fall/winter.

Custom-made/tailor-made, also called bespoke: garments made by tailor or couture house for an individual customer following couturier's original design. Done by either fitting a model form adjusted to the customer's measurements or by several personal fittings.

Diffusion line: a designer's second and less expensive collection.

Ensemble: an entire costume, including accessories, worn at one time. Two or more items of clothing designed and coordinated to be worn together.

Fashion trend: direction in which styles, colors and fabrics are moving. Trends may be influenced by political events, films, personalities, dramas, social and sporting events or indeed any human activity.

Faux: false or counterfeit, imitation: used in connection with gems, pearls and leathers. Faux fur (fake fur) is commonplace today, as is what is sometimes known as "pleather" (plastic leather). Artificial gems, especially pearls, are often made from a fine kind of glass known as "paste", and are accordingly sometimes called "paste" for short.

Haberdashery: a store that sells men's apparel and furnishings.

Knock-off: trade term for the copying of an item of apparel, e.g. a dress or a coat, in a lower price line. Similar to piracy.

Made-to-measure: clothing (dress, suit, shirt etc) made according to individual's measurement. No fittings required.

One-off: a unique, one-of-a-kind item that will not be found in any other store or produced again in the future, e.g. a customized denim skirt or a rare vintage cocktail dress. Can also refer to made-to-measure and couture garments designed for a particular person and/or event, such as a dress for the Oscars.

Prêt-à-porter: French term which literally means ready-to-wear, i.e. to take (or wear) straight out of the shop.

Ready-to-wear (rtw): apparel that is mass-produced in standard sizes. Records of the ready-to-wear industry tabulated in the U.S. Census of 1860 included hoop skirts, cloaks, and mantillas; from 1890 shirtwaists and wrappers were added; and, after 1930, dresses.

5 very good reasons why you should become a *Where to Wear* online subscriber

1. Access the guide online from wherever you are.
2. Take the guide on a laptop or CD ROM.
3. Find a particular designer, type of clothing or boutique easily by just typing in what you want and seeing the result.
4. Results printed out to show information and location, member concessions, special offers and promotions from stores.
5. Exclusive seasonal offers available to *Where to Wear* members only from selected stores.

Visit our new exclusive members website at

www.wheretowear.com/member.htm

How to order *Where to Wear*

Where to Wear publishes guides to the following cities: **London**, **New York**, **Paris**, **Los Angeles**, **San Francisco** and **Italy** (which includes Florence, Milan and Rome). Each edition retails at £9.99 or $12.95.

There is also a gift box set, *Shopping Guides to the World's Fashion Capitals*, available for £29.99 or $49.99 which includes the **London**, **New York**, **Paris** and **Italy** (Florence, Milan and Rome) guides (four books for the price of three).

If you live in the UK or Europe, you can order your copies of *Where to Wear* by contacting our London office at:

10 Cinnamon Row
Plantation Wharf
London SW11 3TW
TEL: 020 7801 1381
EMAIL: wheretowear@onetel.net.uk

If you live in the USA, you can order your copies of *Where to Wear* by contacting our New York office at:

666 Fifth Avenue
PMB 377
New York, NY 10103
TEL: 212-969-0138
TOLL-FREE: 1-877-714-SHOP (7467)
EMAIL: wheretowear@aol.com

Or simply log on to our website: www.wheretowear.com
Where to Wear delivers worldwide.